A Space of Her Own

A SPACE OF HER OWN

PERSONAL NARRATIVES OF TWELVE WOMEN

EDITORS

LEELA GULATI
JASODHARA BAGCHI

SAGE Publications
New Delhi ❖ Thousand Oaks ❖ London

First published in 2005 by

Sage Publications India Pvt Ltd
B-42, Panchsheel Enclave
New Delhi 110 017
www.indiasage.com

Sage Publications Inc
2455 Teller Road
Thousand Oaks, California 91320

Sage Publications Ltd
1 Oliver's Yard, 55 City Road
London EC1Y 1SP

Published by Tejeshwar Singh for Sage Publications India Pvt Ltd, typeset in 10/12 Charter BT at S.R. Enterprises and printed at Chaman Enterprises, New Delhi.

Library of Congress Cataloging-in-Publication Data

A space of her own: personal narratives of twelve women/editors, Leela Gulati, Jasodhara Bagchi.

p. cm.

Includes bibliographical references.

1. Women—India—Biography. 2. Women—India—Social conditions. 3. Sex role—India. I. Gulati, Leela. II. Bagchi, Jasodhara.

HQ1742.5.A3S63 304'.0954'0904—dc22 2005 2004029805

ISBN: 0-7619-3314-X (Hb) 81-7829-444-3 (India-Hb)
0-7619-3315-8 (Pb) 81-7829-445-1 (India-Pb)

Sage Production Team: Payal Dhar, Proteeti Banerjee, Sushanta Gayen and Santosh Rawat

In Memory of Iqbal Gulati

Contents

Introduction 9
Carolyn M. Elliott

1. The Wind Beneath My Wings 21
Nabaneeta Dev Sen

2. A Heritage of Heresy within Tradition 43
Vina Mazumdar

3. A Daughter of Awadh 65
Zarina Bhatty

4. A Struggle for Space 83
Hema Sundaram

5. The Tyranny of Tradition 105
Leela Gulati

6. Wings Come to Those Who Fly 125
Maithreyi Krishna Raj

7. The Times that are a-Changing 143
Priti T. Desai

8. Uneven Earth and Open Sky 165
Saroja Kamakshi

9. Abode of Colour 181
Vijaya Mehta

10. Striking New Roots 203
Sushil Narulla

11. Matriliny within Patriliny 223
Jasodhara Bagchi

12. Three Generations of Women 237
Mary Roy

Afterword: The Colonised Coloniser 257
Arlie Hochschild

Select Bibliography 265
About the Editors and Contributors 271

Introduction*

Carolyn M. Elliott

A seventh-grade textbook on Indian history makes a perplexing pair of observations about the position of women in the Vijayanagar empire of 17-century south India. It observes: 'Women occupied a high position in society. They played an active role in the political, social and literary life of the country.' Then follows the statement: '*Sati* was very common.' This raises many questions about the meaning of freedom for women in the mind of the author. How can one say that ending of one's life because one's social role of wife is over, even if done voluntarily, represents a high position for women? Is personal freedom available only when one is protected by a male? Can this be called a high position?

The narratives in this collection provide insights on many important issues such as these. Eight of the narratives were written for a workshop on women's lives hosted by the Centre for Development Studies in Trivandrum in 1998. Leela Gulati and Arlie Hochschild of the University of California at Berkeley, then a Fulbright Visiting Fellow at the Centre, convened the meeting. They asked the writers to reflect on the lives of their mothers and their grandmothers in relation to their own lives. Four pieces have been added subsequently to expand the range of the volume.

In a society where marriage means a girl leaving her natal family to join another family, this project represents a somewhat subversive voice. It is about hidden relationships, that is, women's relations with each other unmediated by marriage. It is an effort to bring into view the lives of women who, while often treasured in private memories, have been unavailable to us. Some can never be recovered. Thus, Nabaneeta

* An earlier version of this Introduction was published in the *Indian Journal of Gender Studies*, Vol. 6, No. 2, 1999, pp. 177–84.

Dev Sen tells how her maternal grandmother's name has been lost. Even the favoured son who donated to charity in her memory failed to record her name, her parents or her place of origin in the voluminous history he compiled of the family males.

To fill the gaps left in such histories, this project requested the writers to focus on structures that have been hidden by the normative view of Indian family life as patrilineal and patrilocal. Our writers were asked not how they as young wives fit into the duties and structure of their marital families, but what kinds of connections they maintained with the women of their natal families, that is, their mothers and grandmothers. Thus, it asked them to reflect on the emotional lines of matriliny within the social structure of patriliny.

As the narratives reveal, this proved to be an impossible task. Given women's engagements with large numbers of kin, our writers did not find it possible or useful to extricate their relationships with these key persons from a larger narrative of family life. Women's embeddedness in relationships of all sorts is not a unique finding of this project, but it makes more compelling the question posed at the outset: were the women portrayed in the narratives able to find any space for themselves? Or were they so constrained by the social roles of greatest importance to their families—wife and mother—that ending these roles meant some kind of death?

Each narrative may be read as a tale of how the author established her own personhood. As Susan Cahill (1994) observes in her introduction to a similar collection of Western women's writings, 'memory contains the map of identity'. Several of the authors are explicit in recognising what they have accomplished. Thus, Zarina Bhatty looks back over a life that included divorce, raising a daughter alone and discrimination in her search for a job, and calls it a success, for she has now established both a happy family life and a career of her own. So, too, does Saroja Kamakshi in talking about the satisfaction she derives from managing her daughter's dance career. In others, the recognition is implicit in their stories of survival and work. In each case, I suggest, the happiness expressed arises less from having achieved a measure of externally recognised success than from having established a sphere of autonomy where they could make decisions that nurture themselves as well as others.

Four themes emerge prominently in the life stories of the authors. One is the role of renegade predecessors in the family who set out a pattern of independence that paved the way for, or inspired, our author.

Thus, Zarina Bhatty describes her aunt Vakilan ('female advocate' in Urdu), so named because she was an argumentative child who desperately appealed to neighbours to save her from an unwanted marriage and later ran away from the marriage to live an independent life in Delhi. So, too, Vina Mazumdar describes a young daughter-in-law of an earlier generation who publicly challenged a *sati* as she mounted the funeral pyre, arguing that while the *sati* selfishly pursued her salvation, she ignored the impact this illegal action might have on the family. As their families carried these stories through the generations, the young authors found in them suggestions that girls could have their way if they dared.

Less dramatic but more immediately present in the lives of our authors are the mothers or grandmothers who came forward in situations of stress to exhibit unforeseen strengths and flexibility. Leela Gulati tells of her mother's courage in moving her children across India when her husband's death ended all support from his family. Sushil Narulla recounts how her mother emerged during the Partition from wifely seclusion to become the family negotiator with the police and bureaucracy in refugee camps. Jasodhara Bagchi tells how her mother, then old and frail, threw open her house to Muslim strangers from East Pakistan when the Pakistani army invaded in 1971. Even Priti Desai's once suicidal mother is remembered as a survivor as well as a victim. While these are stories of strength on behalf of others, not of self-nurturance or personal goals, they inspired the daughters who cite them as part of their own histories.

Several of the authors recount how previous generations of women found personal space under the 'bushel of domesticity'. Jasodhara Bagchi reports that the 'self-fashioning that went on largely within the four walls' inspired her own efforts to create space for women's studies at Jadavpur University. She cites singing and cooking together, facilitated by humour and grace, as her inheritance from matriliny. Similarly, Vijaya Mehta states how writing plays and acting the roles of historic women introduced her to the strengths of her mother and grandmothers. She argues that while women now have more choices, earlier generations found distinctive and centred identities that made their lives meaningful. Vina Mazumdar recalls how her mother and aunt each located a space of her own, her mother by herbal healing and aunt through education. Speaking for all, Priti Desai recalls her mother as a 'feminist who had quietly passed on the message that a woman had an identity, a will and needed a space of her own'.

Several of the daughters, however, drew from their mothers an unfulfilled demand for personal space that was a source of their determination to create their own lives. Both Leela Gulati and Priti Desai cite their mothers' chafing at being economically dependent on others, with no financial resources under their control. In contrast, Sushil Narulla describes the family jealousy of an aunt whose wealthy natal family enabled her to establish a position of autonomy—even to the point of naming her sons outside the Sikh family tradition—that was unavailable to the other daughters-in-law. And there is the negative image of Vijaya Mehta's aunt who was feared for practising black magic after being discarded by her husband, a charge she never denied.

Then there are the stories of obstacles overcome. Zarina Bhatty's father's opposition to her attending college was overcome only after her marriage to a husband going off to England for higher studies. This is a story not simply of luck, but of her determination to take every advantage of this opportunity. A *zamindar*'s daughter raised in the privilege of seclusion in a Lucknow household, Bhatty washed dishes and sewed garments to earn her education in London. Similarly, Nabaneeta Dev Sen, also from an aristocratic family, tells of supporting her daughters in London by driving her car as a minicab on the airport route. Even more difficult for her was surviving the social criticism directed at her status as a divorcee upon her return to Calcutta. She states her pride in raising her two daughters as a single mother and becoming a published writer and professor in Bengal.

The biggest obstacle of all, however, was being born female in a culture that denigrated, distrusted and ultimately feared women. One must note the bitterness with which most of our authors recall the treatment of women in their lives. With the exceptions of Mazumdar and Bagchi, we see no glorification of women's historic domestic role. And Mazumdar's positive examples are predominantly of women who gently or defiantly pushed against normative structures. Almost all our writers carry in their memories tales of women diminished and constrained by their gender. We learn of the burden of marrying daughters, ill-thought marriages arranged hastily when a daughter reached early puberty, girls withdrawn from school to ensure they would be compliant brides, mothers unable to protect daughters from unwanted marriages, and women hating their sex because it meant entrapment. We see women blamed for family misfortune even into the next generation. Thus, Priti Desai's unhappy mother compared her daughter to a malign incarnation of her hated mother-in-law, establishing an emotional distance between mother and daughter that could never be erased.

Even worse was the sexual stigma of being a woman, manifested most dramatically in the treatment of widows. Nabaneeta Dev Sen provides a poignant portrait of her teenaged widowed mother stripped of all decoration and colours, deprived of food and water, and spied upon by the family—all to desex her and protect the family honour. Her own divorce was seen as the just dessert for her widowed mother's remarriage against orthodox strictures.

Though shelved by the culture, many of these widows found sources of strength and humanity within themselves that inspired our authors. Several of the narratives recount the kindness of widowed aunts or grandmothers, others of their surprising endorsements of our authors' untraditional choices of husbands and careers. Krishna Raj recalls the advice of a grandmother who had spent her life looking after 10 children, 'Don't mess up your life with marriage. What is there to look forward to in marriage?' Others carved out small spaces for themselves. Mehta's portrait of her elderly grandmother smuggling snacks through the barber who came to shave her head is memorable, as is Hema Sundaram's picture of her widowed great aunt wearing diamond studs while handwashing her own clothes to avoid pollution. We can only guess at the emotional cost of maintaining such dignity.

Though internal family dynamics appear to be the most important forces that made our writers who they are, we must also note the effects of external social change. Vijaya Mehta's narrative is rich in locating her family amidst the changes in colonial India: the decline of feudalism with land reform, movement to cities where limited space ended the segregation of men's and women's spaces, middle-class progressive movements for education and social reform, and the freedom movement emphasising citizenship over caste solidarity. Other narratives tell of Partition dislocating and separating large families. It broke patriarchal patterns in Narulla's family and enabled all the girls to be educated. Several other narratives also cite the significance of geographic movement in freeing women from oppressive joint families.

Throughout India our authors note a change in intellectual climate in the 20th century that diminished religious orthodoxy and brought a new rationalism to social relations. Our authors talk variously of the influence of the Brahmo Samaj in Bengal, the Radical Humanist Society in Maharashtra, and general liberal currents in Madras. In the life of Vijaya Mehta, exposure to an uncle who followed M.N. Roy led to her joining Jayaprakash Narayan's Rashtra Seva Dal and rejecting the caste-based rituals followed by her mother. She feels that the tide of progress and women's emancipation in Maharashtra eased her movement into a self-determining adulthood.

But our authors resist interpreting these changes in a simple tradition-into-modernity framework. Jasodhara Bagchi attests to the rationality, efficiency and planning that permeated good housekeeping in her ancestral household, while Vijaya Mehta cites the respect that Maharashtra has historically accorded strong women. Further, Bagchi records how women in her family responded selectively to new opportunities, conscious of resisting Westernising social mores. Hema Sundaram perceives a marked disjuncture between public expressions of liberalism and the continued strength of patriarchy in private family relations. We also see the backlash against liberalising movements in the decision of Bagchi's great grandfather to remove his daughters from school to resist the effects of reforms. The assumption of unilinear progress towards modernisation, as in the model, is more complex in reality.

At the individual level, education is the most significant force enabling our narrators to fashion their own lives. It helped them to perceive new possibilities, find employment, and see themselves differently. Almost all are or have been employed in positions attainable only through education, as professors, writers, researchers, and so on. It is striking that in many narratives, education is the alternative to an oppressive family life. Realising she was smart in school enabled Maithreyi Krishna Raj to overcome psychological neglect and denigration in her childhood. Gaining a college teaching job enabled Hema Sundaram to find support among co-workers and eventually leave an abusive husband. Invitations by universities abroad enabled divorcee Nabaneeta Dev Sen to overcome social censure in Calcutta.

Can these narratives be considered the social history of previous generations? They are not eyewitness accounts of the past, and are clearly mediated by each author's contemporary effort to explain herself. Yet all history is mediated by its teller. I would argue that these narratives contain the stuff of history, materials to be taken along with others, to help construct a portrait of the past.

The narratives' contributions to this portrait are precious. They interpret for us the emotional dimensions of the social structures so well laid out by anthropologists and historians. The various individual reactions to normative structures that shaped lives and consciences can only emerge from materials such as these. It would be even better to have diaries written by each of the women presented, but that would have required a self-awareness and claim of personal space that most would not have made. We can gain important insights from the memories of our present authors, particularly when these memories present us with the richly integrated mixture of character development and plot that many contain.

Priti Desai's description of her grandmother's typical day at home is a full account of women's daily domestic life. It shows women's lives throughout the day, cooking, feeding, organising, washing, all according to the honoured rituals of caste tradition. Krishna Raj's piece describes domestic life from the perspective of an overworked daughter-in-law in an oppressive joint family and then in a separated household living on a meagre salary. And the Mazumdar piece tells much about women's roles in healing. One cannot but be impressed with the significance and burden of marriage and domesticity in the lives of all these women.

High-caste Hindu families, we learn, lived under an unforgiving rule that daughters must be married by puberty. As the puberty clock ticked away, families made greater and greater compromises in the choice of husbands to fulfil this obligation. Thus, we see a number of marriages arranged with completely unsuitable men—old, already married and so on. We also see the role of caste in narrowing the choice of possibilities. Even as progressive a family as that of Vina Mazumdar's insisted on caste status above all.

We learn of the humiliation felt by young girls as they were subjected to inspection by boys' families. Mary Roy of a Syrian Christian family in Kerala vividly recalls her feelings, while Priti Desai complains that the systems of arranging marriages made them feel like defective products on the market. The girls' sense of inferiority was repeated in the subordinate relationship of their families to the in-law families throughout the duration of the marriage. Krishna Raj tells us that her mother's parents were powerless to protect her from her in-laws, one of several authors who show how the economic standing of a bride's natal family affected her treatment by the marital family.

In this strict normative system, it is intriguing to note what people did when the system did not work as it was supposed to. According to the Hindu joint family system, in-laws were supposed to assume full responsibility for the bride upon marriage. Widowhood was common. Most large families had one or more widows needing housing and support, and often young children to be raised. Yet the Sundaram narrative tells of a daughter-in-law thrown out by a father-in-law on the son's death. A young widow might be seen as a 'bad luck' bride who has caused her husband's death. Even her natal family might not want such a bride returned to them, as in the case of Nabaneeta Dev Sen's mother. Women widowed later in life might also be rejected. Leela Gulati's mother was not only abandoned by her in-laws, but also cheated out of property by her own sisters and left to fend for herself and four children. As Krishna Raj observes, 'It is incorrect to assume that it is modern forces that are breaking up families. Families were always fragmented.'

These narratives are littered with failed marriages, not only unhappy ones but many that broke up completely. The Narulla narrative recounts at least three, Mary Roy's mother's is one, Vina Mazumdar's account has two, and there are others. When the failure happened soon after marriage, we see a father receiving the daughter back, perhaps implicitly acknowledging a misjudgement made by his generation. Even later in life, Mary Roy's mother was taken in by her father, though at the cost of a humiliation that Mary Roy has not forgiven.

We also see cases of brothers or sons refusing to support vulnerable women, such as the desertion of their mother by the Narulla brothers after Partition. Similarly, a Gulati widow was left to die in a hospital general ward after devoting her life to raising her stepchildren. With no resources to sustain them and little capacity to do useful work, these women were simply cast off by their families. It happened to sons as well; the Gulati piece narrates the abandonment of her sick father by his family.

We see strong bonds among many, but not all, generations of women. Some of the maternal relationships were so impoverished or poisoned by the treatment they suffered that the mothers had little to give to their daughters. Thus, Priti Desai regrets that her 'mother chose an inner aloofness of cold contempt while always remaining correct'. Mary Roy found her mother unable to nurture, establishing a non-traditional pattern of distance from her children that persisted in Mary's own experience in child-raising, albeit now a more constructive pattern. Saroja Kamakshi simply regrets that her relationship with her mother 'has not worked out'.

Other narratives report very strong bonds between women. Bagchi celebrates how women's singing brought together her maternal line through three generations. Mazumdar fondly recalls the support she received from her mother on many difficult occasions. Even the over-protective mother of Nabaneeta Dev Sen, exhibiting another kind of response to the family system, established a deeply valued if somewhat disabling bond with her daughters. Leela Gulati provides a simple but moving statement of how her mother inspired her, 'She made a success ... of all whose lives she touched.'

At another level, these narratives can be read as material for great fiction. Just as truth is often stranger than fiction, many of the characters presented here are more strongly etched than those created by novelists. Particularly memorable is *Pishima,* the runaway bride in the Mazumdar piece who successfully defied a family that wanted to return her to the in-laws, and went on to become the pivotal manager in the family. She protected her new sister-in-law who arrived into a complex joint family at just 11 years of age and again defied family norms by insisting on the young bride's right to study. Later Pishima led the entire locality as a campaigner for girls' education. We have only a tantalising glimpse of another spirited woman, Kamakshi's aunt, who coped with a conservative joint family by finding within tradition—pilgrimages, visits to holy men, ceremonies of all sorts—opportunities to go out for new experiences.

On the other hand, we have numbers of embittered women portrayed with great poignancy. Narayani in the Sen piece is so unhappy with her status as a woman that she cannot love her granddaughters, and Seetha of the Gulati piece so hated her detested marriage that she tortures the entire family. Both Kamakshi and Desai's mothers adopted the resistance of silence, but paid for it with lethargy or suicidal unhappiness. Krishna Raj's mother quite literally worked herself to death.

On the male side, we have the indulged son for whose education the Narulla family mortgaged major assets, only to be disappointed by his lack of self-discipline and career failure. So, too, is Gulati's brother, who was pampered like royalty and grew up with little confidence in being able take care of himself. There are several wife batterers, most notably the eminent Imperial entomologist of Mary Roy's story who became a demon at home. The image of his newly-grown son confronting him and ending the terrible beatings is memorable. The Narulla narrative portrays a similarly violent father. Their dominance gone, both these men eventually deserted their wives. Others left their wives while remaining at home. Kamakshi portrays her unsuccessful father as so unhappy in his status as a son-in-law living with her mother's family that he moved into one room upstairs and had his food brought up. Mehta provides two portraits of men leaving their wives in mid-life of immerse themselves in religious movements.

The narratives are also full of intrigue. The Gulati piece presents brothers scheming to deprive the eldest one of ancestral land because he fathered only daughters. She also portrays in-laws utilising every opportunity to milk favour out of their relationship with her rich and indulgent grandfather. And Krishna Raj tells of a grandmother selling off baby food that was sent by the mother's family for a newborn.

On the other hand, we also have many incidents of unexpected kindness and generosity. The unknown boatman who brought Mazumdar's fleeing young aunt home to her parents and stayed with her until dawn is a lovely image. The in-laws who took in Dev Sen's teenage widowed mother and allowed her to be as free to go out into society as their son was so as to escape the constraints of high-caste widowhood is another. And there is Bagchi's husband who without complaint moved into his widowed mother-in-law's house to facilitate her care.

It is not surprising that in the present generation several of our authors celebrate non-traditional modes of life. Two of our narratives arise from households exclusively of women—Dev Sen and Kamakshi—while another is written by a woman who, along with all three of her sisters, resolutely remained single, so disillusioned were they by their mother's inability to escape a humiliating marriage.

Several authors have pursued non-traditional public careers. Vijaya Mehta's success in Marathi theatre and Mary Roy's Supreme Court challenge of the Syrian Christian inheritance law that disadvantaged daughters are only the most publicly visible. Vina Mazumdar led the national women's studies movement, to which several of our authors have made important contributions. Leela Gulati became a noted researcher documenting the lives of poor women, calling attention to their double entrapment in unequal marriages and poor labour market conditions.

What do we learn from these narratives of women's lives? Women's vulnerability to the purposes, tempers and fates of their husband and families, both natal and affinal, stands out. This does not mean the women were victims, for most demonstrated great strength of character. But without social and economic capacities to support themselves, which came only in the present generation, even the most determined could only seek to influence the opinion of others.

We see how much women valued their relationships in families. Even into the author's generation the women cite their children as their proudest accomplishment. Oppressed though many were by family relations, they show a deep commitment to human solidarity (Cahill 1994). The memories record, however, the distortion in relations with children and others when women have been denied a personal space of their own. And they record the costs to men of living in patriarchal superiority, deprived of the accountability that mitigates narcissism and anger and produces personal growth. These narratives lament not only lost opportunities and wasted talent, but also the difficulty of sustaining a flourishing personality under the weight of unreasonable obligations and ignorance of human needs.

Finally, we should recognise how these memories helped our authors find strength and self-awareness. I suggest that stories such as they have told, repeated by each generation to its successors, inspired women to survive and create lives for themselves, their families and the women who followed them.

REFERENCE

Cahill, Susan. 1994. *Writing Women's Lives: An Anthology of Autobiographical Narratives by 20th Century American Women Writers*. New York: Harper Collins.

1

The Wind Beneath My Wings*

Nabaneeta Dev Sen

Narayani: 1865–1952

I did not know my grandmother Narayani very well, except that she had no particular interest in me. Whenever I offered a ritual *pranam* to her, as on Bijoya, she offered me a sweet with a blessing, touching my head lightly with the tips of the fingers of her right hand.[1] Did she smile? Was there a caress in her touch? Did she offer me one of her sweet toothless smiles that she reserved for *Dadabhai* (elder brother)? I can't remember. For me she had a grim face, a faraway look. For me she was a ritual. My grandmother was not fond of her granddaughters.

Since I knew so little of Narayani, my *Didima* (maternal grandmother), I looked up my maternal uncle's autobiography to find out more about her. She spent her last days with him, her favourite son, after her husband passed away. *Mamababu* (maternal uncle) writes that he had always been a dedicated son, that there was nothing in the world that he would not have done for his mother. She was given a grand funeral and a magnificent memorial service, and, on top of all that, a free bed was dedicated to her memory at the Cancer Hospital in Calcutta. *Didima* was the daughter of an aristocratic feudal family, the Duttas of Hatkhola, who appear in the history of Calcutta city. The sprawling family mansion in north Calcutta still exists with its stables and garages for carriages, cowsheds and broken palanquins on the ground floor, surrounding the central courtyard which faces

* Originally published in the *Indian Journal of Gender Studies*, Vol. 6, No. 2, 1999, pp. 221–39.

the family temple where the annual family Durga *puja* is held to this day. *Mamababu* had written in great detail about his father, his uncles, his grandfather and his great-grandfather. But not a word more about his beloved mother. Who was she? Where did she come from? Who were her parents? How many brothers and sisters did she have? What was her name? Her dedicated son was not interested in telling us all that. Her name appeared only once, as a caption under a faded photograph, never in the text of the book.

But this nameless person, whose only identity was to have borne a dozen offspring (six of each sex), reigned over *Mamababu*'s household, and kept every breathing creature under firm control. We were terrified of her. She sat cross-legged on the floor in front of the kitchen with an alarm clock, a shiny brass cash box, a basket of vegetables and a chopper, and ran the house. She did not raise her voice but no one could disobey her. Her children used to refer to her as Queen Victoria, a nickname she herself had coined for her deputy magistrate husband, because he was always busy holding court. *Didima*, too, was a dignified presence. Plump and not fair, she wore a white borderless cloth without a blouse, the customary attire for widows who were not supposed to wear stitched clothes. She was dark but pretty when young, and was married at the age of 9. We have a picture of her young days in *Mamababu*'s book.

Narayani was married into another old Calcutta family—there are two streets in Calcutta named after Narayani's father-in-law, Panchanan Ghosh. He was the rebel son of an old *zamindari* (landowning) family from the village Harinabhi, where the water reservoirs, the girls' high school and the community temples founded by him are still functioning. (Incidentally, Radharani, my mother, went to preside over the prize distribution ceremony of the school in 1975, and I did the same 20 years later.)

Narayani lived the life of a civil servant's wife, running a nuclear household in Coochbehar, a native state then, with all her 12 children ably looked after by the elderly widow she had brought with her when she came as a bride from her parental home. This nursemaid, *Khokar Jhi* (child's maid), was referred to warmly in all the childhood stories Narayani's children recounted, in fact far more than Narayani herself did. She had taken the place of a grandmother in the nuclear family set-up.

Narayani's husband Ashutosh Ghosh was an able administrator and an enlightened Hindu. He went to visit the poet Tagore taking along their daughter, the child-widow Radharani, with him because she wrote poetry. He held morning prayers with his children in the Brahmo[2] style, singing Tagore's spiritual songs. He subscribed to a number of literary magazines and encouraged the children to bring out a wall-magazine. Narayani never joined him in his prayers—in fact, she made sarcastic remarks about his weird practices. But he gave Narayani a free hand in tackling family situations: her will was supreme, she was extremely rigid and, unfortunately, rather narrow-minded. She had internalised all the patriarchal Brahminical values and applied them vigorously in her own life and the lives of her children. She was against women's education and widow remarriage, hated girl children in general, doted on boys, and had blind spots and favourites. My strongest memory of *Didima* was also my last.

HOLY WATER

Mamababu was sitting near her head, very gently pouring Ganga *jal* into her parted lips drop by drop.[3] *Didima* was breathing rather noisily. The sound of her breathing reverberated through the house, magnifying the eerie silence that had descended upon it. Yet the house was filled with people, as if there was a wedding in the family—all my uncles, aunts and cousins were there. Only the feeling was different, there was darkness and suspense in the air. It was about 10 o'clock in the morning, and *Didima* had been like this all night. *Mamababu* too. Everyone was waiting for it to happen. I was 14. I had never witnessed a death, and I was curious. *Didima* was not fond of me; in fact, she was not fond of any of her granddaughters with the sole exception of Padma *Didi* (elder sister), the first-born of her first son. *Mamababu* got up to stretch his legs and probably for a cup of tea, relegating his duty to his son by handing the sacred copper spoon to him. *Dadabhai* now settled down in his father's chair and carefully started to pour the Ganga *jal* into *Didima*'s mouth. I was watching. Nobody had asked me to leave. *Didima*'s eyes were closed, her body covered with a blanket, a small *Gita* placed by her head. Her chest was heaving and although her face showed no pain, it seemed a great struggle was going on inside her. *Dada* was also looking at her and his face was tense. Maybe *Dada* loved her. After all, she was very fond of him. On all festive occasions she sent her grandsons new clothes and sweets. But never to me. She made pickles for *Dada* every year, but never for me. It made me sad to think that I did not have one of those storybook grandmas who loved their granddaughters and put them to bed with fairytales. My father had lost his mother before I arrived on the scene and *Didima* was the only grandmother I had, but she did not belong to me. But maybe *Dada* felt for her. After a while *Dada* signalled to me. Poor thing, he was bored with this 'last breath' duty. He had only recently learnt to smoke and badly wanted a puff. So he passed on his duty to me for the moment and stepped out. I sat by her bedside and started to pour drops of water between her parted, shrunken lips very carefully. *Didima*'s eyes were shut, she could not see me; hence, could not refuse my services. I felt sorry for her. Here she was, such a powerful person, whom everyone in the family, male and female, held in awe, lying so helplessly. Mouth half open, eyes closed, chest heaving in a strange irregular rhythm, silently receiving her last holy water from a girl for whom she had no love. And who, in turn, did not love her. As I watched her, fascinated, slowly the struggle ceased. There was a sense of calm, the breathing could be heard no longer. The drops of water trickled down her chin. I knew. I felt a deep sense of guilt for being the only one to witness this moment when the house was full of deserving adults. I stood up, put the spoon down and called out, '*Mama*, *Didima* isn't breathing any more!'

I did not know it then, but I do know now what the greatest irony of Narayani's life must have been. It was the fact that I happened to be the one to offer her her last drops of water, thus endangering her 88 pure years of careful virtuous living. A daughter's daughter, a girl child born out of a widow remarriage. What could be worse? Maybe the remarried widow herself!

GURUDEV'S LETTER

When my marriage broke up, among the myriad reactions in my social circle one was from our family's *Gurudev* (spiritual guide). A decent and affectionate man, a *sanyasi* (ascetic), he wrote a letter to comfort me, stating that it had to happen since I was paying for my mother's sins. It was all Radharani's fault that my husband had deserted me, because when a widow remarries she loses her chastity and the gravity of the sin affects the following generations. What I should do now to put things right was to give up my worldly desires and choose a life of spiritual enlightenment. Although I was passing through a phase of spiritual inclinations, this letter upset me. The accusation against my mother was coming from a person who had shown a great deal of compassion and had not blamed me, unlike my own mother and mother-in-law. But he was blaming another innocent woman for my tragedy. I wrote a 20-page letter to him objecting to his unfair accusation. It became a big issue in the family, and was regarded as an act of rebellion against *Gurudev*. I was amazed to see how many members of the family found nothing wrong in his statement. Strangely enough, my mother herself was not touched by all this. She was neither angered nor saddened, she merely found it amusing. In fact, she tried to find arguments to explain this strange act. She said that since he was fond of Nabaneeta he could not bring himself to blame her, but a reason had to be found, and here was a good enough reason for any Hindu holy man.

For Radharani, the word '*gurudev*' meant the poet laureate of India, Rabindranath Tagore. She needed no religious mentor and neither of my parents was a practising Hindu. In fact, there was an occasion when my mother had a little tiff with *Gurudev*'s disciples. It was in 1966, when my father had a stroke and was in a coma, *Gurudev* came to pay him a visit. A visit from him was regarded as a great blessing. And this was even more so as it was unsolicited. A small group of *sadhus* (ascetics) accompanied him, continuously singing 'Hare Rama Hare Krishna', the holy chant. When *Gurudev* arrived at the door, *Ma* (mother) ran downstairs and urgently requested him to stop the chanting. She was afraid that if father heard it in his subconscious state, he might think he was already dead since it was this chant that accompanied a dead body. This might rob him of his will to live, she felt. *Gurudev* gave her a patient hearing and immediately stopped his *kirtan-wallas* (singers of devotional songs). But he remembered her as an outlandish woman who did not believe in the magical healing power of the holy chant, and who did not hesitate to stop an auspicious ceremony, a ritual service that was being especially dedicated to her husband's recovery. (Incidentally, my father did recover from that coma and lived for five years after that incident.) However, to give the holy man his due, *Gurudev* received my reproach most gracefully, saying that he owed my mother an apology, and soon after paid her an unannounced visit. Mother was happy to receive him, she took it as naturally as she had taken the humiliation. I mention this incident for a number of reasons. It was an example of the kind of humiliation a remarried widow has to face in our society to this day. Even a cultural celebrity like Radharani Devi was no exception. Despite this, Radharani's rational approach to life and her confidence in herself helped her cope. The incident also provided a taste of the kind of complications a divorce used to cause for everyone in the family—even the poor *Gurudev* was not free from it!

RADHARANI: 1903–89

Fifteen days after her marriage, Radharani came back to her parents in Coochbehar, and the young electrical engineer returned to his place of work in the United Provinces (UP). She had to wait to become a mature woman before she could join him. Eight months later, a messenger came to take her to Calcutta, from where she was to travel with her mother-in-law Sushila to UP where her husband had had an attack of the Asiatic flu. Sushila, daughter of a famous surgeon, assisted her father when he went to operate on his patients, was excellent in delivering babies and always available on call. Even the day her youngest son died, she left his body and ran to handle a difficult delivery case, saying, 'But this child and the mother must survive!' A widow with many children, she became legendary for her broad-mindedness and her willingness to help others in distress. Narayani refused to let any of her sons accompany Radharani to UP. What if they, too, caught the deadly fever? Besides, God forbid, if something happened to the son-in-law, the brother would have to bring her back home with him, and she would be a burden for life. But if no one from her parents' family was present then the in-laws would have to take charge of the widow. So, Radharani went to be by her husband's deathbed with her mother-in-law whom she hardly knew. She was 13.

He was already dead when they arrived. Seeing him lying there in his wedding *dhoti-kurta*[4] with sandal paste decorations on his forehead, Radharani felt a pang in her heart. She knew this handsome young man was gone forever and she would never see him again. Radharani felt like weeping. Everyone else was. But Radharani knew it was immodest to weep for your husband in public. Whenever her elder sisters came home from their in-laws, they wept for their husbands in private. You don't express your feelings for your husband in front of other people. Radharani tried very hard to hold back her tears. She fought like a brave soldier. Later, people commented on how astonishingly hard-hearted the young bride was—she did not shed a single tear!

Once back in Calcutta, Sushila announced with rare courage that she was going to arrange a marriage for Radharani. Instead of the harsh widows' diet, she prescribed a normal vegetarian meal for her, and instead of the rough widow's cloth without a border, an ordinary white sari. Moreover, although Radha's *sindur*[5] and the wedding bangles had to be removed, she left some simple jewellery on her and did not allow her hair to be cropped. As soon as the news reached Narayani, she sent a son to fetch her daughter. She could not let this immoral act take place—to allow her own daughter to sit for a marriage a second time. Radharani came back, but not as a financial burden on her father, as her mother had feared. She was earning a handsome amount from her husband's insurance policy. But her presence itself was a strain—an inauspicious presence. Narayani took off all her jewellery, chopped off her thick long locks, enforcing a widow's close crop, made her wear the borderless white cloth, and forced her to wrap a widow's *chador* (long cloth) around herself. From now on she was to eat a proper widow's diet, *havishyanna*,[6] only once a day. Radharani was to eat for the rest of her life what is usually eaten only by those practising austerity during the formal mourning period after a death. And what did Radharani eat on the fasting days, like the *ekadasi*?[7] She ate nothing and she drank nothing. What if she cheated while taking her bath and quietly gulped down a few drops of bath water on a hot summer's day? To stop that, she was always accompanied into the bathroom by an invigilator, like a sister or a maid, who would keep a careful eye on her penance. Narayani was not torturing her daughter. She was merely protecting her from worse tortures in the life to come. Everything Radharani needed, from her clothes to her toothpaste, even the earthen pitcher for her drinking water, she had to pay for from her own allowance. As also for her books and medicines, pens and ink, and notebooks and postage stamps.

Very soon, Radharani realised that she was alone, she was an outsider in her parental home. By reading books, she was told, she had voluntarily courted widowhood. It was no one else's fault but her own that her young husband had to die. She was an inauspicious creature with inauspicious habits. But here she was, still trying to read books and to write in her notebooks. And her father seemed to be encouraging her. Narayani had to put an end to it. She sent Radharani back to her in-laws, confident that with that close-cropped head and those fearful, tearful, lacklustre eyes, no one could get her remarried. Her appearance had changed completely.

When Radharani arrived, a quiet 14-year-old with silent eyes, all bundled up in a widow's *chador* over a borderless white cloth, hair cropped, barefoot and without jewellery, her mother-in-law Sushila ran out of the house refusing to see this cruel sight. Her sons brought her back and comforted her. Looking at Radha's desexed image, they told her, 'Why don't you treat her as your eldest son from today, rather than the eldest daughter-in-law?' So it was to be. Radharani was groomed to occupy the position of the son who was no more. She was put in charge of the household finances and in charge of the education of the schoolgoing children. Though self-educated, she was well read and well informed. With increased responsibilities she became the centre of the family in many ways. Her mother-in-law succeeded in changing her looks once again. She made her grow her hair, put on a gold chain, a pair of bangles and ear studs, forced her to wear at least a black-bordered *dhoti* and sandals. As for her food habits, the *havishyanna* was out, but Radharani stuck to boiled vegetables and milk. She was encouraged to pursue her intellectual and artistic interests, allowed to attend literary and political meetings, the family car at her disposal. Writers, men and women, were welcome to meet Radharani in the house, the drawing room was open to her literary friends. There were relatives who criticised all this, and most of all Narayani, but the family paid no heed.

In the 1920s Radharani's poetry was published in major literary magazines. She was exchanging letters with the top people of the time—not merely writers, but also famous scientists, philosophers and journalists. She gave a speech at the Porabazar Congress Session, and her incisive criticism of Tagore at the Presidency College has been referred to by many. She was building her career as a writer and soon two volumes of poetry were published, illustrated by famous artists of the Bengal school. She edited the first anthology of modern Bengali poetry with the poet Narendra Dev. Her poems were greatly appreciated, but there were strange reviews as well. Radharani's daring articles and short stories were measured unfairly against the backdrop of her personal life by critics who attacked her views.[8] 'Though they are extremely powerful, emotionally and stylistically mature and impressive,' wrote Lilamoy Ray (a *nom de plume* of Annanda Sankar Ray), 'we cannot take them seriously as we know these are all faked emotions, the writer is a child widow in an aristocratic family and the intense erotic tension underlying her poetry is only artificially simulated.' As a matter of fact, what should have been a strong plus point for the artist was for her critic a weakness. The personal life of a woman writer can hardly be kept out of her professional existence—and Radharani suffered for it.

Radharani could not tell her in-laws when she left home to remarry. They had been so incredibly kind and had treated her as a *devi* (goddess). How could she break that image? The next morning's dailies published the sensational news: the poet Radharani Dutta had married the poet Narendra Dev in the presence of Bengal's cultural celebrities. She was supported by Tagore and the novelist Sharatchandra Chatterjee. The papers dubbed them the Browning couple of Bengal.[9] It happened in the monsoons—I do not know which day of the week it was, nor the time of day. I do not know whether it was raining that day. But in my mind I see a dark, rain-splashed night and a slim girl in a stark white sari leaving home to find herself:

> *Unmada pabane* Jamuna *tarajata/ghana ghana garajata meha*
> (In the wild winds, the river Yamuna swells, the clouds roar)

For, when a girl named Radha steps out of her in-laws' place for a rendezvous with her lover, it could only be in a windy monsoon night. I often wonder who had accompanied *Ma* from Bhawanipore in south Calcutta to my father's house in the countryside.

> *Kunjapathey sakhi kaise jawaba/abala kamini re!*
> (My friend, how do I walk down the forest path, I am but a helpless woman!)

Married at 13 and widowed at 13, she had never travelled alone.

Radharani was 28. Narendra Dev was a bachelor and 15 years her senior. The Devs had received their *jagirdari* (land deed) from Nawab Aliwardi Khan, and were among the first students of the Hindu College. For several years their family home in Calcutta had housed the office of the Indian National Congress. The family accepted the son's marriage to a widow without much ado. Her former in-laws were the next to open their doors. Radharani's parents were the last. Her second mother-in-law, Mrinalini, was a shy, quiet and soft-spoken widow from an aristocratic but enlightened Calcutta family. This was the first widow remarriage in the large joint family. Although she was broadminded, in view of the social stigma attached to widow remarriage, Mrinalini decided to leave the family home together with her son and daughter-in-law, and moved to a country house so that the future of the unmarried girls in the joint family would not be affected.

As a famous poet, my father was a cultural celebrity. He was affectionate and friendly with children, and communicated well with young people. Yet he remained distant as a father. A public person, he was very popular for his unassuming nature. He never interfered in my life, never shared my thoughts, never shared his own thoughts with me except twice—and both times it had to do with my mother's health. He encouraged me to write poetry and to study comparative literature. Though he was not happy about my joining a co-ed college, he was proud of me when I won a scholarship to go abroad for higher studies. He happily accepted my choice of husband and our intercaste marriage. He was very fond of his granddaughters, but did not live to see my divorce. He loved books and dogs, and instilled that love in me and my daughters. Narendra was proud of his wife, treated her with the utmost respect, loyalty and love. She was the only one who really mattered to him in the family. I was an extra.

I was born eight years after their marriage, and again the dailies reported it. They also reported that the child was named by Rabindranath Tagore.

What they did not report was the story that lay behind the name. When I was 3 days old, a letter was delivered to our house. The envelope was addressed to Nabaneeta Dev at Bhalo Basa, 12 Hindustan Park, Calcutta. This is still the address at which I live, and the letter said, 'Since you are too young to reject my gift I give you this name which you have inherited from your mother.'[10] When Radharani left home and married Narendra Dev, Rabindranath had given her the name 'Nabaneeta', the newly-taken-in one or the newly-wed one. My mother, a free independent spirit, politely refused this offer, saying that she already had two books under her own name; besides, she liked her name. Radharani was not ready to change her identity. But she was happy to accept it as Tagore's blessing for her newborn. Radharani wrote a poem on her daughter's *anna prasan* (the child's first rice-eating ceremony, when she is also named). It was printed in light green ink on silky art paper and distributed among the guests. The invitation letter to my *anna prasan* read as though written by me, at 9 months, a bright-eyed baby girl doing a *namaste* (greeting with folded hands) in the facing sepia-coloured photograph. Sixty years ago it was a novel idea. Obviously, a great deal of attention was paid to this girl child by her parents. The invitation card was my father's idea, the poem my mother's. The poem is both powerful and beautiful. And it makes me sad every time I read it. It also makes me guilty. Did I deserve such parents?

Unspoilt and tender like freshly opened petals,
Our darling baby girl, forever, smiling, forever matchless,
Sparkling with the purity of a morning-showered flower,
You've stepped into our home and lit it up with joy.

In you lie all our auspicious hopes,
In you is fulfilled the love that conquers pain,
My priceless jewel churned out of life's tears and laughter,
You've opened up in my heart a deathless spring beyond words.

The ideals that I had cherished all through,
The boundless desires and visions that remain
Unfulfilled, and find no meaning in my life,
My auspicious girl, may it all bear fruit in yours.

Flying high the colours of life, unvanquished, Daughter,
May you make your birth meaningful through your hardships,
May the whole world pay its homage some day
To the magnificent moment of your life.

Daughter, dearer than life, at this blessed moment,
Projecting our visions far into the distant future,
Your loving parents' hearts have just one single prayer,
Death-defeating life shines forever in service offered.

That is where we wish to see you, in the hearts of people,
In the seat of imperishable love.
That is where we wish to see you in the wide, wide world.

The hymn that remains unsung deep within our soul,
May it find a clear voice in your life, be a full-bodied tune
Like the lotus in the sun opened out in its full glory.

May you love this world and may the whole world fall in love with you.
May you travel at ease on your life's journey through sufferings
and ecstasies.

May bright lights shine all the way on all your future roads.

Although the poem is signed by both my parents, it was written by my mother. She was 36 then. Radharani became the joint-founder-secretary of Poets, Playwrights, Essayists and Novelists (PEN), 13 West Bengal, along with her husband, and built up an important literary association in Calcutta where writers came not only from other parts of India, but also from abroad. My parents represented the Indian PEN at the Edinburgh PEN Congress in 1950 and I went along with them. The family travelled all over Europe for eight months. We went to visit the British Parliament and heard Winston Churchill. We had also made an appointment with George Bernard Shaw, but he died on the day we were supposed to meet him. So we went to the funeral instead. We visited the homes of famous writers all over Europe and England, and most of the important museums of France, Italy and Holland, saw a war-devastated Germany, experienced the midnight sun in Norway, saw the Pope in the Vatican City (it was the Holy Year), watched the Passionspiele at Oberamergau. Radharani gave her daughter a grand start.

She wanted to live through me, who was less than a year old, and had shown no signs of the expected brilliance. Many times in my life, in the 51 years that we have spent together, she had told me these things in ordinary conversations. These were not my father's words. He was not ambitious, he had always wanted to send me to the neighbourhood school. His wishes for me were safe ones without the element of risk. Mother was the adventurous spirit. I am afraid I have never made any efforts to live up to her expectations. I did not try to protest either. She was too strong for me. She was a fighter. I was a shirker. After losing the guidance of my husband, I once again allowed myself to be guided by my mother for the longest time. And now that she isn't around, I find myself wandering uncertainly without a road map in the world.

She liked to believe that I was too innocent and immature a creature to be able to look after myself, that I would be crushed under the weight of reality without her active protection. Probably I believed that. I depended on her for every decision and had a very poor idea of my own intelligence. Mother told me that I was talented and creative, but clumsy and foolish, lazy and impractical. I believed her. She compared me to my friends and to my younger cousins to show how much superior they were to me. It hurt me, but I could see that she was right. In my teens, when the mirror had suddenly become the most valuable object in my life, mother told me that I was not a good-looking girl, after all, and I should not be standing endlessly in front of the mirror wasting my time. I took her words as gospel truth and formed a very poor image of myself. Only after a classmate fell in love with me and told me that I was the most beautiful girl in the whole universe did I begin to think of myself as less than ugly. In fact, to this day I need only a hand mirror to get ready.

Ma had achieved many small 'firsts' in the family, not only on her own, but also through her daughter and granddaughters. Her daughter happened to be the first woman in both her maternal and paternal families to attend a co-educational college, go abroad for studies, drive a car and get a Ph.D. She was the first to have an inter-caste marriage, get a divorce and bring up children on her own as a single mother. No woman before her had held a paid job, and that too in India and abroad. Mother had given up her literary career soon after my birth and made it her life's work to live through her daughter. She gave the girl all the warmth and honour that a male child receives in society. She offered me all the opportunities she was denied, but no freedom of choice. Being such a possessive and domineering guardian, she rendered me powerless, vulnerable and transparent.

My mother was my best friend and she was also my worst enemy. I am what I am today only because of her, and what I am not, what I could not be, is also because of her. I meekly resisted her overpowering ambition by not being ambitious at all. I followed her dreams, but not with my heart and soul. I applied myself with the minimum effort because I took my career as something that was dear to my mother and did not try to excel. In this way I was resisting *Ma*'s will, denying her what she desired, by not trying for it. Now when I come to think of it all, I feel sorry for both of us. She pushed me too hard. I was too weak to challenge her openly, so I resisted her inwardly, by being foolishly self-destructive. I felt trapped within her dreams. I was smothered by her obsessive love for me. Now I have two exceptionally talented daughters and I hope I do not make similar mistakes with them.

It is rather strange that although Radharani was a social rebel and built her own life by doing what she wanted, not wasting time imagining what others might say about her, she did exactly the opposite when it came to her daughter's life. She was overly sensitive about what others might say about me, and made me value others' views as well. I feel today that all my life I have let my own desires float away from me in order to please others—mother, husband, in-laws, neighbours, colleagues. And now, daughters. Social codes and the public gaze used to be very important for my husband, as it was for my mother. I was not a polished child all through my happily wild childhood, and my mother used to be embarrassed by my words and my acts. And the very same thing happened with my husband. I continued to drop bricks in social conversations well into my 20s and 30s, and neither my mother nor my husband could forgive me for that. (My daughters tell me I still do it and embarrass them, but the world has since adjusted itself to me.)

After my marriage broke up and I returned to my mother, I became totally dependent on her advice for every little thing—practical, emotional, intellectual. She controlled all my activities from within, by being my only source of confidence. I had lost all faith in myself. Nor did my mother show any confidence in me as a dependable adult. She did not disclose her bank accounts to me, for example, even though I was her only heir, was earning enough, and had no abusive addictions like gambling, romancing or drugs. I had a hard time after her death trying to locate her accounts. And this is not a winning combination, either in a marriage or in a profession. Had I been less overpowered by my mother, I would probably have been a different person. Without the strong self-destructive force that makes me leave things to the last minute, lose important papers, forget important appointments, miss deadlines, forfeit offers and ignore opportunities, I would be living a different life today.

At 21, on my way to the United States, I got engaged in England. We informed our parents over the phone. My parents had not met Amartya,[11] but they were happy about it. So were his parents. We were from different castes, but neither set of parents objected as we were probably the most eligible young people of the day. We came from the same cultural and economic background, belonged to the same social circle in Bengal. I already had a book of poems in the market. And both of us had been named by Tagore, if that is any indication of social status. After the engagement party we went off to Wales together for a few days and sent ecstatic postcards to our friends and family. On our return to Cambridge, where Amartya was a Prize Fellow at Trinity, we found a telegram waiting. It was from my mother: 'Do not send postcards. Enjoy yourselves. Blessings. *Ma*.' Only then it struck us that we were not only committing a shameful, sinful act, but also advertising it!

Next summer we came back to Calcutta and got married. Then I returned to my studies at Harvard. Amartya accompanied me with an Assistant Professorship at the MIT. I continued to do a second M.A., a Ph.D. and several years of postdoctoral research while keeping house for Amartya in the USA and in England, at Indiana, Harvard, Berkeley and Newnham College (Cambridge), and Delhi University. Thoroughly supportive of my scholarly endeavours, he took a lot of interest in my research work, believed it to be academically worthwhile and encouraged me to publish it. But he did not encourage me to take up a job as he hopped from one university to another. Unfortunately, he had no interest in my creative life, and did not introduce me to his friends as a poet. He had made a condition before our marriage that there would be either pets in the house or Amartya, not both! He was gregarious, responsible and caring, though too busy to help me out with the household chores or to tackle small children. He was neither dictatorial nor possessive. Completely trusting, he did not try to exercise financial control. He did not interfere in household matters, but never paid a compliment either. He was warm towards my parents until he decided to walk out. A civilised divorce took place after 16 years of marriage. Well, our marriage was good while it lasted. His present wife Emma has excellent relations with both my daughters and with myself.

My Ph.D. degree and my first child came in the same year. I was 25. I rushed back to Calcutta from Cambridge to have my child born on Indian soil. Motherhood was the most magical thing to have happened to me in my entire life. Here is a poem I wrote in Bengali for my daughter, just to give you a taste of my feelings. How marvellous, I thought, that it took only nine months within my womb to make life pass through all those stages of evolution, from fish to man, for which this planet took millions of years.

Antara

Antara, rising from primordial water
As the first sun, forever new, forever old,
You made me the universe.
History and prehistory filed through me.
Hand in hand, in gradual evolution.
Antara, because of you
I have earned the right to enter
The tenfold halls of my foremothers.

Clutching your baby hands in my fist
I have made the future a debtor to me
Antara, in an instant you have filled all time
By your grace I am coeval with the earth today.

When my marriage fell apart I was 34. By then I had lived at 11 addresses with my husband in the United States, England and India, had two lovely children and two heart-rending miscarriages, several degrees and never held a job. I was stupefied at first. I had not realised that it was a bad marriage. I had always taken us to be a happy couple. I thought I had a wonderful husband, and was quite a good wife, mother and hostess, and had gathered some confidence in myself. Though Amartya could not be useful around the house since he was much too busy, he seemed to me to be a loving and caring husband. To my great surprise I was told that he was not in love with me any more. 'Nonsense!' I thought. 'Of course he is!' But he proved me wrong. After several months of looking into shop windows for temporary jobs in London and having driven my small red Japanese car as a private minicab on the London–Heathrow route for two months, I was offered a teaching job in my old university department in Calcutta. I returned with two suitcases and two girls of 8 and 4 to my mother and joined Jadavpur University. My mother-in-law, who is a good friend today, was no friend in those days, and my mother to whom I had come seeking refuge, was hostile. Father was dead, so was my father-in-law. It was hard. People were curious, and they were cruel. Calcutta was brimming with exciting stories about my secret lives, my inadequacies. I had been away a long time. People always blame the woman and sometimes it may be the wrong woman. But, fortunately, I had a few strong friendships among both men and women in Calcutta, which stood me in very good stead.

Mother was terribly upset. It was a social disaster. Divorce was a dirty word. The fault, of course, had to be mine. Mother had a soft corner for Amartya—her first child, a son who died in a week, was born the same year as Amartya. Besides, she now had a world famous son-in-law, a celebrity. Why could I not keep him tied to my apron strings? It was my failure. Being the unworthy creature that I was, I had sent him running into the arms of the other woman: 'Why should he fall for another woman? What were you doing?' (My mother-in-law said, 'Because you had failed to make him happy, so he went elsewhere in search of happiness.') It did not occur to either of the mothers that marriage was a mutual bond, it was also the husband's duty to make his wife happy. Neither of the women thought perhaps that a woman was being wronged here! Ten years later, when Radharani was 80, her views matured with the times. She apologised to me for having blamed me earlier. Incidentally, my mother-in-law, too, has offered her apologies quite recently, at 86, 26 years after the event.[12]

Mother made my life more miserable than it had to be. Thank God I did not agree with her. I knew I was not to blame. A new confidence was slowly sprouting within my heart. I did not feel guilty or ashamed. Mother felt both, and had a nervous breakdown. This was the first time I knew that my mother could be wrong and she could be weak. This was also the first time in my life that I realised that it was possible for Amartya to wrong me and that he was not the strong person I always thought he was. It was a moment of recognition all around, my world was changing shape, and I was struggling hard to adjust to the new realities. It was also a moment of finding out more about myself, the self that no one had told me about before.

I found it amazing that I was being falsely blamed by one who had been a victim herself, falsely blamed for her husband's death in a pan-Asian epidemic. I was beginning to see my mother's faults. There were great scenes in front of the children and the domestic helpers, with mother accusing me and me sobbing uncontrollably in anger and self-pity. When mother was not in a state of temporary insanity (which consisted only of raging against me), she advised me on how to live my life.

She told me to concentrate on my academic career and my children, and to forget about men. Sexual-emotional relationships will always have an element of uncertainty, hence remain out of my control. I might have a second heartbreak, better to be safe than sad, she said. My children's future and mine depended on my own hard work. I should now begin a new chapter as a career woman. She was against my writing in a regional language, 'Write in English,' she insisted. 'Let the whole world read you.' She was not happy with the little bit of regional success that I had. National and international readership was her idea of success. And this was long before the Seths and the Roys, even before the midnight's child.[13] I did not follow her advice. I had a moral and political aversion in those days against Indians writing in English. I continued to write in my mother tongue, and this continued to inhibit my speech, standing over me like my mother.

Mother did not find fault with my way of bringing up children, although it was completely different from her own style. She appreciated me a great deal over this one thing and repeatedly told my daughters, 'If I had a mother like yours I would want nothing else.' With them she had a wonderful relationship, far less domineering, far more sweet, far more equal. They worshipped her, criticised her, loved her and took care of her. Whenever I was busy, Mother told them stories, put them to bed, fed them with her own hands. All the care I did not get from my *Didima*, they received from their *Dimma* (affectionate for grandmother). They had fun together, they joked and sang together. She had a different personality for me.

About 10 years later she came to the conclusion that I was not to blame for the breakdown of my marriage. In her last years she used to apologise to me for having said what she did. As she saw me settling down in my new careers (I had two running parallel, as an academic and as a creative writer), she was less tense about my future and a bit more relaxed. Her obsessive love for her daughter came back as some of her dreams were beginning to come true. I was in the international conference circuit within a year of my return, travelling abroad, presenting research papers, holding executive positions in international academic associations, getting visiting professorships abroad, reading my poetry at festivals and universities, and winning fellowships at artists' colonies. And my position as a creative writer was becoming more stable at home. I had started writing prose and had an adoring readership. I was enjoying the recognition. I wanted it to grow. I worked very hard. The girls needed me. And I had many friends. Life was treating me well and I had no time to feel lonely. Here we were, three generations of single women living under one roof. A widow, a divorcee and two unmarried girls. But the oppressive shadow of Narayani was not over us.

Mother, incidentally, had become bedridden after her nervous breakdown, and never quite recovered from it. She remained an invalid for the rest of her life and had to be attended to by a nursemaid during the day while we were out. It had changed our lifestyle and the basic nature of our household. In the middle of fun and games (yes, we had a lot of laughter in the house, too) there was always a small emergency around the corner. And all three of us were prepared to handle it.

On my mother's 80th birthday, we brought out a collection of her poems. These were written under a pseudonym, Aparajita, and had received a great deal of media attention when they were first published 56 years ago. All three generations appeared in the book, *Ma* as the author, me as the editor, my elder daughter Antara who had just touched 20, as the publisher. And the copyright went to Nandana, the younger one. In 1986 the book was awarded the prestigious state literary prize, the Rabindra Puraskar. When the prize was announced, my mother was an invalid, I was in the USA, representing India at the India Festival, reading my poems and lecturing at various universities. My elder daughter was studying at Smith College in the USA. So it was my little one who went to receive the prize on behalf of her grandmother. Radharani had received many other literary awards such as the prestigious Bhuban Mohini Gold Medal from Calcutta University (which, incidentally, was also received by me 40 years later and which she did not live to see) and the Leela Prize. In 1989 I was holding a visiting professorship (the Maytag Chair of Comparative Literature and Creative Writing) at Colorado College when *Ma* had a stroke. I gave up the job and immediately returned to India. She died after five months.

In her last years, after she was 80, my mother used to tell me that I was her only friend. That the things she could tell me she could not share with anybody else in the world because nobody else would understand her—I was the only one on the same wavelength. I felt both flattered and guilty. I wondered how far she was right. Did I really understand her? Was I her friend? Today, at 60, I feel the same way. What my daughters understand of me, no one else ever will. What I can share with them I cannot with anybody else. The obsessive love my mother had for me, I, too, have for my daughters, for both of them. And in their lives, I know I occupy a very special space. Both are married and with busy careers, but *Ma* remains an important part of their lives. Partly a positive presence and probably partly negative. They are mature, sensitive, honest and intelligent women. And they do not depend on their mother for the decisions of their lives. With lots of creative imagination and empathy for all creatures, they are self-sufficient, confident and outgoing, apart from being charming and beautiful. They are brilliant cooks, too. And they are genuine people. Over time they have also managed to establish a warm and friendly relationship with their father. A name they have a slight problem with—they neither want to hide it nor flaunt it. Their father is gradually getting closer to them as he gets to know them better as grown-up young individuals. My mother saw the beginnings of their careers, but had she been living today she would have recognised a truth, that her prayer has worked, but it has been spread out among the three of us. Her vision for her darling daughter has been partially fulfilled over two generations. There is more to come. Un-confident as ever, I was afraid to ask. I did not have a prayer for my daughters. I just offered them hers. Today the nest is empty, as both my fledgelings have flown away to their workplaces. I miss them every day. But I miss my mother most. I miss her every minute. She was the wind beneath my wings. But I never took off.

NOTES

1. *Pranam* is a gesture of offering respect to one's elders by touching their feet. Bijoya is a Bengali festival celebrated on the last day of Durga *puja*, a festival celebrating the mythical annual visit of the Goddess Durga to her paternal home. It also celebrates the Goddess' victory over the demon Mahishasura.
2. A religious denomination started in 1833 by Raja Rammohan Roy, the 19th-century Bengali social reformer. It emphasised the need to move towards an interpretation of Hindu scriptures according to certain rational principles such as the monotheism of the Upanishads, humanitarianism and the worship of a formless god.
3. The last purifying ritual of pouring holy water from the river Ganga into the mouth of dying person.
4. An ensemble consisting of a long cloth wrapped around the waist and a long, loose shirt, worn by men.
5. Vermillion worn in the parting of the hair by married women as an auspicious symbol.
6. Rice boiled with green bananas and split peas paste with clarified butter.
7. The 11th day of the lunar month, considered auspicious for fasting by widows.
8. Incidentally, it was this attitude of the critics that had led her to perform a most interesting literary experiment. She started writing under a *nom de plume*, in a completely different style and in a different hand, hiding her identity even from the editors. Aparajita Devi's poems created a huge sensation in the Bengali literary world. Here was the genuine feminine voice at last, it was the woman speaking. Here were the voices of the kitchen, of the bedroom, of the girls' hostel, the young bride, the widowed aunt, the rejected wife of the filmstar, the nursemaid, the cook, you name her and she was her. For 12 years Radharani kept her secret. Even Tagore wrote admiring letters to her, but never knew her true identity. Radharani's own poems continued to come out along with Aparajita's. One was serious, an introvert, using the elevated unisex poetic diction of the day; the other an extrovert, light and jovial, speaking in a colloquial female tongue. Then, suddenly, Aparajita disappeared. Radharani has later explained that Aparajita was just a spoof of what men think of women's writing. Women should not talk of elevated matters, but remain housebound even in literature. Then only is it 'genuinely feminine' to the male critics. She only wanted to show that it was not hard to do. It was fun, but not

poetry for her. As a matter of fact, Aparajita had become far more popular than Radharani. She was completely original and without a parallel. But Radharani did not allow her to live.

9. A reference to Robert and Elizabeth Barrett Browning, the poet-couple of 18th-century England.
10. I still live in the same house. Both my parents breathed their last in this house, in the room with the green floor, the room where I was born. Narendra Dev had named it 'Bhalo Basha', meaning love. It also means a good nest. It surely has been both. To me, my mother and my daughters. I grew up as an only child in a pleasant, unconventional home, frequented by creative artists and intellectuals, and inhabited by a variety of animals—rabbits and goldfish, birds and squirrels, kittens and puppies. Father took care of the dogs, Mother took care of me, and I took care of the rest. My daughters Antara and Nandana had been to school in the United States, England and Delhi before settling down in Calcutta. Both won scholarships and went abroad for higher studies like their mother. Antara to Smith College and Nandana to Harvard University. Both are seriously involved with their work as successful career women. Both married their lovers with whom they lived for a while before tying the knot (surely a first in the family!). Antara married outside her caste, and her husband is a few months younger than her. Nandana married a foreigner. In their father's family and in their mother's, Antara is the first girl to work as a private detective, an advertisement copywriter and as a journalist; and Nandana is the first to become an editor in a publishing house abroad, a filmmaker, a scriptwriter and a film actress. The 'broken home' syndrome, however, is not very visible in Radharani's granddaughters. Both are achievers, and seem to be quite relaxed and self-confident, balanced and helpful, with lots of friends and a charming sense of humour. Both use Dev Sen as their surname. The girls grew up in the very same house, also with a load of stray animals, and frequent visits from creative artists and intellectuals, but it was a different home. Mine was a copybook nuclear family with father, mother and child, but Antara and Nandana grew up in an all-female household with three generations of women, where an invalid grandmother and a single working mother were bringing up two girl children. The grandmother was a celebrated poet and the mother, too, happened to be one. Both had a public face and kept appearing on the media. They even had a famous grandfather, also a poet, whose centenary was publicly celebrated for over a year. Their absentee parent was an international celebrity, who kept making news every now and then all around the Western world. (Incidentally, they also have a gorgeous half-sister and a charming half-brother across the ocean, and all four of them are blessed with a genuinely affectionate stepmother—a living disgrace to the age-old image of stepmothers!) I often wonder if, in spite of all the love and attention, it has been hard for my daughters to have a properly private family life. Too many celebrities in the family perhaps.
11. A renowned economist, Amartya won the 1998 Nobel Prize for Economics.
12. My mother-in-law Amita, who is 10 years younger than Radharani, had a formal education at Santiniketan, the university established by Rabindranath

Tagore up to the level of intermediate (arts). Daughter of the renowned scholar K.M. Sen, one of those great personalities who helped Tagore build his institutions, she was a dancer in her youth. She lived happily as Mrs. A.T. Sen for 40 years, but her personality developed amazingly after she was widowed, when she came into her own. To pass her time, she wrote a couple of memoirs of her student days in Saṇtiniketan, started republishing a prestigious women's magazine of older days, and managed to carve out a definite social space for herself after she was 60. It is also amazing to watch the way she has been adjusting herself to her son's changing lifestyle. Her relationship with me has been ambivalent due to her negative role in the breakdown of our marriage, but I admire her strength, her courage, her abilities and her love of life. Incidentally, she, too, like my mother, has always praised me to my children for my role as a mother, and holds me responsible for their success in life.

13. A reference to Vikram Seth (*A Suitable Boy*), Arundhati Roy (*The God of Small Things*) and Salman Rushdie (*Midnight's Children*), important writers of Indo-Anglian fiction.

2

A Heritage of Heresy within Tradition*

Vina Mazumdar

Introduction

My first two stories are set in East Bengal (now Bangladesh). The family and the community from which I come are the Vaidyas of Bengal.[1] The practice of ayurveda died out in the Majumdar family several generations ago. That itself is a story—passed on to our generation—but I doubt if the memory will persist beyond ours. The last of the trained ayurvedic scholar physicians in our family was known as *Kaviraj* (physician) Majumdar. According to the family's oral tradition, this last *Kaviraj* was so engrossed in his books that repeated messages from inside the house that his ailing son's condition was worsening could not break his concentration. The son died. After that *Kaviraj* Majumdar burnt all the books that he possessed—he had quite a collection of manuscripts—and expressed a *shāp* (curse) that if any other members of this family took to the study of Sanskrit, they would become *nirvamsha* (without a male progeny) like himself.

All this happened at least two centuries ago, but may explain why our more recent ancestors did remain without formal education in the caste occupation; they could not take to the study of Sanskrit because of this curse. The first person to break this taboo was my uncle—the historian Ramesh Chandra Majumdar in the 20th century,

* Originally published in the *Indian Journal of Gender Studies*, Vol. 6, No. 2, 1999, pp. 291–309.

because he was determined to read Indian history. RCM and his two brothers were also the first to pursue higher education in the modern English system. They restored the family's reputation for scholarship and pulled the next generation out of the mire of a declining family economy by ensuring its access to formal education.

Whatever property the Majumdar family might have possessed in the distant past had all disappeared by the time my father's generation appeared on the scene. Theirs was a generation of about 15 men and six women (cousins) in a joint family. The six women, my aunts, of course received no formal education. But out of the 15 men only the three youngest ones turned out to be good students. If they had not earned scholarships from primary school onwards, they never would have been able to study further. Education took them out of the village home after primary school. The scholarship examinations at the end of each stage supported very few students. For that generation, for three successive brothers to win these scholarships, go to secondary schools in the subdivisional and district headquarters, and from there to college and university at Calcutta, was a sensational achievement. Each of them used the scholarships to pay for his own maintenance (once they left the village home), buy the required books and still manage to send some money home. That is the background of which I am very proud. It was repeated to us by my mother (Labanya Majumdar) and aunt (Pramada Majumdar—father's youngest sister whom we called *Pishimā*) that the background in which we had to take pride was not one of wealth, but of learning and hard work. My mother used to repeat frequently that she would never want to marry her daughters into either a propertied family (she had a horror of property) or an old *bonedi* (traditional land-owning elite) one, 'because they did not know how to treat their women'.

This introduction is based on the memories of members of the family that I have known personally and what I learned from them. *Kaviraj* Majumdar's story became significant to me because he stood for a lost heritage of learning/scholarship that my father and uncles revived. At least, *Pishimā* and *Mā* (mother) thought so. But the family carried other legacies, too, through some unusual, if not extraordinary, women. Interestingly enough, pride in that legacy reached us not through my usual channel of *Pishimā* and *Mā*, but through my uncle and my grandfather, both men who were otherwise patriarchal in their attitudes. I begin my narrative with one particular ancestor set in the context of the 1830s. I never learned her name, but she was my great-great-grandmother. Not a Majumdar by birth, but through marriage, she too became a source of family pride and reputation, at least for some of us.

I

In 1829, the Government of India banned *sati* by legislation.[2] Two years after that my grandfather's grandfather died at the ripe old age of 105, and his wife (who was in her 90s or 80s perhaps) decided to become a *sati*—a genuine case of a voluntary *sati*. All her sons tried to dissuade her, quoting the law. There was no question of any property being involved since there was too little of it. The sons were more afraid of the repercussions on the family. But she would not listen. People came from five villages nearby to witness the event, and of course all the married women came to receive her *sindur*.[3] The old lady noticed that there was one daughter-in-law missing—my father's grandmother, at that time a young woman in her 20s. From the few accounts I have received from various members of the family, she was called quite a *dojjal* (untranslatable, but comes close to a shrew and a toughie by all accounts). When the old lady who was about to become a *sati* called for her, the missing *bou* (daughter-in-law), we were told, came out with a broom in her hand. She stood before the crowd from five villages, men and women, and told her mother-in-law, 'I don't need your *sindur*. You are busy buying your ticket to heaven. But tomorrow if the police come and put handcuffs on your sons, will you be here to defend them?'[4]

The defiant *bou* was not inventing new values, only reminding her mother-in-law that the woman's role is to protect and hold the family together. She was thus accusing her mother-in-law of having become selfish, placing priority on her own 'ticket to heaven', ignoring possible dangers to the family. The public nature of her protest made me question the reality of the subjugated, *purdanashin* (secluded) higher-caste women of Bengal, whose condition had inspired the social reform movement of the 19th century.

The other half of the story is the way it was handed down in the family. When I heard it from my widowed aunts (some members of that generation of six) and from my widowed second grandmother (my grandfather's second wife—I did not know till I was quite grown up that she was not my real grandmother), they used to speak of it in whispers, and add: 'You know, there were six *bous* in that generation. She was the only one who became a *bidhavā* [widow].' All the others died *sadhavās* (wives who predeceased their husbands). Being victims, they felt it their duty to transmit the horror of widowhood. But the way the same story was told by my grandfather (the rebel's son) and the historian uncle (her grandson) conveyed enormous pride.

I never attached particular importance to this bit of family history, though a lot of it used to be narrated whenever my uncle, the historian—a marvellous storyteller—was in Calcutta during his vacations. Another of his favourite stories was about his own mother, who did come from a wealthy family. She was a descendant of Raja Raj Ballabh Rai.[5] One of that family's last palaces (Ekush Ratan) collapsed into the Padma river in Bangladesh the year my uncle was born. Raj Ballabh's descendant and the Majumdars' grandfather in fact ended his life as a pensioner of my father Satish Chandra Majumdar (SCM). RCM, while narrating the story of the legendary bags of gold coins picked up by a boatman on that fateful night when Ekush Ratan went into the river, used to say, 'Thank heavens! If it had survived, we would be squabbling over the remains instead of getting on with our lives.' This contempt for inherited property was implanted in us from childhood. Instead, there was perhaps a lot of family arrogance—of having pulled the family up through education and through certain other nebulous values—which took me a long time to figure out.

The story of the rebel *bou* resurfaced after decades in my mind when Kate Stimpson, then editor of *Signs*, gave me a paper written by an American graduate student on *sati* which she was going to publish in the journal (Mazumdar 1978; Stein 1978). Kate asked me to read it and write a comment right away. So I spent one hour reading the paper and then sat down, with no idea in my head of what to write. Out came this story straight from my memory, saying there is no way one can defend something which is indefensible, and here is my family legacy that says it is indefensible.

Thinking over this difference in perception and linking it up with later statements by others in the family, I realised that the men were taking pride not in the lady who became a *sati*, but the rebel who could stand up before a crowd of five villages and register her protest against this religiously sanctified action because at that point it had become illegal.

II

The next story is about *Pishimā*, SCM and RCM's sister, mentioned earlier as one of my major sources of family history and tradition, and influence. My father's youngest sister, she was one of the six girls in that generation. The Majumdars were *kulins*, who claimed a special elite status within the caste group.[6] *Kulin* girls had to be married only to a *kulin* boy. This being considered an honour, even for the groom's family, the question of dowry would not arise. It was, however, permissible to marry a *kulin* boy to a non-*kulin* girl in exchange for a dowry. It was only the *kaulinya* (*kulin* status) that had brought my grandmother—daughter of an old wealthy family—to face a marked change in the standard of living which possibly shortened her life.

On the other hand, for the daughters of the family—my aunts—the family's *kulin* pride restricted the choice of grooms; severe but great pride was taken in the fact that Majumdar girls were married only with a pair of cotton saris, a pair of conch shell bangles and a pot of vermilion. In fact, the family could not have afforded anything else. But pride in their elite social status—inherited, but not earned—provided a convenient cover for the disposing of six daughters very casually, with no enquiries about the qualities or characters of the grooms. The only considerations were the *kulin* status of the grooms' families and their readiness to accept an alliance with the Majumdars, whose poverty was no secret.

The net result of such marriages arranged according to caste status, with little thought to the character of the grooms, was a very sore point with my father, uncles and all members of our generation, irrespective of gender who had the misfortune to interact with these uncles-in-law. The common perception was that they were 'specimens' (i.e., types to be avoided for the next generation of Majumdar daughters). One was a drunkard, the other an opium addict and the third a wife-beater (he also had venereal disease), and one kept losing jobs because of embezzling. I never learnt anything much about the man who married *Pishimā* because she never told anyone in the family. If anyone knew, they did not talk about it.

Pishimā or Pramada Majumdar was born in the mid-1880s. She was married at the age of 14 and sent off to her husband's village. Soon thereafter (I think the year was 1902), she left her husband's home one night. Wrapped in a shawl, she walked to the river, got into a boat with an old Muslim boatman, gave him her only bit of jewellery, a bangle, and said, 'Will you row me to the village of Khandarpara?' She was returning home. The old man rowed her through the night and reached the Majumdar family home just before the crack of dawn, where she fell asleep on the verandah. The doors were all closed and the village was dark. This old boatman sat at her head. This is one part of the story that I have found the most moving because it tells me so much about existing community relations in East Bengal at that time. When my grandfather opened the door at dawn he found his daughter asleep on the floor and the old man sitting by her. He told my grandfather: '*Babu* [sir], she is a very unhappy girl. If she had not been very unhappy she could never have taken this kind of a step. You promise me that you will not send her away and you will not scold her or beat her. And please take back this bangle that she had given me.' He got the promise from my grandfather. In reply to my grandfather's efforts to pay him, he said, 'It is enough of a reward that I have managed to reach her safely to you and you have assured me that you will not throw her out. No money is needed,' and went away.

The rest of the family, of course, was not like my grandfather. The uncles and aunts all shouted at Pramada. There were threats of tying her up and sending her back. She had lost her mother when she was only 6 years old and the aunts had prevented her from becoming close to her stepmother. The oldest aunt who loved my father and the baby, Romesh, like her own sons, unfortunately had no love to spare for the female child. I suppose my grandfather and her brothers, very conscious of all this, tried to compensate for this lack.

How did Pramada cope with the family's reaction? The answer was very simple: she told my sister, 'I took a sheet and covered myself from head to foot. Fourteen days I stayed like that. By that time they [the uncles and aunts] gave up.' She had also told them, 'You may be able to send my dead body back but you will not send me.' She never told a soul what had driven her to this step. Family accounts of later events indicate that her husband was quite fond of her. He kept coming back and tried to persuade her to return. She refused to see him. *Pishimā* got away with this defiance, just as her grandmother had got away with hers, decades earlier.

Pishimā died when I was just 5 years old. But I do have vivid memories, not only of what she looked like, but of her tremendous sense of humour, her way of quietly managing the family without making my mother feel even once that she had taken on her job. My mother always said, that *Thakurjhi* (husband's sister) was her second mother. 'Whatever I know of family management, I have learnt from her,' she used to say. *Pishimā* was *Mā*'s guide, philosopher and friend. Above all, she guarded *Mā* fiercely from any criticism by other members of the family. *Mā* was only 11 years old when she came to the Majumdar family as a young bride, straight from the jungles of Burma where she had spent her childhood.[7] She had no formal education and no experience of living in a vast joint family of conservatives. We heard from *Mā* that *Pishimā* used to describe the Majumdar family (with the exception of her own father and brothers) as a zoo with 'many wild animals'. 'I shall teach you who to talk to and how you should talk to them,' she used to say, adding, 'The less you speak, the better.'

Pishimā found that *Mā* was desperate to study. Tutored by her parents, she had become literate and had learned a bit of mathematics, but had no formal schooling. Living in the jungles of Burma the question did not arise. Though her father had no objections to women studying—he educated his two youngest daughters right up to the university level—my mother, the eldest, never had that chance. *Pishimā* got hold of RCM—a college student at the time, to teach both his newly-married 8-year-old wife and his sister-in-law. The former dropped out of her own choice, but *Mā* continued her lessons.

There was a huge row in the family. The aunts and uncles were furious. RCM, though a *devar* (husband's younger brother), was practically like her *bhāshur* (husband's older brother). How can this *bou* be taught by him? Bengali convention permitted a *bou* to have a lot of freedom in talking to her *devar*, whereas it was strictly taboo to talk to the elder brothers of the husband. But for a young bride to become the pupil of a *devar*, seven years her senior, was regarded as intolerable conduct. It is still a mystery to me how *Pishimā* defied all these objections and made it possible for *Mā* to study. What was the source of her courage and conviction that if she showed toughness and determination, the family, however furious, would have to accept? It was only five or six years since she had shocked them by leaving her husband. What gave her the sense of confidence and authority to take charge of my mother, only a few years her junior? In response to the family's reaction when she left her husband, *Pishimā* had said, 'I know you are worried about who will provide me with *bhat* [food] and *kapor* [clothes]. I believe that my brothers will take care of those needs. If my fate prevents that, then I assure you, I will find a way myself.'

At that time only the eldest brother had concluded his studies and was trying for a job. By the time *Mā* appeared on the scene, my father's scholarship and forthcoming specialised studies abroad must have appeared like a pot of gold at the end of a rainbow. Women's education was a hotly debated issue and RCM, having enrolled himself for formal training in Sanskrit, had just discontinued attending his classes after finding out that the Sanskrit teacher beat his wife. He informed his eldest brother and, I am sure, his sister that he *could not* and *would not* accept a wife-beater as his teacher, but preferred to learn Sanskrit on his own.

Ensuring an opportunity for *Mā* to be taught by someone who valued education, along with such strong views against the oppression of women, was only the beginning of a new struggle. As *Mā* expanded her reading ability and was fed with books by her young teacher, the relationship between *Pishimā* and *Mā* became still closer. *Mā* provided *Pishimā* with a window to the outside world. She read out not only whole books but also acquainted *Pishimā* with the ongoing debates on women's education. Very soon *Pishimā* began her own campaign to ensure that every girl in the Majumdar family received formal education. She would get them admitted to a school despite resistance within the family, including from my *Jethamashay* (father's eldest brother), whose daughters became her first concern.

In 1910 my father was back in India and was posted to the Madras Presidency, working on various irrigation and river protection projects.[8] *Mā* was sent to join him after another year, and it became a regular programme for *Pishimā* to go and stay with them for some months in the year. During her absence, *Jethamashay* would remove his daughters from school. The cousins by that time were all faithful disciples of *Pishimā* and *Mā* in this matter, and would promptly inform them of the interruption in their studies. On several occasions, I have heard, *Pishimā* would return and get them readmitted. As a result, the education of the older cousins was sadly erratic, making some of them reluctant to go back after a break to study with younger girls. It was only the younger cousins, along with my sister, myself and RCM's three daughters who were to receive uninterrupted schooling. By the 1920s, when my father returned to Bengal, *Pishimā* had already acquired a reputation in the neighbourhood as an ardent supporter of girls' education. When a new school for girls was established in the area by a group of social progressives, the founders—all men—came to our house seeking her support in persuading local families to send their daughters to the school.[9]

It has always been a mystery to me that *Pishimā*'s socially unexplainable status vis-à-vis her marriage posed no handicap to her growing influence on other middle-class families in the neighbourhood. Everyone knew that she was not a widow because she did not dress like one, nor was she a spinster. I don't know what kind of gossip went on behind doors. The fact remains that one by one all the neighbours with daughters of schoolgoing age agreed to send them to the new school, as *Pishimā* undertook to escort them to and fro every day. The cousins used to go into fits of laughter describing the daily scene—*Pishimā*, with a wet towel on her head, collecting sometimes 20, sometimes more, girls from various households and walking them to the school in the morning, and returning them home after school ended at 4 o'clock in the afternoon. The other mystery to which I never found any answer (because by the time I started thinking of these questions nobody was around to answer them)[10] was how she managed to browbeat her eldest brother—10 years her senior—every time on this issue. *Boromā*, his wife and the mother of the cousins for whose right to education *Pishimā* had fought vociferously, did not share her views either, in spite of her deep personal attachment to *Pishimā*. Since *Pishimā* died when I was only 5 years old, I have had to infer the power of her personality mostly by using my historical imagination and the stories that I heard from *Mā*, my sister and my cousins. Even the lessons and the messages that she passed on to my sister and cousins I have had to learn through their stories. In some cases I have found their echoes in statements made by my mother when I was slightly older.

Some of *Pishimā*'s views, which she articulated forcefully, provoked great amusement among the younger generation, but were apt to embarrass the elders in the family. For instance, 'I find it difficult to stand fools, and I don't like *badmash*es [crooks], but the combination—a *boka* [foolish] *badmash*—is beyond my capacity to tolerate.'

There were many relatives who qualified for this epithet. Whenever they arrived, *Pishimā* used to walk out of the room. Protests from her sisters-in-law and occasionally her brothers were met by flat statements like, 'To hell with them. I don't need to have anything to do with them.' According to her, our large circle of relatives also included many sharks from whom it was necessary to protect *Baba* (father) who was too much of an innocent. My sister and I had standing orders that if we saw anyone in that negative list approaching *Baba*, we had to call *Pishimā* immediately. Many of them were several years her senior, but she had no respect for seniority per se. She would come in just as some wildcat business proposition was being placed before *Baba* to finance and make a cutting remark like 'so and so's brain is circular, like a *jilebi*'.[11] *Baba* would be terribly embarrassed and try to rebuke her, but such statements generally served their purpose in choking off unjustified propositions.

Pishimā was fully supportive of *Baba* helping over a dozen distant relatives to educate their children, often offering the young students a home when necessary. It was she who taught my mother how to assist the widowed aunts living in the village by sending before Durga *puja*[12] the annual stock of clothes that they needed for themselves and their children. The most important of her lessons/messages for all the girls in our generation, which none of us has forgotten, can best be put in her own words: 'I have been fortunate in my brothers. I had the confidence that if I left my husband I would not have to worry about my future. My brothers would take care of me. You may not all be so fortunate. Every girl in this family will get herself trained so that, if necessary, you can stand on your own feet. But no daughter of this family will tolerate humiliation.' She dinned this into the heads of my older cousins and my sister, who passed it on to me. I don't think I even understood at the time what humiliation meant. I had never seen anyone humiliated in our family. But obviously *Pishimā* had often suffered it.

Pishimā died in 1932, about a week before three of my cousins were due to appear for their matriculation examination.[13] Everyone was shattered, but when the girls heard that their father proposed that they should drop the examination in view of the tragedy, all of them decided to appear, crying, '*Pishimā* will never forgive us otherwise.' Two of them went on to college afterwards, when a women's college started functioning in the neighbourhood. This time the initiative was through pressure mounted on *Boromā* by my mother.

Our parents were much more careful in finding grooms for their daughters. Except for two of us in our generation of 10, all the girls had arranged marriages, following all the familial customs and rituals. My father and his brother RCM, however, insisted that after the experience of the six sisters in their generation, they would look primarily for decent boys from decent families, with, of course, an emphasis on educational background. *Jethamashay*, relatively more conservative, still wanted to insist on *kulin* status and follow all the social taboos about not having marriage alliances with families from particular regions and districts. The insistence on sub-caste, language, religion as well as the other taboos reduced options severely for a community that was itself pretty small. As a result, some of my older cousins remained unmarried till their late 20s. The eldest of *Jethamashay*'s unmarried daughters, *Mejdi* (second-eldest sister), was not good-looking. She had to repeatedly face the terrible custom of *meye dekha*[14] before any negotiations could be finalised. The next sister, who was far better looking and had also had more formal education, got married earlier.

My mother forced my father to take a stand against the insistence on all these taboos because she was fiercely angry at the humiliation that *Mejdi* had had to face from repeated rejections. Having found a groom who my father felt was a decent and responsible young man, he advised *Jethamashay* to bury the fuss about *kulin* status and taboos against particular districts. Though *Jethamashay* agreed reluctantly, the remaining unmarried daughters were protected from this kind of humiliation. All of us knew that we had *Pishimā* and *Mā* to thank for this.

III

Many of my memories of *Mā*, going back to my early childhood, are mixed up with the stories of *Pishimā* that I have recorded. As I wrote earlier, the relationship between these two was so close that many of the things that I observed in *Mā* have much of *Pishimā* in them. Thus, I can't always be certain whether memories of my aunt are entirely my own or those seen through my mother's eyes. *Pishimā* died within a year of *Mā* losing her own mother. I cannot remember my grandmother's death, but my memory of seeing *Mā* grieving is during the last few days of *Pishimā*'s life when *Mā* was nursing her. Whenever she came out of *Pishimā*'s room I used to see her crying in her very quiet way. She hated making scenes or a public display of her grief; but I do remember a statement of hers soon after *Pishimā*'s death very vividly: 'She was really like my second mother. I learned much more from her than my own mother ever had the chance to teach me.' I also overheard *Pishimā* telling *Mā* (during those last few days of *Pishimā*'s life), 'I never experienced what mother's love was like. You are the only one from whom I have received that kind of love. I always hated to be dependent on others for my needs, but taking your nursing through this last phase of my life never made me uncomfortable.' Perhaps *Pishimā* did not realise that I was standing in a corner of the room.

Mā's own memories of her childhood were very vague, possibly because from the age of 4 until her marriage at the age of 11, she lived with her parents in the jungles of Burma. One memory of what she experienced when some of my father's cousins came to inspect her while the marriage was under negotiation contributed heavily to her fierce opposition to the whole practice of *meye dekha* in her adult life. Until *Mā*'s marriage in 1907, no woman in the Majumdar household had received any education, but because *Dadamashay* (*Mā*'s father) had informed the family that his daughter had been educated by her mother and himself, *Baba*'s cousins decided to test her; one of them asked her to translate a verse from a very famous epic poem in Bengali into English.[15] Another wanted her to explain Pythagoras' theorem. *Mā* never forgot this experience because she found it humiliating.

The marriage, however, was greatly welcomed by my grandfather (*Baba*'s father). Till the end of his life in 1935, of his three daughters-in-law, he remained extremely partial to my mother. One reason was that she was a *kulin*. The other two had come from wealthy *zamindar* (landed) families with big dowries. My mother had very little, either as jewellery or in the shape of other goods. I suspect that the affection that developed between *Pishimā* and *Mā* had a lot to do with influencing my grandfather's opinion of her, apart from the fact that my father was undoubtedly my grandfather's greatest favourite.

On the only occasion that *Mā* was taken to the village home at her own request, my grandfather went out of his way to provide some extra special comforts so that she could have her bath in privacy.[16] Due to *purdah* (seclusion), she did not speak to my grandfather or *Jethamashay* except through us or *Pishimā* or my father, but she always had a soft corner for the grand old man for his undoubted affection for her and her husband. He was also very kind to her younger brothers and sisters who came to Calcutta for studies when they were still minors and my father acted as their local guardian.

Unlike the Majumdars, *Dadamashay* was considered very much of a *sahib* (Anglicised), and living in Burma gave him the opportunity to discard many restrictive conventions. Serving as an officer of the Public Works Department entitled him to certain modern comforts and amenities even in the jungles of Burma. Why then did he choose a family like ours, which was both poor and extremely conservative for his first child? As far as his own family back in the village, or *Didima*'s (*Mā*'s mother) family were concerned, the *kulin* status was certainly a major consideration. But for *Dadamashay*, his choice of my father, even though he was a widower (his first wife had died within a year of the marriage), was undoubtedly because of *Baba*'s academic record and predictions made about him by Ashutosh Mukherjee, the great builder of Calcutta University who awarded *Baba* a state scholarship to go abroad for further studies. Baba left soon after the marriage and was away for the next three years.

Mā used to tell us that *Dadamashay* brushed aside her mother's anxiety about the poverty of the Majumdars and the difference in lifestyle by saying, 'Never mind. I am looking to the future.' In later years *Mā*'s parents always considered their eldest daughter to have been extraordinarily lucky in having such a 'champion and protector' in *Pishimā*, on whom they depended very heavily when the time came to persuade the Majumdar family to send my mother to join my father in south India. *Mā* always used to look back at the nine years she spent in the south, at various places, with great nostalgia. She managed to learn enough Tamil, Telugu and Kannada to communicate with her neighbours and servants in the places that she lived, and welcomed the opportunities and the freedom that she enjoyed in learning other new things. Since most of my father's income had to be sent to Bengal for the maintenance of the family there, *Mā* had to learn to manage her establishment on a very tight budget. *Pishimā*'s training came in very handy for that. Her only extravagance was buying books. *Baba* had told her that if she managed to save anything from her housekeeping allowance, she could spend it on herself. This enabled her to slowly develop a library of her own.

When my brother was born, *Mā* was only 17 and pretty ignorant about dealing with a baby's minor ailments. But there was an elderly doctor, a neighbour, who taught her many things. Having found an eager pupil, he brought her his own medical books to read. As a result, *Mā* learnt not only basic anatomy and physiology, but became quite an expert in nutrition, childcare and nursing. Till the end of her life, she was the authority in the family for looking after and nursing anyone who fell sick. Every time my cousins or the young wives of our male cousins had a baby, or anyone had an accident, it was my mother who was in demand, rather than their own mother or mother-in-law. *Boromā*, in particular, was very nervous on such occasions and quite content to leave everything in *Mā*'s charge. Compared to *Boromā* or

Pishimā, *Mā* was never an expert at orthodox, fancy cooking, but developed a special expertise in food for growing babies, and sick and convalescent people. I used to enjoy being ill because *Mā* would prepare special light but tasty dishes. She had also learned a few Western dishes from the Tamil Christian cook who worked for her all through her years in the south. My brothers would persuade her now and then to make these on special occasions. Our family doctor developed such a respect for her knowledge of sick people's diets that he used to consult her regarding his other patients and their food restrictions.

In matters relating to health, *Mā* developed a wide catholicity, showing equal respect for traditional ayurvedic treatment, homoeopathy (which she studied on her own) and home remedies developed by women through generations, as long as her experiments were successful and her commonsense found them of value. Her only aversion was to the administration of hard drugs to children. Instead, she preferred developing their natural resistance to various infections and minor ailments. Though her command over theory was not very strong, careful observation of symptoms and extensive reading in homoeopathy enabled her to pull off some miraculous cures, especially of children whose illness allopaths sometimes could not diagnose or for which their science had still not found any treatment. This deep interest and concern for health-related matters and her unstinting nursing expertise eventually won her the respect and admiration of *Jethamashay*, who was otherwise not in agreement with her on many social issues. He, too, had read widely in homoeopathy, was aware of certain preventive, if not curative, ayurvedic remedies and diet control, and came to appreciate *Mā*'s determined application of such treatment in preference to allopathy. Where *Mā* was in doubt, she would seek his advice (via *Boromā*), and *Jethamashay* would read up before giving an answer.

In contrast to *Mā*'s interest and expanding knowledge in such matters was *Baba*'s complete ignorance and dependence on *Mā* on all these issues. His interest in science did not extend to territories outside his own area of specialisation—hydrology and the management of rivers, which he called India's lifelines. He was quite content to leave such matters to *Mā* and *Jethamashay*, and to *Pishimā* as long as she was around. He was healthy, thanks to his abstemious habits (the exception being smoking), a regulated lifestyle and brisk walks, of at least 14 to 15 miles a day, which he used to describe as his recreation. Because he had no experience of feeling ill, he used to get extremely concerned when anyone of us fell ill or even developed a severe headache. When *Mā* fell seriously ill in 1940 and allopaths advised an immediate operation (*Mā* was insisting on homoeopathy), *Baba* felt so helpless that he left the decision to my sister and brother, the only occasion when we saw him unable to take a decision. The specially indulgent attitude towards *Baba*'s reputed 'innocence' or lack of worldly wisdom promoted by his father, sister and brothers was passed on to *Mā* and many members of our generation.

Once *Pishimā* was gone, *Mā* became the confidante of the entire younger generation—daughters as well as sons. She was the one who gradually broke some of the oppressive restrictions against their occasionally going to see a play or a movie. She was the one who took a firm stand against both giving and taking dowry, which even *Jethamashay* was forced to accept. During her years in the south she had the occasion to meet some of the pioneers in women's education and the women's movement. She built on some of these interests when she finally came back to live in Calcutta in 1930 and developed some long-standing friendships with a few leaders of the All India Women's Conference and women teachers, many of them Christians or Brahmos.[17]

Her two youngest sisters were educated in Calcutta along with their brothers. Since *Dadamashay* was still in Burma, they were boarders and used to come to the Majumdar household for short holidays. Later, when my sister and I went to study in the same school,[18] we enjoyed the advantage of having our aunts' friends and contemporaries as our teachers. *Mā* extracted a promise from my father that in education at least there would be no discrimination between the sons and the daughters. She was to draw on this later in my life when she persuaded my father to let me go to Oxford for higher studies. That was in the year of India's independence (1947), by which time many major changes had affected middle-class families in Calcutta. She was very happy that I had inherited her passion for reading and allowed me to read whatever I wanted to, drawing on her extensive collection. Whenever she went out to shop she would bring me books to read. Occasionally, my eldest brother protested that I was reading too many novels meant for adults. She would brush aside the objection, saying, 'Reading will do her no harm and she is reading what I read for my own education.'

For a person who never received any formal education, my mother's views on education were quite extraordinary for her generation. Something she used to tell me in my teens, which I misunderstood at that time, acquired a totally different meaning when I was in my 40s: 'If you see yourself, your husband and your children as the boundaries of your concerns, the older you grow, you will find your mind becoming smaller. Remember you are part of a privileged generation, you are receiving education for which women in the rest of the country have had to struggle for years.' She used to say, 'I see education as a process of ever widening mental horizons and social concerns.'

But if the chance of a good education made any of us too proud or made us change our behaviour towards other people for the worse, she would not forgive us. Being educated, for her, meant being more responsible and more concerned about removing wrongs. On the issue of dowry her position was extremely firm. I remember overhearing a conversation between my father and mother when I was possibly just about 10 years old. 'If either of your daughters ever comes to hear that you are prepared to consider paying dowry for their marriage they will walk out of this house and I shall go with them.'

Baba did not always understand why *Mā* considered dowry such a humiliating practice. Since women did not inherit from their fathers, he thought this was one institution which provided an option—the pre-mortem inheritance theory that we learned about from Leela Dube during the Committee on the Status of Women in India's (CSWI) work (Government of India 1975). *Mā,* however, was adamant. She was equally vehement about the practice of *meye dekha*. She used to quarrel with my aunt for subjecting her daughters repeatedly to this humiliating practice and was determined that she was not going to go begging to anybody to accept either of her daughters as a *bou*. Rather, she would boast, she would find grooms and in-laws who wanted her daughters. Well, she had her own way in both our cases. Another marriage practice to be abandoned in our family on *Mā*'s insistence was that of carrying the bride round the groom on a *pidi* (a wooden plank used for sitting on the floor). Since my cousins were all married in their late 20s, she persuaded my father to raise objections to this custom. She argued, 'Perhaps it had some meaning when girls were married as children. Why should it continue when they are entering marriage as adults? Let them walk.' The practice was abandoned thereafter. Decades later, my sister and I were shocked to see it being revived by my sisters-in-law, during the marriage of their grown-up daughters. *Mā* of course had disappeared long before then.

Unlike *Pishimā*, *Mā* was a very gentle, soft-spoken person who attached a lot of importance to good manners. On issues that she felt strongly about she could be incredibly firm. She was extremely sensitive and affectionate in dealing not only with her own children and other young people in the family, but also with their friends who always felt welcome whenever they came to our house. Many of them developed the habit of calling her *Mā*. When my second brother left to study abroad, he asked *Mā* to take charge of an orphan friend of his. From that day Mukul*da* became a part of our family. We never thought of him as other than a brother, and the grief that he suffered when she died in 1959 was no less than what we felt. It was my familiarity with this characteristic that enabled me to send my student Hassan Ahmed to stay with her when he needed to go to Calcutta for his research in the National Library. My sister-in-law complained to me, '*Mā* scolds Hassan in the same way that she scolds her grandchildren. She forces him to drink milk and eat bland food because he suffers from chronic amoebiosis!' What my sister-in-law did not understand was the impact of such treatment on Hassan. When *Mā* died, it was my other sister-in-law who had to cope with Hassan's grief in Patna as I had gone to Calcutta.

The freedom with which she allowed us to be friendly with all our brothers' friends was often criticised by my aunts. *Mā*'s method of managing her adolescent daughters and sons was not through control and force, but through love. She had the supreme confidence that none of us would ever do anything to let the family down. When she was coaxing my father to send me to Oxford at the age of 20, criticisms erupted from *Jethamashay* and my aunts. *Baba* asked her 'You had agreed to Vani's [my sister's] marriage when she was 20. Why don't you want to do the same for Khuku [my nickname]?'

Mā faced a problem. Apart from being aware of my great desire to go to Oxford, an astrologer had told her that it would not be a good idea to get me married before I was in my mid-20s. But she could not mention this to *Baba*, who viewed astrology as unscientific, as an addiction that could create dependence and prevent the development of mental strength. She, too, valued mental strength and often used to scold my sister for being prone to pessimism. 'If I ever hear that faced with a problem or a crisis either of my daughters had sat down and cried, that day I will know that all the investment on their education and my training has been a dead loss. You must always be prepared to cope.' Years later, *Didi* (elder sister) told me, 'If she had been around today, I would have liked to ask *Mā* why she never taught us the art of helpless femininity? We have been coping all our lives, not only with our own, but also other people's problems. Why don't we find people who will cope with ours?'

But the astrologers' warnings, she felt, could not be ignored, even if she could not tell *Baba* about it. Oxford offered a convenient absence of three years, a delay that would enable her to put a stop to all talk of marriage. *Mā* used *Baba*'s earlier commitment to be non-discriminating in access to education. Since he had already sent two sons abroad to study, and my record as a student was better than theirs, *Baba* was forced to agree. He used to tell us, 'By upbringing and conviction I am a conservative. It is your mother who is the liberal.' But his faith in her knowledge and understanding of her children's needs was such that on most occasions he followed her advice.

Mā had taken on from *Pishimā* the unquestioned role of protecting my father from the nitty-gritty irritations and anxieties of bringing up five high-spirited and often difficult children. Nor would she ever burden him with the occasional hurts she received from some of our more objectionable relatives. The only occasions when she specifically pushed me to *Baba* for advice or a final decision was after I came back from Oxford. *Mā* knew that I wanted to look for a job, but she said I must get *Baba*'s permission. I was frightened as I did not know what I would do if *Baba* said no—it was against our family tradition for women to work. I knew *Mā* had helped a cousin and a niece to take up a job before their marriage by talking to their parents who respected *Mā* greatly. But in my case she insisted that I must get my father's permission. Perhaps she knew him better than I did. It was the end of 1950, when I asked my father about applying for a job. His prompt answer was, 'Yes, certainly, that was understood.' When I looked blank, he laughed and said, 'I expected this when you went to Oxford and I was prepared. But something else has happened during your absence. The Constitution of free India tells me that I cannot discriminate between you and your brothers. I have always told them that my role ends with educating them. After that they have to stand on their own feet and be responsible for their lives. The same applies to you also.' When I still looked stunned, he continued laughing and said, 'Don't you know that I have always believed in the rule of law? When the law changes, I must change, too.'

The second occasion on which my father surprised me was when I was experiencing a lot of confusion and guilt at being unable to do full justice to my two responsibilities—as a mother and as a professional university teacher. There were too many neighbours ready to pity my 1-year-old daughter who was 'deprived' of her mother's constant attention. These views were not shared either by my mother-in-law or my husband, but I was racked by doubts, more because I could not do the additional reading that I ought to have done for my teaching. *Mā* sent me to *Baba* again for advice. It was difficult for her because her standards of maternal responsibility were also very high. She would not encourage me to show any slackness there. *Baba*'s reaction was totally different. 'I feel very reassured that you are doing all this soul searching. It indicates a strong sense of responsibility. But you are trying to balance only between your responsibilities as a mother and as a teacher. There is a third factor. If you introduce it, you will see the equation will resolve itself.' I was forced to ask what the third factor was. 'This poor country has made a major investment in your education. Never mind the fact that the money came from me, it was still this poor country's contribution. Do you have the right to waste that investment?' I was astounded. He was in fact treating me as his equal, because this was the philosophy that he always applied to his own personal career. The 'equation' did resolve itself. After 48 years of working, I can say I have never regretted that decision and have always thanked my stars for that bit of guidance from my father.

From then onwards I felt much closer to my father than I had ever been before. He had always been a distant figure to be revered. It was always *Mā* to whom I could bring all my doubts and confusions. She was the one to whom I introduced the man I wanted to marry. Within a few days she had met his family (she had come to Patna to help me set up my personal establishment, since the university had finally provided me with accommodation). Having discovered that to my prospective mother-in-law I had already become a substitute for the daughter she had lost years earlier, the two mothers settled matters between them. She just told me, 'Now you leave it to me to arrange things with your father.' The downwardly mobile economy of the household of which I wanted to become a member did not matter. The fact that the man whom I had chosen to marry was not a university graduate did not matter either. I do not know what she told my father, but I do know that *Baba* brushed aside *Jethamashay*'s objections to what he thought was an 'unequal' marriage by quoting *Mā*'s opinions. As for the academic discrepancy, *Baba* told *Jethamashay*, 'Khuku tells me that the young man is her intellectual equal, if not her superior. Since she has been trained to assess intellectual abilities, I accept her judgement.'

Baba died in 1956 when my second daughter was only 10 months old. *Mā* never really recovered from her loss, and by the time she followed him, just three years later, she was fully prepared for her departure. Even during this short period she continued to provide the moral and emotional support to enable me to live and work according to my convictions.

I had never questioned the rituals performed at marriages and *shradh* (death rituals), which formed very much a part of the experience of growing up in a large joint family. However, the first time I felt like rebelling was while performing my father's *shradh*. My slight knowledge of Sanskrit enabled me to follow the meaning of the *mantras* (chants) that I was expected to repeat. For a moment I felt like getting up and walking out, but the years of socialisation ('You do not create a public scene which would let your family down') prevented me. It was only afterwards when *Boromā* and *Mamababu* (*Mā*'s brother) came rushing to me to ask whether I was unwell (I was shaking), that the reaction burst out: 'I do not know whether there is any place like *akshyaya swarga* [eternal heaven]. If there is, then my father would have reached there by his own merit. Isn't it audacity on my part to offer all these gifts to some Brahmins I do not know to ensure *Baba*'s ticket to heaven?'

As I should have expected, *Boromā* promptly put her hand on my mouth to stop me from saying any more. *Mamababu*, the most conservative person on *Mā*'s side of our family, was so angry that he could not speak. *Mā* arrived on the scene just at that moment to ask what had happened. *Boromā* burst out, 'I told you repeatedly, do not educate her so much, just listen to her *aakatha, ku katha* [offensive and objectionable talk].' *Mā* asked me what I had said and then wanted to know if any one else had heard me. Had I made a scene at the *shradh* before all the other relatives who were present? When I said no, she said, 'All right, you go upstairs now and rest.' *Boromā* was of course indignant, 'Is that all you are going to tell her?' 'Yes *Didi*, because she is only repeating the value that she has learned from her father—never to do anything against her belief and convictions—but she has said it only before the three of us and has not let the family down. She could tell you because she knows you love her, even if you disagree; so let her be.'

I end my story here. Whenever I have faced a crisis in my later life, the examples set before me by these extraordinary people have been of tremendous help. On many occasions these memories have helped provide new directions and new meaning to my life, and provided the strength to cope with conflicting responsibilities and choice of direction and a purpose. The plunge into the women's movement undoubtedly drew extensively on the lessons hidden in my memories. The need to balance the politics of protest with the politics of construction came from my father. Teaching was a vocation that I chose and faith in education as a process of human and social development was something that I acquired both intellectually and emotionally from the family. But it was only as late as 1991, when I was listening to one of the women in Bankura describing the IPCL[19] method adopted for the total literacy campaigns as a *jilebi*—where you start from something that you know, move to that which you do not know, come back to other things that you know in ever widening circles of knowledge and comprehensions—that I remembered *Mā*'s statement about education as a process of ever widening arenas of the mental horizon and social concerns. Simultaneously, a line from Tagore flashed into my mind: '*Janar majhe ajanare karechhi sandhaan* [I seek the unknown within the known].'

NOTES

1. By tradition practitioners of Ayurveda (the supposed shastric source of traditional Indian medicine among Hindus), the upper-caste Vaidyas soon took to learning and the professions in large numbers. With the introduction of Western education in the last century, together with the Brahmins and Kayasthas of Bengal, they became the lawyers, doctors, teachers and politicians of not only Bengal, but, with migration, other parts of North and South India as well.
2. *Sati* was the act of immolation of a wife with her dead husband, often on the same funeral pyre. This was banned in 1829 through the efforts of Isvarchandra Vidyasagar, Rammohan Roy and Lord Bentinck.
3. The *sindur* or vermillion for the parting in the hair (a symbol of marriage for a Bengali woman) of a *sati* who had chosen *sahamaran*—death with her husband to avoid widowhood—was regarded as auspicious.
4. As working with a broom was regarded as lowly, by coming out with a broom in hand this young woman was expressing her contempt for the *sati* whose act would implicate her family in an illegal act.
5. A leading mid-19th-century landowner of East Bengal.
6. A literal translation of *kulin* is 'of aristocratic and noble descent', the premier among lineages. Initiated as an honour for some learned scholars by Ballal Sen, the Sen dynasty ruler of Bengal, it became hereditary and a stamp of lineage, like many things in India.

7. My maternal grandfather was a Public Works Department engineer in Burma and his job involved building roads and bridges in inaccessible parts of that country.
8. My father, Satish Chandra Majumdar, was an irrigation engineer, member of the Indian Service of Engineers, instituted in 1910.
9. Beltala Girls School, which later added a college, still famous in Bhowanipore in south Calcutta.
10. I was born in 1927 and spent the first three years of my life in Bankura where my father was posted. I have memories of *Pishimā*'s frequent stays with us and the very close relationship between her, *Mā* and my father.
11. Equivalent to today's secondary board examination, after 10 years of school.
12. A sweet which resembles expanding spirals, hence the allusion to a circular *jilebi* to describe a devious brain.
13. A Hindu festival which celebrates the mythical annual visit of the goddess Durga to her paternal home. Also celebrates the goddess' victory over the demon Mahishāsura.
14. The custom of inspecting a prospective bride before finalising negotiations for an arranged marriage.
15. *Raivatak* by Nabin Chandra Sen.
16. The village home had no bathrooms because women bathed in the river or the pond. *Mā* was not used to such public baths.
17. A religious denomination started in 1829 by Raja Rammohan Roy, the 19th-century Bengali social reformer. It emphasised the need to move towards an interpretation of Hindu scriptures according to certain rational principles, such as the monotheism of the Upanishads, humanitarianism and the worship of a formless god.
18. St. John's Diocesan Girl's High School.
19. Interpersonal Communication and Learning (IPCL) was a method of instruction used with great effect in the Total Literacy Campaign of the National Literacy Mission in the 1990s. This particular incident occurred in the Bankura district in the state of West Bengal.

REFERENCES

Government of India. 1975. *Towards Equality*. Report of the Committee on the Status of Women in India. New Delhi: Ministry of Education and Social Welfare, Department of Social Welfare.

Mazumdar, Vina. 1978. 'Comment on Suttee', *Signs*, 4 (2): 269–73.

Stein, Dorothy. 1978. 'Women to Bum: Suttee as a Normative Institution', *Signs*, 4 (2): 253–68.

3

A Daughter of Awadh*

Zarina Bhatty**

I

Lucknow: Then and Now

Now when I visit Lucknow, the city of my birth, my niece greets me with the Arabic salutation, *salaam alai kum* (may God be with you). I reply rather hesitantly, *walai kum assalam* (may God be with you, too), and the words sound strange to my ears. As a child I used the more secular *adaab* or *tasleem* spoken in Urdu, the language of poetry and refinement. This ancient, teeming city has seen much change between then and now. My mother, uneducated and unexposed behind the walls of *purdah,* used to send us properly escorted by a servant to enjoy the festivities of Diwali and Dussehra with our Hindu neighbours. It is a pity that my nieces are deprived of such pleasures now. We grew up without rancour, aware of social and cultural differences that were to be respected but not scaled. I was born into a middle-class Sunni Muslim family in Lucknow in 1933. My parents belonged to *zamindari* families in a *qasba* (small town) called Rudauli in the district of Faizabad, now in Barabanki, in the erstwhile princely state of Awadh. *Zamindars* were landowners with medium-sized estates and were distinguished from *taluqdars*, who were larger landowners. The *qasbati* (town-dwellers) considered themselves

* Originally published in the *Indian Journal of Gender Studies*, Vol. 6, No. 2, 1999, pp. 311–25.

** The author wishes to thank Leela Gulati without whose badgering and help this piece would not have been possible.

superior by virtue of owning land to the *shaharees* (city-dwellers), who were mostly salaried persons and traders. The *qasbatis* also regarded themselves as more cultured and refined. They were very proud and conscious of their language and sophisticated lifestyle, popularly known as *tahzeeb* (culture). The landed aristocracy made a virtue of cultivating the finer aspects of gracious living and an appreciation of the finer things of life.

My Father's Family

Although of the same social class and background, my father's family considered themselves superior to my mother's by virtue of their education. My paternal grand-uncle was the first graduate from Faizabad and my father studied law at the Aligarh Muslim University, a Mecca of learning in his days. Being the only son, he was spoiled a great deal by my grandmother. She provided him with the best she could. I am told my father was very sociable, and used to have many friends and entertained lavishly, a habit that he continued in his later life as well. Looking after his guests was his religion, he would say.

My grandfather died an early death in 1903 in a plague epidemic that swept India. At 18 years of age, with a young son of 6 months, my grandmother faced the grim realities of widowhood. Convention and custom imposed on her an inflexible set of rules. She wore only white throughout her life, but she detested this imposition on her. She was not allowed to participate in any ceremonies or rituals. She could not wear any jewellery or flowers, and personal adornments were forbidden. Such deprivations had their impact on her, and she had nervous breakdowns twice in later life and suffered from high blood pressure. These restrictions, it may be noted, are against Islamic teachings: they were adopted by Muslims from the customs of Hindus. My grandmother was not remarried, although Islam allows the remarriage of widows. In accordance with the Hindu customs of the region, some of which they adopted, Muslims also disapproved of the remarriage of widows. Muslims, however, did not succumb to the pressure of accepting pre-puberty marriage, and my grandmother was married at the relatively late age of 16.

With my grandfather's untimely death, Sirajul Haq, the youngest of my grandfather's brothers, accepted the responsibility of caring for my father and providing protection to my grandmother. In any event, she was financially secure as she was given a share in her father's property according to the Islamic law of inheritance, which gives a daughter half of what it gives to sons. She did not inherit any land from her family, but was compensated in cash. It was indeed my father's good fortune that his mother inherited enough to take care of him financially.

Mahjoob

In accordance with Islamic tradition, with the death of my grandfather, my father had become a *mahjoob*, which means a person who is deprived of his father's property. According to Muslim personal law, if a son dies in the lifetime of his father, the grandson is disinherited and the property entitlement goes to the remaining brothers of the deceased. The rationale for this is that a son is more closely related than a grandson.

My father's three living uncles benefited by my grandfather's untimely death and inherited a larger portion than what they would have had grandfather lived. My benevolent youngest grand-uncle prevailed upon his older brothers to voluntarily give up some share of their property in view of the tender age of the widow and the child. They did so reluctantly, but one of the uncles, being more cunning and devious, planned a strategy to take back the property that he had given to my father at a later date.

My grandmother wanted my father to be highly educated, and her desire was shared by the benevolent uncle, who himself was a graduate and valued education. My illiterate grandmother was a socially and politically aware woman. I remember her singing a song about Khilafat, an early independence movement in India inspired by the Turkish revolution. Two lines from the song still ring in my mind:

Boli amma Mohammed Ali *ki*,
beta jaan khilafat par dena
(Mohammed Ali's mother said, 'Son, you must sacrifice your life for the Khilafat Movement.')[1]

My Father's Half-sister

My grandmother had been the second wife of my grandfather, whose first wife had died in childbirth after her daughter Vakilan was born.

My father's half-sister was a very intelligent and courageous woman. She was raised by the joint family, and was nicknamed Vakilan, which means a female advocate in Urdu, since as a child she was very argumentative. She was an extraordinary woman, who was not only beautiful but capable of a great deal of fortitude. One of my grand-uncles decided to marry his son to Vakilan in order to claim her share of property from my father, thus taking back a part of what little he had given my father earlier.

Vakilan refused to marry her first cousin, who was neither handsome nor bright. Her reluctance was not taken notice of and the marriage was arranged. Her refusal was kept a secret as it was most disgraceful for a girl to express her disapproval of an arranged marriage. In her desperation, a few days before the wedding, she decided to get the support of her neighbours and wrote on pieces of paper, 'Save me from this marriage' and pasted them on the doors of the neighbouring houses, quite reminiscent of Mariana from the *Arabian Nights*. She came up with this unique idea as she was literate, having learnt Arabic to read the *Koran*. Since Arabic and Urdu scripts are somewhat similar, she had taught herself both languages and was proficient in them. However, the marriage took place as arranged.

She could not reconcile herself to this marriage, and had the tremendous courage to leave her husband, her family and the village, and move to Delhi after a couple of years. She earned a living by teaching the *Koran* and by reciting hymns at *milads* (religious gatherings). After some years she obtained a divorce and remarried in Delhi. Needless to say, she was totally abandoned by the family and as children we were not told about our aunt's existence. Occasionally, I used to get a toy from this aunt, but I was not told where it had come from. I think my aunt must have been very fond of my father and his children, and tried to make her presence felt from time to time. But her efforts went unheeded until in her later years one of her sons was posted in Lucknow and she came to live with him. She was by then an old woman and made fresh efforts to become part of our family. Fortunately, by then my father and also my grandmother had softened, and they accepted her back. I remember enjoying her company enormously as she used to tell me interesting stories of her adventures. She was probably the first woman in our family who had empowered herself.

My Parents' Marriage

My father's uncle Siraj, who had looked after him with so much affection, wanted his eldest daughter to marry my father. Marriages among lateral cousins are very common among Muslims. Despite the fact that he was very close and felt highly obliged to his uncle, my father politely refused to marry his first cousin. It may be noted here that a man's refusal to an arranged marriage was not considered disgraceful. This was a great blow to his uncle and his family, and she was quickly married to another cousin, fortunately, the relationship between uncle and nephew did not sour because of this and my father continued to play the role of a son to him.

Since my father's marriage to his cousin did not materialise, my grandmother had to look for another match and found a young attractive girl from the same village and from a similar background. My mother was never sent to school, but could read Urdu and the *Koran*. She was 16 when she was married. Her dowry included a large quantity of gold. She was not given her share of the inheritance despite the Islamic law in her favour.

My father, at 28, was 12 years older than her. He had delayed his marriage as he had wanted to complete his education and was considered to have married late. My maternal grandmother had died early and my mother was brought up by her older sister and father. Her father did not remarry and devoted himself to his three children. My mother's only brother led a life of leisure in the true style of his feudal ancestors, dependant on his father's landed property, while her older sister was married to her cousin and continued to live in her father's home.

I was the eldest of nine children and am 22 years older than my youngest sister. My parents had a traditional yet not an overly formal relationship. There was a happy informality between them, and my mother's attitude, although respectful, was never servile. She lived in *purdah* at home and wore a *burqa* in public. Her visits were limited to those of her relatives, and in the village she travelled in a covered palanquin.

I was born a year after my parents' marriage. Although a girl, I was welcomed into the family as my grandmother had no daughters of her own and longed for one. As my sister was born soon after me, my grandmother raised me and I regarded her as my mother. The relationship between my mother and her mother-in-law was extremely cordial. Grandmother was very helpful at all times. After her death my mother often wept for her. Children were born at home and custom demanded that the first child be born at the paternal home. Although Barabanki was a district town, my mother moved to my father's *khala*'s (maternal aunt) house in Lucknow for her delivery, and qualified nurses attended on her.

Life in the *Zenana*—Or the Women's 'Domain'

Women lived a life of seclusion, confined to the four walls of the home, in *purdah*. Male first cousins and uncles closely related by blood were allowed access into the *zenana*, but male relatives by marriage were not accorded this privilege. Women did not go to shops and travelled little, but traders often visited the house. All transactions took place through a third person, usually an old servant's son with whom *purdah* was not observed. The social structure within the *zenana* was hierarchical, the mother-in-law being accorded great respect and after her time the wife of the eldest brother took her place. Although confined to the home, women were often very busy with stitching and embroidery—outlets for their creativity. They used their imagination and their hands, and made beautiful covers for *khosdaans* and *pandaans*.[2] These artistic covers formed part of a girl's wedding trousseau.

The chewing of *pan* (betel leaf) was a common habit in *zamindari* households. The lady of the house was always seen with the *pandaan* even when she moved from one room to another, offering its contents to visitors. The *pandaan* was a dome-shaped container, the size of which expressed the social standing of the family. The very rich had silver *pandaans* with elaborate filigree work. The *pandaan* had two compartments, the lower, smaller one held the condiments that were placed in the betel leaf—lime, *kattha* (catechu), crushed betel nuts and cardamoms. The betel leaves were placed in the upper compartment. They were filled with the right proportion of spices, painstakingly wrapped into precise conical shapes known as *gilouris*, and elaborately arranged by the women before they were offered to guests or sent to the workplaces of the men. Paper wrappers for the *gilouris* were fashioned by the women of the household and this, along with the crushing of betel nuts, formed an important activity for women of the *zenana*. Married women were encouraged to eat *pan* as it reddened the lips; red being the colour of *suhag* (married status) was, I suppose, desired. So essential was the culture of *pan* that migrants to Pakistan had betel leaves sent from India in the early days following Partition.

We wore flowing *gharara*s (long divided gathered skirts), which were stitched by hand at home and made from 5 to 6 metres of cloth. The old ones were recycled to be ultimately used as *razai*s (quilts). The older women taught us to sew and embroider and make our own clothes, apart from teaching us cooking and other domestic skills. Interaction between members of the extended family was frequent and there was always a birth or a wedding to attend, often accompanied by elaborate rituals. Women took part in these festivities in a big way.

During the month of Ramzan,[3] relatives and friends were invited and the family observed fasting. In each family about four to five children fasted for the first time and waited in great anticipation to be woken at four in the morning to take part in the *saheri.*[4] When I was made to fast for the first time, my sister, unknown to the family, also kept the fast with me. As a result, much to my anger, the gifts given to me at Ramzan by friends and relatives had to be shared with my sister. She was spiritually inclined, and observed the *roza*s regularly, something I found difficult.

On their infrequent visits to the world outside, women travelled in the covered *doli* (palanquin). It was curtained on all sides and carried by four men on bamboo poles. Every house had an anteroom where the *doli* was lowered, after which the palanquin bearers would go out, and then we would alight from it. Wrapped in our *burqas*, we would be seated in the *doli* before the men were called to carry us back to our homes. When we had to travel, I remember in vivid detail the number of *dolis*, the attendant noise and clamour at the railway station, and our undignified haste to enter the compartment, for the train waited for only a few minutes at the railway platform. The *doli*s were carefully positioned at the entrance of the ladies' compartment from where we stepped into the train. During the journey we sat covered in our *burqas*.

I often travelled in the palanquin with my grandmother when she visited her family in the village where the landed gentry continued to live as a joint family to retain the property within the family. Her four brothers lived in a mansion divided into six apartments, one for each of their wives, two of them having married twice. The apartments were connected by doors, some of which were permanently closed, signifying the lack of interaction between the occupants. The six women quarrelled amongst themselves, and the misunderstandings and rivalry were mostly over gifts from parents and husbands. The co-wives were segregated in the second floor of the house with little or no interaction with each other. They were, however, curious about each other and about the other children of their husbands.

My grandmother maintained good relationships with all the women, and whenever she visited them, she asked them to open the doors and helped settle their quarrels. The biggest change in this cloistered lifestyle was brought about by two events. One was the Partition of India, which resulted in the break-up of the joint family as many young men moved to Pakistan in the hope of getting better jobs. The second was the abolition of the *zamindari* system, which compelled youngsters to take to education, leading to professional or salaried work. Lucknow remained free from rioting during the Partition years, but many parts of western Uttar Pradesh witnessed the conflagration.

II

CHILDHOOD

Not a very successful lawyer, my father was unambitious, but handled the legal cases of his relatives, the *zamindars*, who were endlessly involved in litigation. Not only did he refuse to accept his professional fee from them, he also provided them with hospitality when they came from the village. Eventually, he gave up his practice and took up a job in Lucknow, saying he did not appreciate the half-truths and dishonesty that were part of his profession.

When I was about 12 years old, we moved to Lucknow. My father joined the Sunni Waqf Board,[6] which acted as a trustee for the property belonging to mosques and shrines, and rose to become the director of the Uttar Pradesh Waqf Board. We found a house close to the Justice Karamat Hussain Muslim Girls' School, and I used to walk to school wearing a *burqa*. Justice Karamat Hussain was an enlightened Muslim lawyer and a promoter of Muslim women's education in Uttar Pradesh. He had founded two girls' schools in the 1920s in Lucknow and Allahabad. The school in Lucknow was essentially a boarding school to cater to the daughters of rich *taluqdars*. When I joined the school in 1942, the school was run in the British style, offering liberal and Westernised education, although the medium of instruction was not English. The school has now grown into a degree college affiliated to the Lucknow University, admitting both Muslims and non-Muslims. In my time, more Muslims were encouraged to join the school. Thus, the move to Lucknow meant better education for all of us.

When I joined the school, my father had stated my real age, though I had been advised by the principal to understate it. This was a common practice in those times.[7] My father did not see the purpose of understating my age as he was certain that his daughters would never work for a living. In school, my father wanted me to be named Zarina Khatun, but the principal persuaded my father to change it to Zarina Farid, saying it was more modern.

I started wearing the *burqa* a year later when I was 13 years old, but I resented wearing one and thought it was old-fashioned and unnecessary. I felt oppressed and hot in it, but wore one at my father's insistence. I was in the company of upper-class Muslim girls from convent schools, who spoke English and did not wear the *burqa*. The Lucknow *burqas* came in two pieces—one was the flared skirt and the other a top worn over the head. A netted veil covered the eyes. It was difficult to walk in this as one could see only straight in front. Actually, once you have taken to a *burqa*, it is very difficult to walk without one. When I travelled I wore the *burqa* over my *gharara*, but always kept my face exposed so that I could see better. My younger sister, Sufia, often asked me for my clothes to wear only to be met by my refusal. Undeterred, she would slip into them, cover herself in a *burqa* and leave for school. Once there, she would remove her *burqa* and I would find her in my clothes, which I found infuriating.

In Lucknow the younger Muslim women wore *ghararas* and the older ones the usual ensemble of *churidar, kurta* and *duppatta.* My grandmother abhorred white, the colour of widowhood that she had had to wear all her life, and never let us wear white *duppattas* of which I was fond. She would always have our faded *duppattas* re-dyed in bright colours.

Puberty

I was unprepared for the onset of menstruation. We were a nuclear family and although I was the eldest, I had no knowledge of it. I had noticed that the teachers in school excused some girls from reading the *Koran* on certain days. As I disliked reading the *Koran*, I told my teacher one day that I too was not going to read it Very rudely, she told me to get back to my recitation and for a long time I could not understand this discrimination. My mother was inhibited with me, and when I started menstruating I did not know how to deal with it. I was also curious to learn more about relationships between men and women. When my cousin got married, he gave his wife two books in Urdu on marriage. Curiously, the book for men was informative about sex, but the one for women only told them how to be attractive to their husbands, advising them to refrain from expressing pleasure. I read the books hidden in a comer room and became better informed. Girls were usually counselled on the eve of their wedding day by a close aunt or a relative. During menstruation, we were not segregated, but were considered impure, so we were not expected to fast and handle the holy books. So much shame was attached to menstruation that during those days we discreetly abstained from these activities.

My Teenage Years

I led a very sheltered life, protected from the outside world and confined to the bamboo-curtained household. The atmosphere was very stifling and constraining. It made me feel backward and I disliked it. Within the household, I was always protesting against discrimination between us sisters and brothers. I still recall my mother often scolding me and expressing the fear that I may take after my aunt Vakilan. Maybe I did inherit her genes. As I grew up I became disinterested in housework and my mother would often say that my wedding palanquin would come back the same day as I was not domesticated.

After I passed my intermediate examination, I had hoped to join the Isabella Thoburn College in Lucknow and on the quiet applied for admission there. When my father came to know of this, he firmly put his foot down and did not let me join the college as it was regarded as modern and not suitable for *purdah*-observing daughters from 'respectable' Muslim families, although my aunt Hamida had studied there. She used to go to college in a *burqa*, which I refused to do.

Marriage

At 18 I was married to a cousin who was nearly 12 years older than I. He had been married before and was divorced with two children.

His first wife was young and illiterate, and theirs had been a marriage of convenience. A generous father-in-law had financed his education and he had graduated from Aligarh, later taking a postgraduate degree from Calcutta. His father, a miserly person, had been unwilling to spend money on his son's education. His family was descended from a *pir* (religious guide) and my father-in-law's older brother officiated in the *pir*'s *dargah* (mausoleum) on holy occasions. The *dargah* was frequented by wealthy disciples, one of whom offered to finance my cousin's travel to England for further studies. Although married for five years, he had found no companionship with his first wife. Being a close relative, he was allowed into the *zenana* and was attracted to me and my urban mannerisms. I agreed to this marriage as I wanted to study and was fascinated with the idea of studying abroad, and it was decided that we both would go abroad to study. My parents and in-laws, however, advised against my going abroad. My husband-to-be believed in women's education and advancement, but could not take it when confronted later with an educated wife.

A *mehr* of Rs. 10,000 was fixed and some new clothes were stitched for my journey to London.[8] The wealthy disciple at the *dargah* had presented my husband with an ancient book, which he sold in England. The money that was realised supported our stay in London for six months.

When my parents learnt that I was to go to London, they were apprehensive. I was given a crash course in cooking and taught special dishes. My parents were also worried as to what would happen if I were to have a child there. They had underestimated my inner strength and resourcefulness. We were married in 1951 and left for England by boat within a month of our marriage.

III

LIFE IN ENGLAND

In London we arrived unannounced at a friend's house, much to his dismay. For the first time, I saw a man in the kitchen and my efforts to help out with the work were a total disaster. I burnt the rice and broke the glass bowl by washing it in hot water. The change in lifestyle was hard and painful. Coming from a large family of nine children, I would often feel lonely. I would sit on top of double-decker English buses and weep when I thought of my home and family. Some minimal contact was always there through letters and visits of friends who came over with small gifts and eatables once in a while. I came out of the *burqa* even before our journey to England at my husband's insistence. I started wearing saris in London and had to buy warm clothes when I reached there. In those days in England women were not allowed to wear trousers to college.

I disliked the cold and so did my husband. He would often sit by the fire and send me out on errands in the bitter cold. Looking back, it was more a result of his socialisation, which made him feel that the needs of men were supreme, rather than deliberate selfishness.

As my English was inadequate, I applied to a tutorial college that prepared me for entrance to the university. I sat for the General Certificate of Education (GCE) within six months. This was immediately after Indian independence, and I received a lot of encouragement from liberal English teachers. I did not have a very clear idea about the subjects I wanted to study. I had heard about the London School of Economics (LSE) and, fascinated by the institute's great reputation, decided to join it. I was admitted to LSE for B.A. with honours in social anthropology. My husband, who had a master's in psychology, was admitted as a Ph.D. candidate to the University College of the University of London. I enjoyed my years at LSE, and it was a rich and fulfilling experience.

At LSE I showed a lot of potential for leadership. I was elected secretary of the Indian Association there. I also became secretary and later president of the London Majlis, an organisation of Indian students spread all over England. This brought me in contact with a wide variety of people and also broadened my horizons. I was introduced to Marxism and attended evening classes on it. My activities kept me busy and I had no time to think of my personal life. Although most men of my acquaintance in England knew of my strained relationship with my husband and were attracted to my good looks and vivacity, they never tried to take advantage of me. They were my biggest support. Our lives revolved around the college and the library. Often, my male classmates would drop in at our place and I would cook Indian food for them in what was almost a nightly ritual. My husband encouraged this as he did not feel threatened by it at that time. There were only three Indian girls studying in LSE during my days there.

My husband, who had selected psychology, did not pursue it and gave it up for English literature, which he soon dropped for sociology. We sat for the sociology exam together, as I had studied it as a subsidiary subject. I passed the exam while he failed to do so. This was the beginning of a deep sense of insecurity that started brewing in him. He was the spoilt and only son of a feudal family, and was particular about his food and other comforts, and soon gave up his job that he had held for a while at the Indian High Commission. He eventually took a degree in history. I studied social anthropology, attended class in the mornings, and washed dishes from 2 to 8 P.M. at the LSE canteen. On holidays I sewed six dozen aprons a day at a tailoring establishment. I had six months to go before the final exams, when I was expected to sit for 10 papers, two a day, for five days. Such was the system at that time. I had saved money so as to get time to study during those crucial last months. In the meantime, watching my progress, my husband had become insecure and jealous of my achievements. I was 22 years old and he forced me to have a baby. I did not accept my pregnancy and suffered from pregnancy-related sickness so severely that I was eventually hospitalised. A matron at the hospital encouraged me to knit a frock for the baby and when it was complete, she held it up and asked me if I could see my baby in it. I still remember her holding up the lemon yellow dress that I had knitted. That was the turning point, and I started accepting my pregnancy and looked forward to being a mother. It was a hard life, with work, studies and the baby, whom I used to leave in a day creche.

At my professor's insistence, I eventually took my final exams in June, when I was six months pregnant and, much to my surprise, I passed. I could now take up a job as a supplementary teacher, a post that was well-paid. I also started broadcasting in the Urdu and Hindi services of the BBC. My colleagues were helpful. I worked at least thrice a week and the income was enough to pay our rent.

My daughter Huma was born on 24 October 1956 in the fifth year of our stay in England. My husband took me to the hospital and returned home to sleep. I was extremely happy to have a daughter, but was upset with my husband's callousness and neglect. He slept late into the morning while I lay in labour in the hospital. Only when my friends inquired about me did he call the hospital to ask if I had delivered. While in the hospital I kept asking the nurses whether my husband had inquired about me.

During the long stretch of time that I spent in England, I lost several female members of our family, including my grandmother of whom I was very fond. I remember her crying bitterly at my departure and I still recall running back to her before I left for London to see her one more time. That was the last time I saw her. Other losses were caused by the deaths of two aunts, Vakilan and Safia, the mother of lyricist Javed Akhtar, who were my role models. My poet uncle Majaz also died in my absence.

In London I cooked, washed and kept house, which I considered my duty as I was not yet acquainted with feminism. In addition, I was earning a living. All this took its toll. When an X-ray showed an infection in my lung that was diagnosed as tuberculosis, I left the baby in a residential nursery and admitted myself to a sanatorium. At that time, my husband took loans from the Indian High Commission and from various friends on the basis of my illness and spent it all on liquor and women. I received free treatment from the National Health Service and I reacted well to the drugs. After a year at the sanatorium, I returned home on my own as my husband did not have the courtesy to bring me back. I remember returning from the sanatorium, standing in the middle of my bedroom, watching my husband asleep, and stunned beyond belief to find contraceptives in the drawer that he had used with other women.

My Return to India

In 1961, after 10 and a half years, we returned to India on receiving the news that my husband's mother was suffering from cancer. Our return to India was unplanned, and between us we had only £100 and two degrees. Both of us managed to get only fellowships. I got one from the University Grants Commission and my husband got the Chinese History Fellowship from Sapru House. We found it difficult to rent a house in Delhi on account of our being Muslims. We finally got a house in Model Town, but there were many restrictions. The landlord's wife did not like Muslim tenants and we could not cook meat in the house. I found that I could not get a job in the university with three things against me: I was from Uttar Pradesh, I was a Muslim and I was a woman. I thus found that I had a triple disadvantage: I came from the wrong province, belonged to the wrong religious group and to the wrong gender. I had no patrons in Delhi and Delhi University provided employment only to its own students.

The Break-up of My Marriage

Insecure and uncertain of his abilities, my husband soon became envious of my success and resented my friendships with male colleagues. I was frustrated with his attitude and this resulted in further domestic discord and tension. Once, soon after our return, we quarrelled. He started beating me; I was furious and gave him an ultimatum. 'If you raise your hand again,' I told him, 'I will walk out.' His callous response was, 'You can go.' The curious neighbours were told that *I* had beaten him and locked him in. When this episode was repeated, I did leave, never to return. I left with Huma for a friend's place. And they let us stay. Huma was 5 years old at that time. My husband went to Lucknow and complained to my father. My father retorted, 'There must be a reason for my daughter to leave you after 12 years,' and did not entertain him.

I looked for a *barsati* (a studio apartment on the terrace) and found a place in Nizamuddin West in Delhi. Finally, I found a job as a lecturer in Delhi College, now known as Zakir Hussain College. To get there, I had to walk to Nizamuddin East station, take a train and then walk again. It was cheaper than taking two buses—such was my financial condition. My husband wrote to all our relatives that I was a call girl, and had become very modern and liberated and so on. Only my daughter Huma, a silent witness to the violence that had unfolded in front of her, knew that I had been beaten and injured.

During one of those last unhappy days with my husband, I met an acquaintance from Lucknow who invited us to dinner. We went, my husband and I, and that is where I first met my present husband, Idrak-ul-Zaman Bhatty. We exchanged telephone numbers. We were to meet several times after that. Once I arranged a dinner at my place and invited Idrak to meet my friend Saida for a possible match between them. We had a nice evening and she looked very beautiful that day, but I was unsuccessful in my efforts to get them together as Idrak did not take any interest in her.

After moving to Nizamuddin, I used to meet Idrak frequently in the market as he lived in the same neighbourhood. He was very solicitous and protective. He loved children and became a friendly and patient companion to Huma. One day he picked up my daughter from the school bus stop when I was unexpectedly delayed in college, and took very good care of her until I returned. Huma mischievously kept dropping a towel from the parapet so that her Uncle Idrak could jump down and pick it up.

Talaq, Talaq, Talaq by *Khullah*

During this period my husband wrote a note addressed to me saying, 'I divorce you by *Khullah* and I am not responsible for paying any maintenance,' and gave it to a friend asking him to give it to me.[9] He also told him, 'Let me see who will marry her, I have destroyed her.' He had also added that if I were to remarry, he would take my child away from me. My lawyer explained that in a *Khullah* divorce the husband cannot place conditions and I should not worry about losing my child to him even if I remarried. I agreed to the divorce as I felt that my marriage with him was over and told him in no uncertain terms that if he took my daughter away he would have to provide for her education and maintenance. After this he never raised the subject, although I did remarry. However, I did not object to his keeping in touch with Huma.

After my divorce I was confronted with new problems. Being a young woman and alone with a child, there were obstacles on all fronts. In England, Indian men had been very supportive, but it was different in India. Even my colleagues, educated and respectable men, harassed me. One day I could not find Huma and when I finally found her I was so furious that I slapped her. I found pieces of paper in her hand which were invitations to a fete in our house. She said to me that since no one ever visits our home she had decided to invite all my friends. It was then that I realised that we needed a proper home with a man in the house so that Huma and I could feel protected.

A Second Marriage

Idrak was around 37 years old and we grew fond of each other. I was then 29. Huma grew very fond of him, too, and started expecting him to visit every day. I did not know then that Idrak was a Christian. He and his family members had Muslim names and he even had a servant Anwar, who was a Muslim. It was only later that I learnt that his uncle was a scholar of Persian and a priest, and had decided to give all the children Urdu names. I was surprised to learn that Idrak was a Punjabi whose grandfather had converted to Christianity. He made it clear that he was a 'believing Christian' although he was not a regular churchgoer. I was not a practising Muslim.

When he proposed to me I discussed this matter with my father. He felt that marriage was sacred and that I must have a religious wedding, even if it was in a church, as he considered a civil marriage tantamount to living in sin. I was in a dilemma with many questions crowding my mind. Would I have to go through a conversion ceremony? What would happen to my *bachchi* (daughter)? How does one reconcile with all the changes, including the change of social identity? But all these doubts vanished when Idrak convinced me that as I did not practise my religion I had nothing to lose by having a Christian marriage, but, on the other hand, I would acquire something. However, I did not change my social identity.

When we were married a new chapter opened in my life. Our marriage was a meeting of minds and, after my two daughters were born, I took a lecturership in Jesus and Mary College. I devoted my time to the study of social and economic issues relating to poor Muslim women. Opportunities for work and my talent in fieldwork opened up enormously with the declaration of the International Decade for Women. The three handicaps of belonging to the wrong sex, the wrong state and the wrong religion suddenly became assets. My expertise was sought after for understanding the social and economic problems of Muslim women. I was able to establish myself well as a scholar and had several opportunities to work both at the national and international levels.

I have two daughters from my second marriage, but all my three children have been raised as one family. We have raised our children with a liberal education and all the freedom that goes with it, and they are professionals today. They have married men of their choice from different religious backgrounds. They have made their choices and live more easily for it. The three young men who have entered our family are very liberal, and religion does not play a divisive role at all; in fact, they have enriched our lives. I have been proud of my cultural and linguistic heritage, and one of the pleasant aspects of my marriage with Idrak has been our common interest in Urdu poetry. Idrak writes poetry in Urdu.

So, in conclusion, I can say that I have been a woman both of my time and of the future. I made a success of my life against all odds and many setbacks, and I look back with a sense of achievement, coming as I did from a traditional Muslim family, rooted in orthodoxy and bound by the rules framed centuries ago that made a woman a possession of her husband, unheard and unseen behind the walls of *purdah* that allowed her little or no access to modern education and made her silent and servile. I could have followed the path that my mother and grandmother had unquestioningly trod.

But early in my life I looked ahead and viewed education as the door of opportunity that would unshackle me from the fetters of orthodoxy that have bound so many before me. My personal sacrifices have been many, the hurt I have felt deep, and the silent memories of the past painful, but I feel they were justified for a worthier cause—my personal freedom. My struggle has been a source of inspiration for our three daughters who have grown up as enlightened and liberated persons with a deep sense of human values derived from both Christianity and Islam.

NOTES

1. Mohammed Ali was a prominent Khilafat Movement leader.
2. A *khasdaan* is a container for keeping *gilouris*, and a *pandaan* is a container in which betel leaf and other spices and condiments used to prepare *gilouris* are kept.
3. Also known as Ramadaan, the holy month of the Islamic calender, which is marked by fasting and prayers.
4. The ritual meal partaken of before sunrise, prior to the morning prayers (*fagir*) in the month of Ramzan by those who keep the *roza* (see Note 5).
5. The religious fast observed in the Islamic holy month of Ramzan.
6. A board that oversees the social welfare of the Sunni Muslim community, along with the management of common property according to Islamic law.
7. As the age of retirement for government servants was 52 years and there were age limits for taking the civil services examinations, it was common for the age of children to be understated while enrolling them in school.
8. The amount fixed at the time of a Muslim marriage to be paid to the bride by the groom.
9. A form of Muslim divorce that is initiated by the woman and where the man is not required to pay the amount of *mehr*.

4

A Struggle for Space

Hema Sundaram

The Brahmins of Mylapore (a suburb of Chennai), known for their enterprise and dynamism, were perhaps among the first communities of Tamil Nadu to avail of modern education and the opportunities offered by the British. In India's elaborate system of social hierarchy, the Brahmins have historically occupied the top tier. They have monopolised access to formal learning for centuries. This was particularly true of the Brahmins of the city of Madras (officially renamed as Chennai in 1998). Many of them entered government service, medicine and law, professions in which many of them excelled. By and large they were an elite and prosperous community, patrons of classical dance, music and arts. The many *sabhas*[1] and cultural centres founded and patronised by them to promote specific causes, played a key role in the revival of the classical arts of Bharata Natyam and Karnatic music in the former Madras Presidency.

It was a dream of perhaps every middle-class Brahmin woman to be part of this ambience, as is illustrated in a film song of the 1940s, which says, 'I shall become the daughter-in-law of a Mylapore advocate and visit Kutralam during the months of Vaikasi and Ani.'

This is the story of a woman from a middle-class Tamil Brahmin family of Mylapore born just a few years before the Indian independence. The years immediately following independence witnessed changes not only in the political system, but also in social practices. It was a period that gave importance to education, especially women's education; and saw the enactment of the Hindu Code Bill, which conferred on women rights regarding marriage, divorce and adoption. The Brahmin middle-classes were deeply influenced by all these liberal ideas, even while adhering strongly to traditional patriarchal ideas of male domination and superiority. These conflicting ideas affected many individuals in these families, into one of which I was born. My life experiences bear testimony to these conflicts in inherited social values.

I lived with my paternal grand-aunt (my father's aunt), not exactly in Mylapore, but very close to it. My grand-aunt's house was actually mid-way between Mylapore and Mambalam, another area in south Chennai where a considerable number of Brahmin families lived.

My Great-grandmother's Determination

On the paternal side, my father's family hailed from a village in what is now Thanjavur district. My grandfather was the only son of a small landholding family. My great grandmother, given in marriage as a second wife, was widowed at a relatively young age. She had three stepdaughters and probably was married to a man several years older than her, resulting in her early widowhood.

She was a lady of great determination and courage, and eked out her livelihood by working as a domestic help in affluent Brahmin houses. I have no idea as to whether she was educated at all, but her only objective seemed to be to bring up her son and launch him in life. She doted on her *payyan*.[2] My grandfather was fed almost solely by the householders of the *agraharam*[3] everyday by turns. Much against the wishes of his mother, my grandfather went to town to complete his schooling and from there to Madras to take his degree in law with the help of a few well-to-do relatives.

My great-grandmother lived to see her son establish himself as a leading lawyer, married and settled with a large family. While she lived, grandfather took good care of her and had the greatest regard and affection for her. He often told his own children that if it had not been for his mother, he would never have been what he was.

My Grandmother

My paternal grandmother was married to my grandfather as his second wife. His first wife had died young, having borne him three sons. Given the high incidence of maternal mortality in those days, there was a high prevalence of second marriages leading to a high incidence of widowhood. My grandmother was the daughter of one of grandfather's benefactors, a common practice in those days. She was an interesting contrast to my grandfather in appearance and temperament. He was a tall, well-built, very fair, short-tempered, strong-willed patriarch. She was short, stocky, dark, quiet and homely. Allowance for my grandmother's dark complenxion in this alliance was made, as he was obliged to her father.

In this marriage my grandmother had her own tale of suffering to tell. She looked after her mother-in-law and her two widowed sisters-in-law. As already mentioned, the incidence of widowhood was quite common in those days and every household had to accommodate one or more widows at any point of time. My grandmother herself had a large family. She lost several children born to her due to lack of proper medical care, even though there was always a lady doctor to attend to her deliveries. She had a hard time with her children. Her daughters, my aunts, were married quite young. My aunts were very talented women, but they were also quite egoistic and difficult. They were taught to sing and play the violin, as was the custom then.

Of my aunts, the story of Sarada, the eldest, merits some attention. Married to a lawyer and initially settled in the same town close to her parents, she had a son after several miscarriages. Her husband turned out to be a gambler and lost all his money at the races. He died leaving my aunt and his son almost penniless. Undaunted, my aunt took shelter with Lalitha, my grandmother's younger sister, and educated her son. Her son did not fail her. He went on to enter the administrative services.

My paternal grandmother Sundari had to endure the temper of a husband who took his frustrations out on her. I still remember my mother recounting the incident of my grandfather throwing the *uppuma*[4] in grandmother's face because it was served late and he was in a hurry to leave for his village. Very often such rejection or throwing of food was an expression of male anger. Sundari had to face the death of her elder son, a bright young student, and then litigation from his wife on the division of family property. This was something very common in middle-class families. She endured all this with a patience expected of women from such families. She never seemed to have even complained.

She was perhaps convinced that it was her *karma*,[5] a belief usually dinned into the heads of millions of men and women of this country. This belief, accepted by many in Indian society from top to bottom regardless of caste or class, led to the downtrodden, lower castes and classes and women putting up with unimaginable humiliation and oppression. While the knowledge of reading or writing or the performance of sacred rituals were all closely guarded secrets to be taught only to males of the upper castes, the doctrine of *karma*, the clever invention of the priestly class, was consciously and universally inculcated, thus justifying the existence of all kinds of inequalities and unjust practices.

Grandmother, of course, was able to find solace in coping with her difficulties in this highly reactionary doctrine which served in her case as a psychotherapeutic remedy. As a mother-in-law, my grandmother was perhaps exceptionally kind to my mother, her daughter-in-law for whom she was almost a foster mother. My mother had several times talked to us of the concern and love she had for her own daughter-in-law and the grandchildren, and in particular for my mother since she had lost her own father while she was young. The fact that my mother was young and innocent and that my father was so short-tempered probably made her feel protective towards her.

MY SUBSERVIENT MOTHER

My mother was born in a family of modest means. My maternal grandmother Rajam was thrown out with her three little girls by her father-in-law as soon as her husband died. For had not Manu, the great lawgiver, claimed that the father-in-law was not bound to support the wife of the deceased son? My mother was the eldest of three daughters.

My father's parents had been impressed by her good looks, which compensated for her lack of money, and had decided on the alliance. She was a woman of great charm and had a keen sense of humour, which I learnt to appreciate only much later in my life. Petite, fair and good-looking, she was at once friendly and warm even to a total stranger, and fond of children. She would tell them stories, play with them and be one with them. She had great admiration for my father, not only for his efficiency in running a large establishment, but also for his skill in his profession. But, more than anything else, she feared him, and there were times when I could see how deep-seated this fear had been and how it slowly led to revulsion.

There is nothing much to be said for the relationship that existed between my parents. My father was domineering and tough, respected and feared as the patriarch of a large family. My mother was expected to be docile and submissive, ever ready to do his bidding. In the earlier days of marriage, whenever she tried to assert herself, she was silenced by a stinging slap across her face, the typical male chauvinist style of demonstrating superiority. It was perhaps this understanding that united the two women, my grandmother and my mother, in a special bond—that both were enslaved by the men in their lives.

Bringing Up Children

My mother bore 11 children, of whom one girl died when she was just a few months old. Whether it was neglect or sheer ignorance or both, I am not so sure. All her children proved to be very bright and exceptional in their studies. Most of them were quite successful when they grew up. But how much my mother had suffered in the process of bringing them up is something that I could not imagine. We were a handful, always up to some mischief. With so many highly individualistic and assertive children, there was always chaos of minor or major proportions, with some youngster screaming for his/her rightful share and someone else staking his/her claims.

But mother bore all of these patiently. Her world consisted of her children. She was an ideal mother in that she would eat only after feeding her children and would sleep only after every one of us had gone to sleep. To us children, mother was a person who fed us, cheered us and nursed us when we were sick. I wonder at that stage whether we even realised what life would have been without her. We did not appreciate her talents till much later. My mother could sing well, play the violin, and she read the English newspapers. But I never saw her well dressed or heard her sing when I was a child. She was too busy for that. But we always noticed how shabbily she was treated by her sisters-in-law. It may be because she was from a humble family and that she had lost her father when she was barely 13 years old.

Relationship between the Two Families

Since my mother was from a modest family, the relationship between her family and my father's was never very pleasant, though my grandmother Rajam *Patti* was supportive of her. She had a melodious voice and a gift for narrating the *Bhagavatham*[6] beautifully. She was a great favourite with all of us grandchildren. But neither Rajam *Patti* nor my mother were treated warmly by my father's people. This made a very deep impression on almost all of us. My mother was taunted, insulted and humiliated by her in-laws on every possible occasion. My father never gave her the kind of respect that was due to her as the mother of his children; never consulted her on any matter concerning the family, not even regarding the marriages of her own children. In middle-class south Indian homes, the woman has to be from a wealthy family of high social status to deserve respect and consideration among her in-laws.

I would never forget my mother standing in a corner, usually holding the youngest of her children, dressed in a simple sari, with hardly any jewellery. She would stand unnoticed, while my aunts and others in her home strutted about swathed in their Kanchipuram silks and flashing their diamonds. It was this treatment meted out to my mother that made me furious. The anger and hurt used to rise, but I would never question the injustice aloud, for I knew that everyone would blame her saying she had instigated me. But I was determined that I would not allow anyone to insult and humiliate me in my life and I would not allow myself to be enslaved.

A GIRL MUST BE RESPONSIBLE

As a child, I spent only my first five years with my parents. They were then living in a small provincial town in what is now the state of Andhra Pradesh. The town was known for its lovely jasmines and unbearable summer heat. My father was particular that at least some of his children—the elder ones—should go to Madras for their schooling. We were thus sent to our grandmother's youngest sister Lalitha, who lived in her palatial bungalow designed and built to resemble a feudal manor house. The bungalow was set in the middle of a beautifully designed garden, occupying nearly an acre. She was married when she was 9 years old and widowed when she was hardly 30. I remember her as a strong woman, fair and thin, a person of few words, a strict disciplinarian and an efficient lady. In relation to her wealth, she led an austere life. For as long as I can remember, she washed her clothes herself, in spite of the fact that she had domestic help. It was perhaps due to the Brahmin concept of 'pollution', or perhaps her own sense of discipline. She ran the house with clockwork precision and efficiency.

We, the children, had the luxury of a car to go to school. There were servants to do all the work. However, this did not mean that we were allowed to idle our time away. My sister and I were kept busy with lessons in classical music after school. I did have plenty of time in the world to roam the garden, which was almost neglected by the time we children came to live there since Lalitha could not find proper gardeners to tend the place. However, the sturdy trees and shrubs survived with the minimum care shown to them. I spent delightful moments watching fish swim in the huge pond and listening to the chirping of birds or plucking jasmine. My happiest moments were spent in the garden on the swing, with the breeze blowing in my face, and my skirt swirling, as though I was flying, flying far, far away from the suffocating world of elders and siblings who sought to control my life. Being born in a large family might be a blessing. To me, however, it was a mixed blessing. All the time I was told that as I was born into a large family I should learn not only to share but even to deny myself things that I would like to have. I could not even ask for simple things, for if everybody started asking for whatever they fancied, then it would be a burden on my father. Not only was it impressed upon me that I was born into a large family, but that I was a girl, which meant I had to be much more responsible than the boys. Even when I talked or laughed aloud, eyebrows were raised and I would see grandma frowning or my father lecturing me, saying that loud laughter was what destroyed Draupadi and Seetha. Of course, I would sulk and demand logical explanations, but my questions were ignored as the impertinence of a conceited girl.

Comparisons might be odious, but you cannot escape them when you are born in a large family such as mine. Comparing girls with boys, how much of a responsibility girls are. About how to find them bridegrooms, how to settle them; boys, after all, will take care of themselves once they are qualified. There were also comparisons between girls; Mythili, my elder sister, was held out as a model young girl—friendly, bright, hard working and helpful. She was full of life and gregarious. She knew almost all our relatives and never missed a single function. I, on the other hand, ran and hid myself in some corner when I encountered a stranger and was tongue-tied even in the presence of relatives. I was awkward and shy. Physically, Mythili and I were poles apart—she was short and dusky, and I was tall, fair, broad-shouldered and athletic. However, we both had large dark eyes and thick hair and there was enough resemblance between us for one of us to be mistaken for the other. When we sang together, even though we had our training at different times, our voices blended beautifully. But the consensus was that I had a remarkably good voice, that I showed promise! This was one field where I drew attention and appreciation, but otherwise I was considered quite slow and dull.

School, like home, was uninteresting, but in some respects it was better since there was no frowning grand-aunt, finding fault with whatever I did. At school, I was a chatterbox and irrepressible. I was fairly good in studies and the teachers always had a word of praise for me. Though a little lazy, I was never spared by my *physical director*. I was always in some team or other, and played badminton and throwball. When the school started recruiting students for the National Cadet Corps (NCC), I was excited. I wanted to join by all means. When I approached my grand-aunt for permission, she astounded me by granting it without a second thought! She said, 'You should learn to be on your own; you are so used to getting everything done by others, even washing your plates and clothes. If they take you out for camps, it is all the better!' She further said that it would be a good exercise.

I knew that despite my grand-aunt's generally conservative outlook, she was liberal in some respects. Nevertheless, her granting me permission to join the NCC so readily did surprise me. I was thrilled. I just loved to wear the khaki uniform with divided skirts and shoes, and to parade. We were even taken for target practice once and I did fairly well at shooting. I was selected to participate in the Republic Day Parade in Delhi, the high point of my school career.

Grand-aunt's house was the meeting place for all our relatives. During the summer, the house was usually filled with aunts, uncles and cousins. The strain of taking care of all the guests used to tell on her, for she used to be quite irritable and take her irritation out on us. We used to have a riotous time, singing and playing cards. Usually a dozen of us had to manage with just two packs of cards. But grand-aunt's most admirable trait was her charitable disposition. I have seen Dr Muthulakshmi[7] and sister Subbalakshmi[8] visit us periodically. We also visited the Awai home where Dr Muthulakshmi stayed. My grand-aunt never refused anyone who approached her with a request for help for a charitable cause.

It was during those days that I could see what it was to be a girl in a middle-class family. It began with Mythili, bright and fired with the ambition to join a medical college. The elders did not take her seriously, but she applied and got a seat since her grades were quite good. To her utter dismay, all the elders in the family including father and grandma were against it. The reason given was that as the eldest daughter she should think of settling down. Poor Mythili. For days she could not eat or sleep, she was just not herself. It was heart-rending to see her walk about trying to control her tears—Mythili, whom I had never seen shedding a tear, Mythili, so sure of herself, so confident, looked defeated because she was born a girl. She could not choose her profession because she was born in a middle-class Brahmin family. She chose Zoology as her subject and completed her graduation with a university rank.

My own college life was quite uneventful. Somehow, my father thought I would do well as a medical practitioner (or was it a sense of guilt at having denied Mythili the chance which was at work?), but I refused and chose history. College was more interesting than school because students had greater freedom and flexibility. I was called a bookworm and the subject I chose required a good deal of reading. I was quite happy reading history and political science. When I completed my bachelor's degree, I decided to do my master's. My father also thought that I should be allowed to take my master's degree. In middle-class families, education was considered necessary for girls. My family was no exception. In fact, father was very particular that all his daughters should be well educated. All the girls were expected to take at least one degree. In the case of my sister Mythili, she was allowed to do her postgraduate studies. But working and earning were not considered necessary for women. Education was necessary to help the woman to be an enlightened wife and mother. An educated woman would be an efficient housewife with her knowledge of health and hygiene. She would be better equipped to bring up her children. As an educated woman, she would be a fit companion for her well-educated husband. The purpose of educating girls had only such limited objectives. My family was no exception. While I was busy filling in the application for my postgraduate course, the elders in the family, especially my grand-aunt and my aunts, were busy casting my horoscope. Even though my father did not seem to be in a hurry to get me married, he did not stand in the way of these preparations. In fact, he appeared to be a curious mixture of traditional and modern ideas. While he wanted his daughters to be well educated, he was also keen that we should get married and settle down as soon as possible. He thought he would fail in his duty if he did not get the daughters married at the proper age. He was no believer in horoscopes, but believed in elaborate ceremonies and rituals connected with marriage, and believed in giving gifts and presents, since he thought these helped elevate his own status in society.

Just when I thought that I had settled down to study, marriage proposals came from my in-laws-to-be. My father initially did not show much interest, but when he heard of the phenomenal wealth and the position of the family, I think he was quite determined that I should marry into this well-known industrial family. When I heard that the boy's parents were coming to see me, I was quite shocked. I never thought that my wedding would be settled so soon. Like many girls in our society—perhaps even more so—I was completely unprepared to get married. The very idea made me wince. Marriage meant, for me, more or less life-long imprisonment. As I saw it, it was one monotonous round of cooking, cleaning, childbearing and forever trying one's level best to please the husband and in-laws. I never thought I would be successful in the role of a housewife. But my protests and pleadings were ignored. When I said that I was not interested in marriage, people thought I was irresponsible. In middle-class upper-caste families, the older men decide everything. How much education a girl should receive, when she should get married and to whom—all these were questions in which the concerned girl had very little freedom to express her opinion. I had no choice. My father decided that I should marry this particular boy, and that was final. I knew I was fighting a losing battle. Being a girl in a large family, without any support from any quarter, I had to submit. It is painful, even at this distance in time, to think of all the discussions, the amount of coaxing and threats that were used to break my resistance. My mother, who had never had a voice in anything, could only plead her own helplessness to me. It was finally Mythili who spoke to me for nearly two hours. She said that my father's decision was final and that I must have noticed that in the battle that raged, I was alone. I could see that she herself was quite unhappy, that she would rather this match did not take place, but so strong was the authority of my father and grand-aunt over all of us, that she was forced to talk to me and had been assigned the painful task of convincing me. She accomplished it well. Very gently, with an understanding that I found quite unusual, she made me agree to the marriage. At that point in time, neither she nor I had a clue as to how stormy my marital life would turn out to be.

Looking back, I wonder whether any two persons could have been so mismatched as Raman and myself! He loved all the pleasures, pomp and luxury that money could buy; loved get-togethers, parties and spending time with friends. His ultimate God was money. As for me, I preferred to read, listen to good music and, when time permitted, sing. To me, the daily routine of cooking, cleaning and scrubbing was quite boring. I hated people dropping in to see us since I used to be tongue-tied, not knowing what to say, unless the conversation was about some serious subject. But Raman enjoyed showing me off, at least that is how it struck me. I was a graduate (which was a rare phenomenon in those days) and accomplished in music, which perhaps made him feel quite proud. But it is not enough if a woman is accomplished and intelligent; she should be a good cook, a good housekeeper and a good entertainer. Though I was no great cook, I somehow managed housekeeping. I was disappointed that no one took notice of my accomplishments, but only of my inadequacies. My in-laws did not believe that I was capable of running a house and have always lamented that I was no good as a housewife. Before I could settle down, I had my two boys within a short space of time. The arrival of two children did not bring any special joy to me, though I grew fond of them over the years. Bringing up children, I knew, was a difficult task, but how very difficult I found it to feed them, take care of them, as well as nurse them though every illness, and through major and minor accidents! There did not seem to be any respite from these enormous responsibilities. By the time the boys were 3 years old, I had moved from Hyderabad to Kumbakonam, a very conventional city, where I felt alienated and alone. But there were further moves. We kept moving from one place to another—like gypsies, I thought—and I did not really enjoy it.

Parents' Neglect

In all this moving and travelling, there was practically no help from my parents or from my in-laws. Hardly any family members visited us. During all these years, I tried to complete my studies and successfully took my master's degree, but not before encountering mild opposition from my in-laws. They first could not comprehend the reason for my desire to take my master's degree. In fact, I myself realised the underlying reason for completing my studies only much later. I also managed to continue my music practice. One advantage of my stay at Kumbakonam was that I met and learnt from the unforgettable

Rajagopalan—Raja Sir as he was affectionately known—a great exponent of music, who had taught and shaped some of the outstanding musicians of the contemporary period. Raja Sir was the father figure at that time. I not only learnt my music from him, but drew a great deal of emotional support. He always used to say that before he came to teach me, he spent at least half an hour brushing up his theory, since he expected me to suddenly come up with some questions regarding musical traditions. I used to drive through the unmanageable traffic of Kumbakonam in order to drop him at his house after music lessons. I still remember the singing lessons and the long discussions we had during those evenings. I even started the boys on music lessons, but they did not seem interested enough and subsequently the lessons were stopped. Raman hardly noticed anything. To him, only his office and work mattered. During those early years, both of us pursued our own separate interests, and so there were not many causes for conflict. I immensely disliked his habits of excessive spending and drinking. Whenever I started questioning him, he used to end the argument with the remark that smacked of male chauvinism: 'After all I am the male, I shall decide.'

We had moved from Kumbakonam to Coimbatore. There, for four years, life was quite hectic—it was one long chain of parties and dinners. I had a glimpse of the glamorous world of city: the ladies, busy with their visits to beauty parlours, cooking and cleaning, and men whose only ambition was to make money and have a good time; the parties where liquor flowed and the whole house reverberated with the shouts and laughter of the boisterous crowd. With shock, I realised how bankrupt these middle-class men had become; they had nothing serious to discuss except their own business, and their attitude to women was patronising. All that these people wanted was to have a 'good time'.

There was again another move from Coimbatore to Tirunelveli, a town where life was more relaxed. There was little that was exciting about Tirunelveli. Things moved more or less quietly till we came to Chennai. This move turned out to be a turning point in my life. I joined the local college as a lecturer. That was a new experience. Significantly, while working in the college, I had the chance to get involved in the teachers' movement. It was an exciting experience. I learnt of the injustices inflicted on teachers. In many institutions, including the one in which I worked, teachers did not even have security of tenure; there were no benefits such as maternity or medical leave. Teachers, especially the women teachers, were mere wage slaves. The involvement in the movement taught me that one had to struggle to win one's rights.

This involvement led to harassment. My colleague and Leftist friend Indira and I were interrogated and abused as being disloyal to the institution. Our own colleagues would not talk to us. At the same time, the teachers' movement also brought me and Indira into contact with other leaders of the trade union movement. I learned that only an organised struggle could help us achieve a change for the better. Even the harassment was helpful. I felt that I would be able to face problems with greater confidence. As a working woman and a housewife, the pace of life was hectic, but I managed both roles cheerfully. Raman initially did not seem to mind my taking up the job, but what I did not realise was that the process of our separation had already started. On establishing my own friendships and my own interests, we started falling apart, and whatever complaints he had seemed to worsen.

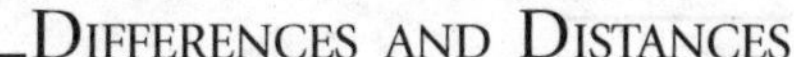

DIFFERENCES AND DISTANCES

During this time, Raman started complaining of all kinds of aches and pains. At the same time, his office began to complain about his temperament. Life with him became quite intolerable. Despite all my protests, the boys were taken to Madurai and left at their grandparents' (my in-laws) house. My work at the college and my friendship with Indira were the consoling factors during those times. But my friends were not welcome at the house. When I went out with them for shopping or for movies, I had to face recrimination and abuses for being irresponsible.

Perhaps Raman was also feeling that he had psychological problems. It was by accident that I once overhead his conversation with his psychiatrist. Much later, I found the card of the doctor and learnt that Raman was suffering from depression. I wanted to ask him, but did not, since I thought it would make him furious.

Matters were gradually getting worse. Arguments between us were an everyday occurrence. The only way to avoid arguments was to keep absolutely quiet even in the face of wanton provocation. Sometimes, Raman got violent and it led to physical abuse. It was then that fear started gripping me. It was the fear of living with a maniac: I did not know what would spark off physical violence as even a chance remark was sufficient to rouse his temper. He was never considerate to the servants at home, but now it was intolerable. As I have noted earlier, I later found out that he suffered from manic depression.

Raman suspected every move of mine. He hated my independence. My involvement in the teachers' movement was resented. He tried dissuading me indirectly, but I would not budge. I went ahead and tried to form a teachers' union in the college. Indira faced harassment in the college because of me. Even Indira's husband Satish came in for abuse from the college management for supporting the teachers' struggle and Indira's involvement in it.

As part of the teachers' struggle, I had to interact frequently with male teachers. My colleagues would not even talk to me.

My husband could not tolerate male lecturers talking to me. He even went to the extent of accusing to me of having affairs with every man with whom I spoke.

Violence

During one of those days when Raman was indulging in verbal abuse, he started shouting and physically threatening me. I just got into the car and drove to the college. I simply decided that I would not go home. The next day was a nightmare. When I came home and he returned from work, the servants were sent outside the house. When I asked for the key of my room, the answer was a flat refusal. As I watched him, he ordered the servants out and closed all the doors and windows in preparation for beating me up. I realised this when he took out his broad belt. My immediate reaction was to try and force my way out of the house, but I was pushed inside a room. I started pleading that I would leave, that I wanted nothing from him except my freedom. I feared that in his anger he might do anything. As far as he was concerned, I was his slave and whatever happened to me, no questions would be asked. Just then, I heard the noise of a vehicle, a very familiar sound, and at that moment a most welcome sound, as Indira and Satish alighted from the vehicle. I ran to the door. Very reluctantly, Raman allowed them in. I was sobbing, terror-stricken. I just grasped Indira's hands. In a voice hardly audible, I mumbled, 'Take me with you, I won't stay here. He will kill me.' Indira was calm. In fact, she appeared the tougher of the two. Satish was worried and asked Raman as to what had happened and the curt reply was that it was something personal.

That same night Raman left for a wedding. As soon as he left, I packed my suitcase and left with my friends. I did not want to stay in that house a moment longer. I feared that in a fit of rage Raman might even kill me. After a couple of days, Raman came back and saw that I was not at home. He came to fetch me from Indira's place. I refused to go with him. I told him that I was unwilling to live the life of a slave any more. It was a shock to him; he could not believe it. Though he went away that day, he tried to get the members of his family to persuade me to go back. He tried through my natal family as well, but I refused. I was not prepared to lead a life where I would be constantly under threat of physical violence, and without any self-respect. The fact that I had a job made a huge difference. Without a job, I would have been completely dependent on him, making me utterly vulnerable.

IMPACT ON THE CHILDREN

The attempts at reconciliation continued. Finally, I decided to take a flat and live with my younger son, who was then 14 years old. I rented an apartment in the same building as my friends. To start with, for a few weeks, everything went smoothly. But when Raman started visiting us during the weekends, trouble erupted again. He would pick up a quarrel on trivial matters. My son was so upset about the visits that he used to disappear from sight the moment he saw his father coming. During the course of the year, I had to face my colleagues in the workplace. People around did not ask me directly, but news spread of this rift between Raman and me. All his friends and our old acquaintances stopped calling on me. Satish used to counsel me patiently through all these tension-ridden times. But the difference in gender gave rise to gossip about us.

There was much gossip connecting me and other men, especially Satish. I could make out meaningful glances being exchanged, and notice the sudden silence on seeing me. As for the college, my colleagues in my own department were wonderful. Whatever reservations they felt, they did not show them. They were polite as usual. Only once or twice, in confidence, did they ask me what had happened. When I told them what I had been through, I remember one of them saying, with tears in her eyes, that I had suffered a lot. There were, of course, others who were not so kind. However, it did not matter, since Indira and Satish were there. They were a pillar of strength and stood by me like a rock.

In all this turmoil, my sons, especially the younger one suffered a great deal. The periodic visits of his father and the scenes and tensions, that accompanied his visit seemed to have left a deep impression on him. Though very bright, he had never been much above average academically, but now his performance at school was going from bad to worse. There were complaints that he never finished his work properly. His father did not seem to be aware of these problems. Whatever he saw in it, all that he did was to indulge him occasionally by taking him to expensive hotels and buying him junk food.

Raman's visits and the quarrels were also making me tense. I used to dread the weekends. During one such argument, he, as usual, tried to hit me. I walked out of the room and went to my neighbour's apartment. After half an hour when I came back, to my dismay, I saw that the lock of my bedroom door had been opened and he had walked away with all the clothes and my personal belongings. It was too much. I immediately contacted my family and informed them of what had happened. They in turn told me that they were with me and that the harassment had to stop forthwith.

ADVICE TO ADJUST

Even though my family came to my support, all my siblings did not have the same opinion with regard to my decision. While the elder brothers sympathised with me, they felt that ultimately I should try and adjust at least for the sake of the boys. They felt that perhaps a temporary separation would help us get over some of our differences. It was difficult for them to accept the idea that, though their own sister was suffering so much, a woman could even think of walking out on her husband. The younger brothers, on the other hand, were clear that if I decided on a divorce, they would support me wholeheartedly. As for my parents, it was naturally difficult for them to think of divorce. Of the two, it was my mother who supported and accepted my decision to live separately. Whatever reservations he may have had, even my father decided not to question my decision.

I had more or less decided to move the court formally for a divorce. However, I had to abandon the idea when both my sons pleaded with me not to be hasty. I was unable to gauge fully the nature and extent of the impact these developments had on them. Though the elder one appeared quite confident, it was obvious that he was unhappy. The younger boy did not discuss anything with me, but seemed quite confused. But when I came to know that the boys were not for a break between the parents, I decided to wait. At least, I thought, I shall not make the first move towards a divorce.

For the time being I decided to move to the working women's hostel. The college where I worked had its own hostel. Initially, they refused me accommodation, since they feared there would be criticism from the public when a woman like me, who was separated from her husband, was allowed to live with other young lecturers. After a while, they let me stay.

I knew hostel life would be boring. I hated the food, the rigid rules and regulations regarding when to report to the warden and when to go out. But I had no choice, and I had to endure it, since it would be helpful later on if I decided on a divorce. During this period, my in-laws died. The future of the boys, especially the question of where they would stay, became a question mark. Their father decided to leave them in Madurai, in a small apartment, which he would visit periodically. I was not consulted by anyone in this matter.

Even if I had offered to accommodate them, I wonder if the boys would have been prepared to live with me. They knew that I would not be able to give them the kind of creature comforts they had got used to. Life would be somewhat spartan for them if they chose to stay with me. They would have to work hard. All this must have weighed heavily against living with me. Moreover, the gossip about Satish and me, and the criticism of my in-laws, could have influenced them.

Living away from their parents, without any older person to discipline them, had its effect on the boys. They lost interest in studies. The younger one especially was totally confused and disoriented. During his school days he was extremely good in sports, but there was no encouragement from any of us to help him concentrate on sports. He seemed to have been deeply hurt by the break between the parents and by his own academic failure.

Everything seemed quiet for a few months after I moved into the hostel. But soon Raman started indulging in threats. He even spoke to the hostel management and told them that I should be asked to leave the hostel. On one occasion, he sent a few thugs to threaten my friends to face the consequences for supporting his wife.

When I found these harassments unbearable, I approached the All India Democratic Women's Association (AIDWA) for help. It was my first encounter with some of the women leaders of the Left movement. After their intervention, the harassment was mitigated. Nevertheless, I had to file a police complaint on a couple of occasions. From the way I handled the whole problem, Raman seemed to have understood that I would not be cowed down easily and that I had the support of an organisation that could not be treated lightly.

While I went through all these problems in my personal life, I was also getting involved in the women's movement through AIDWA. It was during this time that I met some of the top leaders of AIDWA. Their work in the movement was a source of inspiration and their support gave me a lot of confidence. Activists at various levels of the leadership of the organisation gave me support. I also met many other women—ordinary women, who had fought their own battles in their personal lives, deserted by their husbands or harassed by their in-laws who had approached AIDWA for support and had subsequently become members and activists of AIDWA. These women had struggled to make their lives meaningful, and I spent long hours talking to them. Their lives and their struggles had a profound influence on me.

Getting involved in the women's movement gave me a chance to read a great deal about the position of women, of the condition of our own society. I started writing. I handled classes for activists of the women's movements on history, political economy, the challenges before the women's movement and many other topics. The experience of working in an organisation gave me greater confidence in myself. In addition, involvement in the teachers' and women's movements led to an encounter with Marxist philosophy. The philosophy itself was quite difficult for me to understand. I spent time reading a great deal of Marxist literature, which influenced my perception of everything round me. My own problems, I understood, were part of the larger problems existing in society. I understood that as long as this system of unequal relationships existed, there could not be equality of the sexes. In the present setup of society, I could see that everything, even human beings, were just commodities and personal relationships were not based on considerations of natural respect. As one among the millions of women who suffered injustice, I learnt to connect my own problems with the larger social and political milieu and its contradictions.

While I was going through these new experiences, and when I thought that things were slowly setting down, my younger son suffered a nervous breakdown. This was a shock. Earlier, the passing away of my sister Mythili had been a great shock to all of us. My parents were heartbroken. It was a loss that left a void in the lives of those who were close to her. I took quite some time to recover from it. But my son's illness caught me totally unawares. We had all noticed that he had not been quite himself for a few months. He had withdrawn himself completely from all activities. But nobody knew what exactly the problem was. He never left the room in which he stayed, nor spoke a word to anybody. All of a sudden, he became violent and was uncontrollable. Clearly unable to handle the crisis, Raman got in touch with me and requested me to go to the hospital to take care of him.

The reaction of my own family was quite predictable. The boy's illness, they felt, was mainly due to the break between the parents, and because I failed to take custody of the boys. All of them forgot that I had no say in the matter. In fairness to my parents, it must be said that they supported me. Strangely, it was my father who felt guilty, since he thought that the marriage into which he had forced me had only brought me trouble.

ATTEMPTED SUICIDE

I spent weeks in the hospital with my son, taking care of him, taking charge of his medical treatment and discussing his case with the doctors. There were moments when he would turn violent, and hostile to everyone, including me. Still, at such moments, I was the only person who could control him. It was once again Indira and Satish who told me that only work could lead to a cure. Within a few years, he attempted suicide twice. He was in the hospital for several weeks and had to undergo major surgeries. Once again, I was with him day and night. I do not know how I managed to go through the nightmare, but then I was determined that I would not be defeated with each crisis. I felt my determination growing stronger. But it was not easy. Sometimes I found it really difficult to cope and when I went to college to settle my leave, it was one of my friends who pulled me out of my depression. After one look at me, she said, 'You look defeated, please pull yourself together don't forget, there are many in the college who gain confidence by merely looking at you—at least for the sake of those women, fight back!' That was enough. I decided I would not give up the struggle. I would fight back, by all means.

In this crisis, too, it was friends, more than relatives, who helped. I could not even get half a dozen of my relatives to visit my son regularly. It was my friends who visited him and spent time with him. As for my in-laws, I hardly had any help from them. As for Raman, he was only too happy to be relieved of the responsibility of looking after his son.

It is said that even the darkest cloud has a silver lining. In all these stages of turmoil in my life, I reminded myself that I was highly qualified, and that I had many sources of support. My friends have been the greatest source of support and joy. I have been with my niece Akila ever since she was born. We enjoy a special relationship with each other. At one level, I am her '*athai*' (paternal aunt). At another level, I am her friend. When she was a child, I had sung lullabies to her and had told her stories as she grew up. I used to tell her about all kinds of things; she used to say that she developed an interest in life sciences because of me. In moments of crisis she was a source of great solace to me. Now, as a young girl, she shows a greater understanding of my son than even the grown-ups do.

It has been now almost 20 years since a serious crisis erupted in my marital life. Raman has more or less become reconciled to our living our own separate lives. However, my younger son still continues have his periodic tantrums and is still unable to get into any routine work. I try to accept these problems. I am much more fortunate than many other women—I am educated, I have a job, I have friends. I remind myself that for many women, their day-to-day life itself is a struggle. I see that my own problems were due mostly to the fact that I was born a woman in a patriarchal society. Since a woman was expected to be primarily only a wife and mother, and to subordinate all her interests to those of her husband and children, even holding a job was hard work. I needed the job so that I could be independent, and it was this need for independence that was resented by our patriarchal society. In this struggle to retain my independence, I had to pay a price. The taunts and insults that a patriarchal society reserves for independent women, the sustained harassment from my husband, the illness of my son—all these challenges had to be faced and met. If, in all those crises, I was able to retain my sanity, it was because of my job and due to my involvement in the women's movement.

There are scores of women who are oppressed due to their caste, oppressed in their workplace and in their families. If I can contribute a little towards helping those women in gaining their freedom, I would be happy. I would consider my life and my own personal struggles meaningful if I could contribute in some way to making this society a better place for human beings to live in. My own struggles in my personal life have enriched me and helped me to achieve great economic and personal security and stability. They have helped me to try and understand society better and equipped me to work with other women and men, to make this world a better place.

Notes

1. *Sabhas* refer to voluntary organisations formed to promote classical dance, music and the arts.
2. A colloquial expression in Tamil meaning son, or more generally, a boy.
3. A colony of houses exclusively occupied by Brahmins.
4. A cereal-based preparation eaten as breakfast.
5. The theory of *karma* argued that one's lot in life was the consequence of one's actions in the previous birth, and could not be changed by one's efforts in the present one.
6. A popular text in Hindu mythology.
7. Dr Muthulakshmi was a well-known fighter for women's rights. She was in the fore front of the fight for the abolition of the *Devadasi* system.
8. Sister Subbulakshmi, an educationist, established a home for the training and education of young widows.

5

The Tyranny of Tradition*

Leela Gulati

Ponnamma (1866–1932)

Our story begins with the life of Ponnamma and her husband, Balakrishna, my maternal great-grandparents. They lived around 1860, in a small village called Kadathur, in Coimbatore district of Tamil Nadu, formerly part of the Madras Presidency. Ponnamma, which means 'golden girl' in Tamil, was born into a very rich landowning family living in the village of Kolinjawadi on the banks of the river Amaravati. (There were actually six such villages, all beginning with the letter K, located on the banks of the river Cauvery and its tributaries, of which Amaravati was one.) As Ponnamma's family had won scholarly distinction, the Sanskrit title of *dikshitar* was conferred on its members in recognition of their abilities in the Sanskrit language and their performance of special rituals.

Ponnamma was born around the year 1866, one of five children—four daughters and a son. She was married before she was 12 to the third son of another Brahmin landowning family in the neighbouring village of Kadathur, also located on the Amaravati. Her husband Balakrishna or Bala, as he was called, was six years older than her, and the marriage was performed after their horoscopes were matched.[1] Bala was not only well versed in Sanskrit and Tamil, but was also a matriculate and hence literate in English, for English education had already come to his village by 1870. Ponnamma, too, was proficient in Sanskrit, having learnt it at home. Western education was acquired

* Originally published in the *Indian Journal of Gender Studies*, Vol. 6, No. 2, 1999, pp. 185–201.

solely for the purpose of getting a job, and since Ponnamma, being a girl, was not expected to work, she was never sent to school. Her husband taught her some English, which came in handy later in her life when she had to move to Burma. The couple lived beyond the normal span of life for men and women in those times. Ponnamma lived for 67 years and died in 1932 in faraway Burma. At the age of 73 Bala died there, too, within a year of her death, grieving for her.

Bala's family was involved in paddy cultivation. The land was planted and harvested three times a year. For some years their land was cultivated with the help of hired labourers, mostly tribal; at other times they leased the land out to other socially inferior communities. Rice was grown twice and a crop of lentils the third time. The joint family also lent money on the basis of collateral—usually land or gold jewellery—and probably usurped the land of those who failed to repay, a common practice in those days. In the middle of the 19th century, the Brahmins, by virtue of their literacy, religious scholarship and ritually superior social status, were feared, trusted and held in awe by the rest of the population.

Ponnamma and Balakrishna lived in the exclusive Brahmin neigbourhood usually referred to in all south Indian villages as the *agraharam*, consisting of a single row of houses in which 60 families lived. The canal to the Amaravati river was just a kilometre away. These Brahmin households were connected to one another through marriage and kinship, and other social and economic ties.

Being the eldest son, my great-grandfather was the head of the extended family. The ancestral land was jointly held. He and his brothers lived virtually under the same roof. Their houses were adjacent and had common walls, such that there was ventilation only from the front and the back. All the doors were constructed in a single line of vision; a person standing at the front door could see right up to the yard where the well was located. The pillared front porch connecting all the houses was exclusively for the men. This is where all the moneylending, leasing and repayment transactions took place. Women were confined to the interior parts of the houses and only elderly women could come out to the main porch. The houses, though dark, were cool, with air flowing in from the common front porch into the shared inner courtyard called the *muttam*.

The family was rigidly patriarchal, with lineage and property passing through the male line. Ponnamma and Bala had four daughters and no son, a repetition of the pattern in Ponnamma's natal family.

Later, Ponnamma had to adopt the second son of her first daughter to make up for this lapse for the purpose of funeral rituals.[2] While otherwise life was fairly easy and smooth, the family moneylending business, which they called a bank, met with a crisis. Some form of Western banking had reached the villages by 1870, and was beginning to provide competition. The family's lending operations collapsed in the 1890s, a decade of depression, famine, pestilence and great impoverishment in the south Indian countryside. The brothers, who were the real managers of the bank, approached Bala for help. They asked him to forfeit his portion of the ancestral property in return for lifelong support and help with the dowry payments for his three unmarried daughters. (Only one out of their four daughters was married by then.) The argument was, 'Give us your share of the land and do not worry about the debts. We shall pay them.'

Bala's loyalty to his family was very strong. He had no reason to suspect his brothers' bona fides. A verbal assurance was more than enough for him—after all it was his family and he was the head. Ponnamma, who was practical, shrewd and cautious, asked Bala to be responsible for only a part of the debt so as to keep a share of the ancestral property. But he would not hear of any of this. Unlike his wife, Bala was 'God's own good man'—very trusting. Here we see that women had very little say in the decisions men made. If Ponnamma had made an issue of it, she would have been considered an outsider showing her true colours. So Bala signed away his share.

It did not take long for things to go from bad to worse. Bala's brothers could not stem the tide of debt. As things deteriorated, Bala and Ponnamma felt increasingly isolated and found themselves totally destitute, with no means whatsoever to fall back on. They were financially deserted by the joint family, and finally Bala had to take up a job as a primary school teacher in a neighbouring village—something considered humiliating for a family who were landed gentry. This was around 1900.

Ponnamma's first daughter had been born after many prayers and vows were made. Since the snake goddess had been propitiated, the child was named Nagamma after her. Three more daughters followed her. The fact that they were all girls made things very difficult, deepening the family's economic crisis. If there had been even one son, there would have been no question of forfeiting the ancestral property. While the economic situation of the family was deteriorating rapidly, the girls were fast reaching the age of marriage.

With the pressure on Bala and Ponnamma to get the girls married before they attained puberty,[3] the stress within the household increased. Ponnamma's ill luck in having only daughters came in for much caustic comment. In the early phases of their married life, when things were moving smoothly, Bala was central and Ponnamma on the periphery of family affairs. When the family fortunes collapsed and Bala could not cope, it was left completely to Ponnamma to negotiate the family through the crisis. Ponnamma was considered a practical, intelligent and helpful woman of great compassion. She was knowledgeable about ayurvedic medicine,[4] often helping other Brahmin households with their illnesses. She had a good reputation in the village and the esteem in which she was held helped her now.

SEETHA (1885–1964)

The marriage of the second daughter, Seetha, who was to become my grandmother, now had to be arranged. She was already 10 and would soon reach puberty. Though fair-skinned by Tamil Brahmin standards, she was severely handicapped by poor eyesight. In addition, there was no money for dowry or marriage expenses. In this predicament, Ponnamma set to work with all her resourcefulness and networking skills, and began searching for a groom. Through word of mouth and marriage brokers, one was located. He was 20 years older than Seetha and had been married twice already. His first wife had died within days of the wedding ceremony in an accident. He had been married to his second wife Akka for six years and the couple were childless as Akka could not conceive. Monogamy had already become a well-established practice. It was the Hindu ideal, and Rama and Sita were considered the ideal couple. But when a woman was infertile, a man was permitted to take another wife.

If my grandfather had not married at all he probably would have joined a Hindu monastic order. Unfortunately, the Ramakrishna Mission,[5] with which he had close ties, admitted only the unmarried. So he was definitely in no frame of mind now to accept an additional wife. But his mother was bent on forcing her son to marry a third time. He even ran away to Agra to pursue his academic interests and take up a job. The family would not hear of this, and forcibly brought him back and exerted pressure on him to marry. So he finally agreed, provided Seetha's family consented to some conditions of his own. The principal one was that he would not abandon his existing wife or send her back to her parents. Ponnamma was so desperate to marry off her daughter that she agreed to this. And so the marriage was solemnised.

It was not a good match—the groom was much older than Seetha, already married and had wanted to become an ascetic. To top it all, he had a family of 11 younger brothers and sisters, and a widowed mother to look after! Except for his educational achievement (B.A. in mathematics) and a steady government job, nothing else was attractive about him in traditional marriage market terms. Did the girl have a say? Was Ponnamma more anxious to get rid of her daughter than to consider her happiness? Unfortunately, yes—beating the puberty deadline was more important than anything else.

However, Ponnamma did win some concessions from the groom's family. Seetha's near-blindness would be ignored, the marriage would take place at the bridegroom's house, all expenses incurred would be borne by the groom, and no dowry or jewellery would be demanded or given. While Ponnamma and Bala thought they were getting a good deal, Seetha did not think so at all. To be the second wife of a man 20 years older than herself and to have to agree to live with his previous wife were humiliating conditions of marriage. Why did she have to be subjected to all this humiliation? Obviously, being a girl, she was a burden and not an asset to the family. The discussions within the family that preceded the marriage dwelt obsessively on these themes. These ideas became permanently ingrained in her mind, and left deep scars and negative feelings about her sex. For the rest of her life she detested women and made no secret of it. She would always regret the fact that she was born a girl and would say it was a curse to be a woman—first as a daughter, then as a childbearer and finally as a widow.

The marriages of Ponnamma's other two daughters, Seetha's younger sisters, were of the same order: the family's bankruptcy meant it had no bargaining power. The third daughter married a man whose father was in debt. In addition, the groom was shorter than the bride—something traditionally considered embarrassing. The last daughter was married into a very poor family.

After her wedding, my grandmother Seetha, at the tender age of 11, moved into her husband's house. She had to cope with and take care of 11 brothers- and sisters-in-law, all older than herself but younger than her husband. She had to share the economic resources of her husband with them, and the emotional ones with the other wife. Her status was low in the eyes of the other female family members. She was much younger than all of them. Since she came from a very poor family and could not contribute much to the housework due to her near-blindness, her position was marginalised even further.

The management of the kitchen and the day-to-day affairs of the household were left to the senior wife. Akka had good support from her family, who always sent her gifts and clothes. Seetha's parents not only did not have the resources to do likewise, they had, in the meantime, emigrated to Burma in the hopes of recouping their fortunes. Seetha was, therefore, generally jealous and miserable. She did not endear herself to anyone. Her resentment and bitterness were revealed in her caustic remarks and unpleasant nature. She was considered a terror by all. Even her husband tried to avoid her. In fact, he kept a safe distance from both his wives. He never took them out and expected them to live frugally, discouraging them from acquiring and wearing jewels. He passed derogatory remarks about women: 'what do women know', 'women are mad', 'women do not have any brains' and so on. The house was so built that he had an entire apartment to himself with a separate entrance and exit.

The economic status of the family improved enormously with his success in the world outside. He was tutor in philosophy to the *Maharajas* of Mysore, attended discussions at the Ramakrishna Mission where he was revered, and in the scholarly pursuit of philosophy met and corresponded with other philosophers in India and Europe. The status of his two wives reflected his status and prestige.

Meanwhile, Seetha had four children, three daughters and a son. She grew obsessed with money and continued to scorn girls. She got along only with her son. She overfed him and pampered him beyond imagination. By the time he was middle-aged, he was obese. His lack of interest in studies and his obsession with food distanced him from his father, but his mother doted on him. He was able to find work only because his father asked the *Maharaja*, as a favour, to give him a job in the railways. Seetha's world was limited to the house with its various religious rituals, and her son. Supervising servants, deciding menus, feeding her husband's students and arranging the marriages of her children were all part of it. To have an income of her own, she tried to save some money out of the housekeeping allowance. She also ran a small business selling saris by mail order to her relatives and other Indians in Burma. Her obsession with money led to her being completely in awe of rich women. She lent money at interest to her own servants.

What was life like for Seetha? She had very little education and had never had much emotional support. Relegated to household duties, religious rituals and thrown into the circle of hostile relatives, she was a non-entity in the eyes of her husband's extended family. It was only after she became widowed in 1949 and after Akka died in 1954 that she started to matter.

Akka, who had quietly served the family with great affection and efficiency, was ignored after my grandfather died. She survived him by only five years. When she died, her jewels, including her diamond earrings, were distributed among Seetha's children. Rumour has it that she was moved to the hospital's general ward, with few people to care for her. Seetha's daughters, whom she had helped raise, had moved away and it was left to the resentful junior wife, Seetha, and her son to care for her.

SARAS (1913–93)

Seetha's two older daughters—my mother's elder sisters—were married off to relatives. Now it was the turn of her last and youngest daughter, who had been born after a gap of eight years. Actually, her arrival had been a great disappointment to her parents, as they had not wanted a fourth child, and definitely not a daughter. However, when the child arrived, her father doted on her. She was named after the goddess of learning, Saraswathy, a name that suited her well as she was not only learned, but also respected learning.

Saraswathy, or Saras, who was to become my mother, grew up in great comfort. Although she was disdained by Seetha, her mother, she received much affection from her father and other relatives. My grandfather now had a prestigious job as registrar at the new University of Mysore. Since the major part of his economic and social success came after my mother's birth, she, too, was held in high esteem. My grandparents had by now built a very modern and spacious house.

The family had close connections with the Mysore palace and was showered with gifts. Every day, when the palace car came to pick up my grandfather, it was loaded with exotic fruits, nuts and sweets. Since, being a Brahmin, he could not partake of any food or drink in the palace, these gifts were sent to him. The Muslim driver who came to pick up my grandfather was given a cup of tea, in a special ceramic cup, washed and placed outside the house in accordance with the rules of pollution and purity. A Brahmin widow usually cooked for the household. She commenced cooking only after a bath, wearing clothes she had washed and dried on a bamboo pole close to the ceiling. No family member was allowed to go into the kitchen. The vessels washed by women of other castes were rewashed before use.

My mother's happy childhood in these surroundings lasted for only 11 years because she, too, had to be married off before puberty. During these brief childhood years, my mother travelled to Burma to visit her grandparents, enjoyed the bounties of the Mysore palace and met many distinguished people. In Burma she noticed that women had a high status. Burmese women were well educated, controlled the economy and were more prominent in their culture. Back in India, she observed the differences between her very orthodox Brahmin home and those of other families. Meanwhile, my grandmother was making desperate attempts to find a groom for her. She finally located one in a village called Nanjangud. Though the families were equal with regard to caste and religious credentials, the groom's family was not interested in this marriage since our family had travelled abroad and had become ritually polluted. Also, the bride was dark. Once again, as had happened in the previous generation, the bride's family was at a severe disadvantage during the marriage negotiations.

As the puberty deadline approached and time was running out, my grandmother begged the other family to accept her daughter. Her pleas finally got the family to agree to the marriage, but for a price. It is interesting to consider that men played very little role in these negotiations. Why did my grandfather not take more interest? Why were these negotiations left to women? Several offers of marriage came from Kannada and Telugu Brahmins settled in Mysore, but my family was not willing to consider any of them because of caste restrictions. Like her mother, the bride-to-be had no say in any of this and remained a passive witness to the negotiation of her future. The demands were: 10,000 rupees in cash, a lavish marriage and the girl should stop going to school. The notion that an educated girl would be dangerously emancipated had obviously gained currency. My mother was very sad at having to leave school at the age of 12. Schooling had been free, and a palace vehicle, a cart enclosed on all sides with curtains, had come every day to take the children to school. It was agreed, however, that after marriage she would be allowed to learn music to keep herself occupied. These lessons, given by a man, were conducted in the presence of a chaperone. My father was then studying for his degree in history and economics.

A Lavish Wedding in 1925

My parents had an extravagant wedding. Part of the dowry was given by my grandfather to his daughter's father-in-law in cash. The marriage expenses, the cost of the furniture, utensils, gold and fireworks—considered an unnecessary waste by us—were borne by the bride's family. Although it was she who had pleaded and begged my father's parents to accept the proposal, my grandmother was heartbroken at the thoughtless expenditure of her husband's hard-earned money and hated the bridegroom's family thenceforth.[6]

A bride's family is subservient for life to the family of the bride-taker. My father visited Mysore frequently and, as a son-in-law, had to be received with honour. His brothers, nieces and nephews, too, had to be lodged and entertained frequently. After the wedding, my grandmother would have liked my mother to move in with her husband or at least be supported by her husband's family. Once my grandmother discovered that my mother did not enjoy much support in the house of her in-laws and also did not have any space in that house to take in the gifts she received as dowry, she decided to take firm steps. She asked my mother to hand over all her gold jewellery so that it could be sold to buy her a piece of land in Mysore.[7]

My mother was unhappy at being forced to leave school in her early teens. She tried to while away her time learning music until she became pregnant in 1927. She was embarrassed to be pregnant at the tender age of 14. Some of her friends were still in school and her two sisters, married into more enlightened families, were able to remain in school after marriage and complete their 10th grade. By the time she was 18, she had gone through three pregnancies, two in very quick succession. Her second child, a daughter, was born very weak, was severely undernourished and probably premature. In addition, her own health was depleted and she found the responsibility of the care of three children enormous, more than she could cope with.

In all she had nine pregnancies, of which two were miscarriages. Of seven babies, three died in childhood. My father sent her to her parents' home in Mysore for all her confinements. She resented this because he would not give her any money for expenses. Each pregnancy was thus a long-drawn-out period of boredom, trauma, humiliation and dependence on her embittered mother. My mother was an easy target for my grandmother's wrath, which was not really financial in origin, even though these were the terms in which she expressed it. The fact was that my grandmother did not want the family's resources to be spent on my mother. She felt that my father's family ought to bear some financial responsibility. My grandmother found the financial liability excessive and made no secret of her utter disgust at this state of affairs. She grumbled about delivery expenses, the cost of maintaining the grandchildren, the care to be given to the newborn baby, the special dietary restrictions, traditional baths and medicines, all of which she found terribly irritating.[8] The message was that with a daughter one's responsibilities never ended; they only multiplied and gave one pain throughout one's life. How did my mother survive this ordeal for almost 20 years? Fortunately, she would steel herself to ignore her mother's taunts and sharply remind her that it was all her fault for having arranged such a marriage. Besides, she had strong support from her father. She also learned to immerse herself in painting, music and sports, talents that were unappreciated.

Culture of Silence

My mother seems to have made no attempt to convey her unhappiness to my father, who had no inkling of what she was going through physically, emotionally and financially. My mother rarely raised the issue of money, fearing unpleasantness and rebuffs. She also felt it was beneath her dignity to talk about money, preferring like many others of her time to suffer in silence. On the other hand, it is also possible that my father felt that my mother's parents were so well off that there was no need for him to give her any money. This was reinforced by the fact that whenever he visited them he never felt any of these tensions as he was treated with the respect due to a son-in-law. Most of her life my mother had to grapple with a complete lack of resources.

For my mother, marriage essentially meant being sandwiched between her own hostile mother and the need to cope with a highly intelligent but emotionally insecure husband who found it tough to deal with her affluent family. The economic status of men was very important in negotiation with family members. If one were on top of the heap financially, things moved smoothly for the wife and children. My parents set up their own household first in Madurai, the temple town of Tamil Nadu, around 1928 or 1930. My father was a lecturer in economics in a private college there. The college could never pay its staff members regularly and they were always short of money. It was, therefore, not a good job, but work was very difficult to come by. My grandfather visited my parents once and saw my mother taking care of two small children and expecting the next. It was at this point that he persuaded the couple to send their first two children to live in Mysore. He said that he was very lonely and that the Mysore home was a madhouse with the two wives quarrelling all the time. He felt it would be a real pleasure for him to have two growing children in the house. My grandmother had no role in this particular decision.

My brother and older sister thus went to live in Mysore. My brother was the apple of my grandfather's eye and the entire house revolved around him. My sister, who was totally ignored and uncared for by anyone, was not only sickly and weak, but also dark—again the issue of colour among people of colour! As they grew up, my brother got all the attention, while my sister felt discriminated against and humiliated, and she grew jealous and rebellious as a result.

My grandmother complained bitterly whenever my mother visited. To the children she also spoke badly of my father for not sending money for their care. Consequently, they grew up with negative feelings about their father. My brother referred to his father as his 'mother's husband' in one of his letters. With very little nurture or love, the two children grew up with little confidence and emotional security, posing real problems in later life. My grandmother, violent and verbally cruel, was fundamentally responsible for destroying the minds of two young children.

Strangely enough, the senior wife of my grandfather, Akka, was a picture of warmth and affection, and served the family till her last days without any complaints or bitterness. Akka was extremely fond of my mother and her children. She knew that my father was a foolish man with no clue about financial management. She was also very fond of my brother and even bequeathed her final savings to my mother and my brother. She often felt sorry when my father was humiliated. She supported my mother all the way and gave her the necessary sense of self-esteem, and respected her very much.

My father was the most brilliant man in the family, but the other sons-in-law had property and families to fall back on for support. He would do something extravagant and in the process embarrass my mother. She was at times ashamed of his behaviour and foolishness. Luckily, my mother had no inferiority complex, and the family respected her and admired her courage and sense of humour, though it did not always tolerate her boldness.

The job my father had in Madurai was really a dead end, and after 10 years, in 1938, the family moved to Belgaum. He continued to teach. When she set up her home in Belgaum, a cantonment town close to Bombay, my mother tried to improve her existing skills and learn new ones. It was an interlude during which she learnt to paint, play the flute and violin, read English literature and play badminton at the women's club. My father taught her English, and both were in favour of Western education and ideas. My father encouraged her to attend ladies' clubs, participate in women's conferences and to become a voluntary civil magistrate. In her later years she frequently remembered with gratitude that it was her husband who had exposed her to the outside world. The problem was that they had too many children and inadequate resources. My father's struggle to keep up appearances forced him into expenditure that ruined him, and my mother was angry because he would not consider any of her suggestions in times of trouble. My mother would also recall how my father would not take care of the children even when she was seriously ill because men were clueless about childcare. We lived in Bangalore from 1939 to 1942. Finally, my father found a better job in 1942 in Indore as director of industries. Later, he held several important posts enjoying the privileges due to a senior government official. This lasted for only three years. Then my father fell sick, with a kind of bone cancer in the ankle that threatened to spread all over his body. He stayed for two years in a nursing home, but was desperate to return home.

My older sister had meanwhile moved in with us in protest against the discrimination she faced at my grandparents' house. She was 16, but the move did not solve her problems of loneliness and hunger for affection. She grew attached to one of our drivers, which caused a furore and led to her confinement and humiliation. In 1945 my father went on long leave without pay and we returned to Bangalore, never to return to Indore. My father's father was in no mood to help. His parents-in-law, too, cold-shouldered him. Life took a downward plunge financially, socially and psychologically. The move from Indore to Bangalore created immense problems for my mother. She had a sick husband on her hands, a young, weak infant, unhelpful and hostile relatives, dwindling economic resources and an uncertain future. We children were malnourished on account of poor availability of food during wartime. To add to these were the hospital visits to her husband and the unpleasantness of my maternal grandmother who, on the pretext of helping us, came to boss over us and made life even more difficult. She was bored in Mysore and when she came to our home in Bangalore she would exert her authority.

My mother spent nearly six years nursing her sick husband, both at hospital and home, and taking care of her three surviving daughters. In his terminal stages, my father moved to my grandparents' house in Mysore with my mother. There, he underwent ayurvedic treatment as a last resort. But the oil massages and the strict diet with its innumerable restrictions only served to aggravate the pain and the disease, virtually killing him. By the time the family discovered the mistake and moved him back to a hospital, it was too late. My father died in 1948, and my grandfather took the responsibility of his daughter's family into his own hands. For the first time, he had the courage to depart from rigid Brahmin tradition and orthodoxy. Death in Brahmin households is steeped in expensive rituals and ceremonies. He felt that enough was enough and decided to take some bold steps. A significant gesture was to refrain from asking my brother to light the funeral pyre, the chief duty of a Brahmin son. Another departure from custom was to send my mother away to Bangalore to prevent too many mourners from coming home. In this context, it is pertinent to remember that a widow is not allowed to leave the house for a year, the statutory period of mourning. My mother was also spared other horrors in terms of the changes brought about by widowhood.

My grandmother seemed totally unmoved by her son-in-law's death and had little to say about it. Her daughter had been married for 22 years and had a respectable number of children, so it did not matter now. In fact she was glad it was all over. The only sign of affection for my mother I ever saw in her was when she quarrelled with my father's uncle, who had matched the horoscope for the wedding. My grandmother took him to task for not forecasting the disaster 22 years earlier.

My grandfather often came to Bangalore to stay with us. His presence was soothing, unlike my grandmother's. Once my grandmother brought a distant relative with three daughters to live in the house and to 'help' my mother. This was the limit; the house seemed like an orphanage. My mother complained to my grandfather, probably for the first time in her life, and normality was restored. A new home was found for these relatives.

The father–daughter relationship was exceptional. My grandfather loved my mother and took care of all her needs. He had constructed a small house for her to stay in Mysore, on the land bought for her with the gold she had received in dowry. He had expected my father to be an invalid for a long time and wanted us to be close by, but in a separate house. He was constantly doing something thoughtful for my mother. As long as he lived, he took good care of her and all of us. He was attentive, in particular, to my brother as the future breadwinner of the family. He was shocked that a huge insurance policy due to us after my father's death had lapsed because the last instalment had not been paid.

My grandfather died within a year of my father's death. He was 82. After his sudden death my grandmother took over again and resumed making life difficult for us. She was probably jealous of her husband's extraordinary affection for my mother and brother. My mother tried to keep her sanity and that of her children in as many ways as was possible. She paid special attention to my brother, decided to get him music lessons, a record player and a motorcycle to commute to the Indian Institute of Science, where he was studying. Needless to say, this was a major drain on our dwindling resources.

THE ESCAPE ROUTE (1951–52)

We continued to live in my maternal grandfather's house in Bangalore without much help or support. My brother got a small job in Ahmedabad and the family felt encouraged. My brother went to Ahmedabad alone. He could not cope with the loneliness, the unbearably high temperature in summer, the indifferent food and so on. I remember we had to send bread by parcel post from Bangalore to Ahmedabad. His letters would move us to tears and my mother decided to go and help him out. The argument was that he was the only son. He might fall sick, and a mother's duty was to look after him. Also, escaping from the clutches of her mother had become very important to her. Any place away from relatives seemed worth trying out. The crocodile tears, sarcastic comments and false pity that she was subjected to presented a situation to be avoided at any cost. Bangalore, a place my mother loved, seemed to lose its attraction in 1950. She did not stop to consider the consequences of this decision. The question was: could the girls manage without her? We could not, and after my 10th grade we joined our mother and brother. Ahmedabad was different from south India, and we found it a very trying and unpleasant city. My uncle did express his displeasure that my mother should think of moving on the basis of a small, unsteady job her son had. But the women, my aunt Rukmini and grandmother, tried to push her out saying, 'You cannot stay here forever.' The role played by my aunt was not a very pleasant one.

The implications of this change were many. First, our standard of living fell. In Bangalore, despite all the sarcastic remarks from her mother, my mother lived in a style that she was used to, the outward semblance of respectability and family prestige being maintained. Second, my uncle from time to time had helped her out with firewood from the railways and other home-grown products. By moving away Saras became dependent solely on her son's income. Still, she was relieved to be thousands of miles away and not be pitted constantly against her family and compared to others who were doing well.

Both the families—natal and affinal—found it convenient to forget her at this stage, leaving her to fate and God. My mother found herself responsible for four adult children and not much to fall back upon. Her young son, though educated and brilliant, had grown up with little confidence and capacity to cope with the world. He had led a sheltered life and was used to being treated like royalty, so he was no help. Her second child and first daughter was a nervous wreck, having faced severe discrimination in the house of her maternal grandparents. She would always recall how badly my grandmother treated her and the way she humiliated her in front of relatives. The impact of those early days could never be erased. She would get into tantrums or deep depression. It was only with the psychiatric help of a visiting Swedish psychoanalyst that the damage was contained.

My mother felt she must try to undo the effects of all the mistakes in her life, starting with her early marriage, incomplete education, superstitions and ritualistic religion, and now, regional prejudice. How could one demolish so many barriers at one stroke? First, we decided to confine our daily worship to a lamp lit before an altar and did away with all other rituals and *pujas* (worship). Then we rejected all the superstitions observed so far and retained only some basic principles pertaining to right and wrong. We also eschewed what had caused too much pain to earlier generations of women in our family—arranged marriages and dowries. By taking these risks and putting herself into rather humble surroundings, my mother tried to create a better life for her children. And in this effort she succeeded.

My brother wanted to get married and out of sheer fun placed an advertisement in the paper. When my aunt came to know of it, she suggested a suitable match. A girl from a less educated but wealthy family, in good health and with a lot of relatives was chosen, precisely because our family lacked all three. There was a grand wedding in 1955, which all our relatives attended.

Soon after this we moved to Baroda because my brother got a new job there. But the households were separated when he moved back to Ahmedabad owing to better job prospects. We three sisters and our mother remained in Baroda. Within months it was clear that the household in Baroda would have to function on its own steam and would receive no financial support from my brother. I decided to take up a job as a library assistant and attend graduate school, the popular idea being that one did not have to attend graduate school full-time and that attendance was not important! Then I graduated to a market research job with Hindustan Lever.

When around this time I fell in love, my mother, who had only negative feelings towards marriage until then, felt that I should get married since the man in question was educated, as well as a good person. She probably also realised that it was difficult to go through life without strong male support. My mother followed commonsense and gut feeling. Quite remarkably, she agreed to my entry into an entirely different religious, ethnic and regional group. My fiance Iqbal's family were Sikhs who had migrated from Pakistan at the time of the Partition. My family and his knew little about each other and, apart from my mother, who was supportive, there were many misgivings on both sides. My people regarded them as a family of truck drivers, while all they knew of us 'Madrasis' was that we were dark. My mother consulted her brother and sisters about her decision to give her blessing to our marriage. Her brother came down heavily against it. My aunts, however, felt it was all right for me to marry out of caste, but my grandmother said bitterly: 'What else can you expect?'

The only conventional thing my mother did in connection with our marriage was to ask if the groom had a horoscope. The joke was that his family did not know the exact date of his birth, though they knew the year he was born. In any talk of birth dates, his family would go into a long discussion trying to place various events around the time of his birth. Finally, a meek and nervous astrologer was given the task of finding out the date of birth merely by looking at his face, something unheard of among Brahmins. Whatever happened to the horoscope matching we do not know.

My mother travelled to Mysore to buy clothes and to ask for her house back to live in—the one that had been built by her father on the land that had been bought with her gold. Her mother and siblings refused either to transfer the money or to grant her the right to the house. Some steel utensils and one sari were all that were given to her. I was married in 1957. One of my sisters went to live in a students' hostel, and for a year my mother and younger sister moved in with me.

Both my sisters had degrees and could get jobs, and things started looking up, especially when my younger sister, an invalid with a collapsed lung, managed to get a job with the faculty of home science at the University of Bangalore. It was a relief for my mother to go back to familiar surroundings and to stay with an elder sister of hers. The two sisters had time to talk about problems. My mother told her about the refusal of the family to surrender her property and land that had been bought with her jewels. Even more than my aunt, her husband was furious at this injustice and decided to take it upon himself to set things right, for my mother needed a place of her own. It is not clear whether my uncle took up my mother's cause out of a genuine sense of outrage or because he wished to put his in-laws in their place. There were always tensions between her sons-in-law and my grandmother as far as I can recall. To settle the matter, other family members were called in. To our surprise it was decided that since the land was not documented in her name, my mother was not entitled to anything.

MY MOTHER'S STAY IN THE USA

In 1963, after my younger sister underwent major lung surgery, she went abroad to study at Columbia University and married a mathematician there. My mother went to the US with her after spending a year in Switzerland where her son-in-law, the husband of my elder sister, was working as an accountant. My mother was quite excited about travelling abroad, something she had never imagined she would do. She had a glorified and positive image of the West. She thought Western society was more just towards women. The first year went well, and she improved her health enormously and spent time taking care of two grandchildren. She travelled on to the West Indies where Iqbal and I were then living. Saras had come a long way from an arranged marriage at the age of 12.

My mother's stay in America, where she lived for almost 20 years, first with one and then another of my sisters, was in fact very complicated. While all her basic needs were met and she felt that in the eyes of relatives and friends she had really arrived, day-to-day living posed peculiar problems. Although food was abundant and the country had a cool efficiency, she found some things difficult—the kitchen had to be kept spotlessly clean and there was not much space to do elaborate cooking. If you did, you had no one to help you clean up. Next, because of fire hazards, one could not even light a lamp. You could only hang up a few pictures of Hindu gods. Family members rushed about with little time for social life. Moreover, you were totally immobile if you did not know how to drive a car. Finally, there was no company—no one in her own age group. However, my mother gradually became accustomed to life in the US and found it difficult to adjust to India on her visits. The dirt, diseases and problems with water and electricity were too much for her. Her relatives now looked up to her in admiration, for they had aged and were now much poorer than her. The tables had turned and they did not have access to the resources my mother had. Because her children were living abroad, she now had an independent income that far exceeded theirs.

My sisters found it convenient to have my mother live with them as long as she was physically fit. One of them wanted her help in raising her children and the other sent for her whenever she had problems with her husband. Once the children grew up and the marriage of my elder sister got stabilised, both of my sisters found an ailing mother a liability. An old age home did not seem a good option. A lack of resources or space was not the problem. This issue assumed problematic proportions because my mother was not keen on returning to India. My elder sister's husband was determined not to allow my mother to stay on with them. She continued to live in Chicago with my younger sister, where, too, she was very unwelcome. My sister refused to cook special food for her and would not even talk to her. There was much resentment and tension in the house. My sister's loyalty was to her husband and her children. In spite of the fact that her house was a virtual guesthouse for Indians from overseas working in the mathematics department, there was no room for my mother who spent all her time cooking and coping with the feudal lifestyle of her son-in-law, and received no appreciation.

Finally, she had to leave the US and come to India, and she came to me in Thiruvananthapuram. I was delighted, but she found the journey difficult and was soon sick. She said that she had not suffered as much in the USA as she did in the few months in India. One infection after the other, the heat, the mosquitoes, lizards, cockroaches, water, electricity, uneven roads—the problems were endless.

She had to be moved to hospital and, for a brief period, became all right and for a few months she enjoyed life in comfort. The problems of food and heat persisted, but she managed. In April 1993, after being back in India for eight months, she passed away on the Tamil new year's day. With very few family members present and in a new city, she was cremated in the Kerala tradition with coconut husks. The Brahmin rituals were accompanied by a Sanskrit poetry reading in the presence of close friends.

CONCLUSION

Saras was an extraordinary woman, of great personal courage and confidence. Her remarkable self-image and assurance were the products of happy and good personality formation in childhood. She had the strength to face life without ever losing heart. Her good looks masked an indomitable spirit. Unperturbed by the challenges she faced, Saras consistently devised ways to cope and succeeded in changing environments. She understood very early in life that society was rarely compassionate, and often harsh and unforgiving to a vulnerable woman. The 'mistakes' of her life, she realised, were not of her own making but were the products of institutionalised discrimination against Indian women. Adversity only strengthened her character, for she constantly analysed and learnt from the injustices she encountered. In her mind she was clear that education and empowerment were of great importance, and early marriage and frequent child-bearing were the hazards that impeded the progress of women. Her introspective nature helped her live the life of a practical philosopher and take life as it came, without losing her equanimity and sanity.

Life for her was dynamic and ever-changing. She believed that the final truth and challenge is that no one is shielded from death. Meaningless Brahmincal rituals and prayers found no place in her life, which she approached with a cosmopolitan and humanitarian outlook. In essence, she shaped the lives of three daughters and a son, and all her grandchildren, making a success of not only her own but of all whose lives she touched.

NOTES

1. Horoscopes are read basically to predict compatibility and to check that both partners will not have an inauspicious period at the same time. There are 36

stars that need to be matched, and if two-thirds of them match then the prognosis for the marriage is considered good.

2. According to Hindu scriptures, only sons can performs last rites for their parents.
3. This custom gave parents of sons great advantage as they could marry at any age, but it placed the parents of girls in a subservient position and rendered them socially weak. The practice of dowry was strengthened by this custom. If you were anxious to get your daughter married off, you had to pay a price. It was a question of supply and demand.
4. A traditional school of medicine based extensively on the use of plants, roots and other natural substances.
5. A monastic order founded by Swami Vivekananda, the 19th-century religious leader.
6. Stories were repeated in the family ad nauseam about diamond shirt buttons presented to the groom at the request of his parents, which he lost in the excitement of the wedding. Fortunately, the diamond studs he received as per wedding norms were not lost and were later given back to my mother to be made into a pair of earnings.
7. The gold given by my mother's family and gifts received from relatives amounted to about 150 sovereigns, each sovereign weighing 8 grams. Gold was cheap, costing only Rs 13 a sovereign and was popular as a wedding gift. The entire range of silver *puja* vessels and kitchen utensils were not sold. Brahmins used silver for its attribute of purity.
8. Unfortunately, my grandmother had to cater to her daughter-in-law also, who did not go to her parents during pregnancy since she came from a village, and Mysore was a modern city with all amenities. There was a special room in the house for pregnant daughters and daughters-in-law, which was originally my mother's room. It had full occupancy till 1949 and was sometimes over-occupied. I was born on the same day in 1936 as my cousin, and in the same room.

6

Wings Come to Those Who Fly

Maithreyi Krishna Raj

The Early Years

My sister and I were very attached to our mother. We loved her deeply. Her death was a terrible blow to us. I can still feel the pain of it. After 40 years, I can still remember the tragedy and oppression of my mother's life as if it happened just yesterday. I remember my mother. She was thin, worn out with work. At 32 she looked ancient. Her day began long before we were up and ended long after we were all in bed. My memories of her are very vivid—a frail figure, clouded by the swirling wood smoke of the kitchen fire that stung our eyes. She staggered under pots of water fetched from wells near or far. We saw her bent over endless household tasks. All rituals were scrupulously kept, for she was 'upper caste'. The daily worship was never skipped. She ate after all the family had eaten, from the father-in-law down. She had no time to read a book, listen to music or just relax. I never knew what she would have looked like with a smile, for all we saw were layers of sorrow in those black eyes. In time the sorrow had turned to gentle resignation. My feminist consciousness developed as I grew up mainly in the world of women and witnessed their daily oppression.

Beginnings

My mother was married at the age of 14 and my father was only 17 years old. He was still in college then. Theirs was a typical south Indian Iyengar Brahmin joint family. My mother was married off in haste as she had attained puberty and in those days it could cause a scandal if a girl had matured before marriage. Her parents were scared that the news would come out. My father was the eldest son of a large family. He had six sisters and three brothers. There was a world of difference between the two families. My maternal grandfather was a deputy superintendent of police in Coimbatore. They were highly cultured and soft-spoken. My father's family was more worldly-wise.

My mother's parents thought that my father had a bright future as he did well academically and was planning to sit for the prestigious IAS (Indian Administrative and Audit Services) competitive examinations. In fact he did take the examination, but missed being selected by just one rank (11th, and only 10 were selected) and so his father made him switch to law much against his wishes. He really wanted to become a scientist and teach after his MSc. Throughout school and college he did outstandingly well in academics. He was brilliant at mathematics and a gold medallist in all the public examinations. His father forced him to take up law. My paternal grandfather, the principal of a high school, was a strict disciplinarian.

Part of my mother's difficulties lay in the fact that she had to cook for such a large family. She was by nature very meek and submissive. Her mother-in-law used to ill-treat her, denying her food and rest. When she fell ill she was accused of malingering. I vividly recall my grandmother dragging her and locking her up in a room because my mother said she had a fever.

My mother was hardly ever sent to her parental home for a holiday. Whenever her parents sent one of her brothers to escort her to her natal home after getting due permission from the in-laws, they sent my father by the next train to bring her back. Throughout my childhood I kept hearing from my aunts, 'Poor Kokila [that was my mother's name]—her mother-in-law is awful.' I could not understand why her parents let her go back each time. Though they sympathised with her but there was nothing they could do about it in those days. Once married, the daughter must stay with her in-laws. Although my mother was given all the customary gifts at the time of her wedding, her in-laws felt it was not enough. The second daughter-in-law was very rich and in comparison had brought in more *streedhan* (wealth and gifts endowed by the bride's parents) and had a lavish wedding. She was arrogant and more assertive than my mother. My father was terrified of his parents and could not withstand their pressure. My first uncle was very different from my father and usually did what he wanted, ignoring his parents' orders. My father was very sensitive and took their orders seriously. He hardly ever played games as a child as he was expected to be home by 6 P.M. to attend to household chores. While going to college he would even carry his younger brother's lunch box as the younger brother thought it infra dig to do so. My father was very fond of music but as his parents would not give him money, he would save money from his lunch allowance to attend concerts. We learnt all this from my father, who was very bitter about his parents' treatment of him.

Later on, my sister's unhappy marriage strengthened my conviction about the need for women to be strong and independent in every way. Often she wanted to break away, but there was nowhere she could go. I was still in college, and not earning. Whenever I tried to intervene, it did not help. Not only did my sister's husband have few interests of his own, he also prevented her from developing hers. Very few men understand the importance to women of avenues of self-development, of the need to have contact with the world beyond the home, and hardly any of them understand how repetitive, confining and unrewarding domesticity is. My sister's life was a classic case of a middle-class woman's oppression.

On the subject of oppression, I recall the sad plight of one of my father's sisters who was married to a musician. He was a drunkard and finally died of alcoholism. She, too, was a singer and gave performances on the radio. She came to stay with her parents after her husband's death. My mother was the only one who was kind to her. There was an element of suspicion about my aunt's chastity. I heard family rumours that she had some abortions which were whispered about. That was probably why my paternal grandfather used to beat her and ill-treated her children.

I spent my early childhood shunting between two households. My elder sister was brought up in my maternal grandparents' house, but I was moved around. I do not know why. My maternal grandfather was an unlikely policeman. He was a highly learned scholar, proficient in Tamil and English literature. He was very fond of me and made me aware of my potential. When I was about 5 years old, I was sitting on his lap when he received a visitor in his room. The visitor, when he heard my name, jokingly said, 'Oh indeed, and what kind of Yajnavalkya is she going to get?'[1]

Another person who was very supportive and influenced my life's goal was my maternal great-grandmother, who was widowed early and wore the traditional white sari of widows. She was the one who gave me my name. She used to tell me that I should live up to my name and that I ought to be a scholar. This great-grandmother was certain I was uniquely gifted. She would often say in the presence of others, 'This child will be a great scholar and do great things.' As a child I used sometimes carry out small acts of mischief and attempt to break accepted rules. The family was very orthodox and particular about pollution norms. Once my great-grandmother had just had a bath and changed her clothes. I ran up to her to hug her. She immediately had to take another bath and change her clothes. I felt very repentant and never did it again.

I disliked my paternal grandmother whom I held responsible for my mother's suffering; yet as a child I am told I was fond of this grandmother, too, and would cling to her. Maybe I needed the reassurance of adults. I remember an incident. There was a family friend, a doctor, who used to visit us. He would call out in a loud voice, 'Come out, grandchild.' This scared me so much, I would run and hide behind my paternal grandmother. This became a big joke in the family and whenever he came he would repeat this performance. Years later, when I was ill, it was this doctor who examined me. He asked my father, 'Is this the child whom I used to delight in frightening?' My subsequent prejudice against my father's mother probably grew from the stories I heard from other adults, especially my mother's sisters. I was told that as a child I did not receive enough nourishment. It was believed that my grandmother sold the baby food sent to my mother by her parents. I believe I used to cry a lot as a child because I was probably weak and undernourished. I was about 2 or 3, and crying for something when my father got so angry with me that he caught hold of me and said that he would throw me into the well if I cried any more.

My maternal grandmother owned some land called 'turmeric land'. This gift to a daughter was in those days termed thus because it would help her meet her essential needs in her in-laws' house. From this income, my grandmother sent us gifts. My maternal grandmother was tall, well built, fair skinned and very aristocratic looking. My paternal grandmother's family members were temple priests and were not considered 'cultured'. Children in my paternal grandfather's house were terrified of him and scampered away whenever he approached. In fact, his fourth son ran away and joined the army. He did not do well in school and was wayward. His father used to beat him with an umbrella for his transgressions. Many years later a Kannadiga woman claiming to be his wife turned up at my grandfather's place with two daughters in tow. My grandfather had to accept her and her family. She was made to wear a 9-yard saree and was passed off as an Iyengar woman. My father supported this brother's family till the very end. While none of the other brothers took any responsibility, it always fell to my father as the eldest to help everyone. I felt he was taken advantage of by his family members.

The two households where I spent my childhood were different in their basic ethos. In my paternal grandfather's family there was music and laughter, but also a great deal of gossip and wickedness. There were six aunts to play with as well as bully us. Both my sister and I were scared of them. My maternal grandparents' family was principled and very restrained. I never saw the gaiety, gossip, friends or enjoyment of life as in the other house.

I could sense contradictions in my own personality. On the one hand I have strong values, a great deal of determination and an inner strength. On the other hand I am emotional, timid and insecure about relationships with people. My *periamma* (mother's sister, *mausi*) often described me as a lighted lamp inside an earthen pot. After my mother died I became increasingly introverted. This shyness and timidity clung to me for many years. Even now I know I am not assertive or forceful.

When I was in the third grade my father finally broke away from the tyranny of his parents and went to Nagpur, taking his family with him. There he got a job in the Nagpur High Court. He earned a very meagre salary, but we were happy and my elder sister joined us then. For the first time, we were all together. My most precious memories were the five years before my mother's death. My mother loved us greatly. She was very protective towards my elder sister and did not allow her to do any house-work. I was somehow thought of as 'tougher'. She had high hopes for me academically. She used to speak of getting my sister married after high school, but for me she dreamt of academic honours as I used to win a lot of prizes in school.

Mother used to prepare delicacies for us every day. I remember my mother working very hard, doing everything herself to make both ends meet. We had no servant. She used to stitch our clothes and our bedsheets by hand. My father continued to meet the demands of his family on his meagre pay. My grandfather had retired at the age of 55 and lived up to the age of 90. He had to be supported till then. Furthermore, my father's six sisters had to be married and settled. He paid for his youngest brother's foreign education, too. We could not afford many things. My mother was also quite orthodox and religious. She used to make cowdung cakes for fuel and carry water from an outside tap. She was scrupulously particular about cleaning everything herself on account of pollution norms governing a Tamil Brahmin household. It was only after we moved to Nagpur that I could understand something of my parents' relationship with each other. My mother had a strong desire for learning. She had studied up to the seventh or eighth standard. She knew English and Tamil, and she would get my father to set exercises for her. When father came home late, she would complain and my father would get annoyed. She felt he was not sensitive to her needs, though I think they were quite fond of each other in their own way.

In spite of her heavy schedule, my mother would find time to knit sweaters and would try to learn Hindi from my school books. Perhaps I have inherited my sensitive nature from my mother. She could play the violin, but as her mother-in-law and sisters-in-law teased her about it, she gave it up. They used to object to her having a hot bath so she switched to cold water or stopped having it all together. I think the reason why they were able to bully her was because she was very mild and submissive, and my father never stood up for her in his own home. In his turn, my father had an inferiority complex as he was not as rich as the other sons-in-law in his wife's house. He felt that they looked down on him, but in reality they thought very highly of him as a learned person. Perhaps he sensed this in a way. My mother was always pitied by her family because she was not as well off as the other daughters.

My father moved up in his career when he got a government posting to Shimla. Those were happy days. We used to go for picnics every weekend and had lots of fun as a family. My father unfortunately contracted typhoid and was hospitalised in a government hospital in Shimla. There were no antibiotics then. My mother nursed him day and night. In those days there was no road transport in Shimla. She had to climb the hilly roads everyday. My mother faced great difficulty in managing the house and looking after my father. She was very religious and people said that it was Kokila's prayers that pulled him through. She was spoken of by my grandfather as Savitri who brought her husband Satyawan back to life.

We then moved to Delhi where my mother fell seriously ill. I think she contracted TB. Unfortunately, she conceived as well. I was immediately packed off to my *periamma*'s house in Madras and put in school there. During this time I spent a lot of time with my mother's sisters. My eldest aunt was childless and she was supposed to have spiritual powers. She suffered from rheumatism and various forms of psychosomatic illnesses. She was said to be possessed by the *devi*. She lectured to us children a great deal about neatness and modesty. Later my mother too was sent down to her parent's house at Coimbatore to have her baby. She was moved immediately back again to Madras for treatment where she died. My sister had to give up her studies in order to look after my baby brother and join my father in Bombay where he was now posted. She really had a tough time. There were always relatives dropping in and expecting her to provide them hospitality. What they did not seem to realise was that she was just a 15-year-old girl managing everything. My sister brought up my brother till he was 5, and much later I took over when my father moved to Delhi as a joint secretary and my sister was in Bombay. My sister felt immensely responsible for us as my mother had asked her to look after us. I was unable to openly express my sorrow on the death of my mother and people got the idea I did not feel her loss, but I was really inconsolable, watching my mother slowly sink and die. Her death occurred just a few weeks before my school final examination. The grief was overwhelming. I used to go to the terrace and cry inconsolably. Nobody in my aunt's place knew about it.

I joined Queen Mary's College for Women in Madras to study science but attended only one semester. I started getting fevers, but I told no one about it. I ate very little, but no one noticed even when I started losing weight. It was only after some months when I collapsed that my aunt realised how ill I really was. I diagnosed with TB in a galloping stage and was given only a month to survive as both my lungs had extensive cavities. I was sent to Coimbatore to my maternal grandparents' house for rest and ayurvedic treatment. For a short while my sister came down to look after me. She must have found it very difficult to manage both me and my baby brother. This was the time when my maternal grandfather spent a lot of time talking to me and encouraging me. He used to speak of his childhood and early life. I was given medicines, but I only kept getting worse. My father was informed, and it was decided on the advice of a doctor to send me to a TB sanatorium in Ghataprasha (called Hukeri Road then) in Belgaun district. I was admitted there.

I continued to run a high temperature—104 degrees every day for several months. Just when the doctors had given up hope, streptomycin and PAS became available. I was given four daily injections of streptomycin (in those days that was the dose) for several weeks and tablets of PAS. The doctor would joke that there was no space left to give the injection! After some weeks the temperature began to drop.

The sanatorium in those days consisted of isolated little cottages where the patients had to be nursed and cared for by their own relatives. In my case no relative was willing to go with me. Finally, my father's mother was sent for and she accompanied me, but just after a month or so she suddenly decided to go back to Madras saying, 'Your father is rich enough to keep a servant for you. Why should I look after you?' She also packed up all the Horlicks, biscuits and all the other things my father had kept for me. I had no strength to do things for myself and was still completely bedridden. This was the last attempt of the doctors to save my life. They were not sure I would live and I felt so totally abandoned when grandmother just left.

The hospital sent a wire to my father. He did not come, but sent a servant to look after me. He was a cook—a 17-year-old boy. The hospital nurses came around only once a day. The cook slept in the kitchen and served me food. I was getting better, but was still very weak. A few days after the cook had come, when I was sleeping in the afternoon, I felt him push my skirt up. I was 16 by then, but knew nothing at all about the facts of life. Something alerted me, even as sheer panic gripped me. With a superhuman effort, I jumped out of bed, unbolted the door and ran out. What gave me such strength I do not know. The boy, too, was probably very surprised. I ran to the next cottage as fast I could, pounded their door, loudly and collapsed. I do not know what happened afterwards. I was totally unconscious for several hours, but I must have said something to the person in that cottage.

They sent a telegram to my father, but he did not come. The boy was kept in detention for some days and then sent away. The hospital authorities shifted me to a new cottage that was not so isolated and a woman was hired on a daily basis to look after me. This woman would go away, locking me in from outside so that I did not have to get up to open the door. This arrangement was satisfactory on the whole, except once.

There was a terrible storm one day. The rain came lashing in and I tried to close the windows, but could not reach the bolts. The rain water flooded the whole room, soaking my bed and me. I felt utterly deserted and helpless, and waited soaked to the skin for several hours till the woman returned and opened the door. That day is still fresh in my mind. Those four years were years of utter loneliness. My father visited me only once a month. He never talked to me or sat with me. He never asked how I was doing. He would visit the doctors, sleep in the next room, get up and go away next morning. He made no emotional contact with me. He also complained a lot to every one about the enormous drain on his finances by my treatment cost. This was, of course true, as apart from all hospital and nursing charges, streptomycin in 1949 was very expensive and my treatment caused him to go into a lot of debt. My doctor told him: 'Your daughter is a precious person and very brave. You should be proud to help her back to life.'

During this bleak period I remember a few bright patches that helped me to continue to fight for life. Before I came to the hospital I used to pray that I should join my mother. One evening, as I lay in my room in Madras and there was no one around, I suddenly saw my mother's figure standing close to me. She said: 'Your time has not yet come. Keep up your courage and live.' Perhaps it was a hallucination, perhaps it was real, but it lasted just a few seconds. It is a question of whether one believes in these things, but after that I stopped praying for death.

My maternal grandmother used to write me a postcard every week when I was in the sanatorium. She always added a sentence: 'You are an unusual person, intelligent and good. Take care of yourself.' This message coming to me regularly in the hospital every week gave me great emotional support. My grandmother was very ill at this time in Coimbatore with asthma, after having lost three daughters in a row.

Last but not least was the unremitting care and encouragement of the doctor who treated me. He was responsible for my complete recovery. He would say to me, 'What do a few years matter in a whole lifetime?' He was soft-spoken and gentle and I worshipped him. Several years later, when I was going to America to study and had trouble getting a visa because of my medical history, he wrote an enthusiastic and commendatory letter to the consulate saying, 'The fact that she has done so much against very great obstacles should be admired and supported.' Years later, when I had got married and had two children, he happened to come to Bombay. He sent word to me that he wanted to see the lucky man who had married me.

Today I lead an active, normal life. When my recovery was complete and I left the hospital, I felt that life had been given back to me as a very precious gift. I felt obliged do something worthwhile with my life. I am not a religious person in the sense that I perform no religious rituals, but my whole being was filled with a deep conviction that some greater power is beyond us and we are bound to it and shaped by it. It inspires us to do something beyond and above ourselves.

The scars of my disease remain. My left lung has extensive fibrosis (scar tissue) that covers the cavities. This prevents proper breathing; I cannot speak for a long time or sing. It makes me cough. In fact, one of the doctors in Bombay advised that this lung be removed, but my doctor at the sanatorium said it could remain. The only discomfort I would face was some breathing difficulty and some phlegm formation, which was not a big price to pay. I went for regular check-ups, but I had recovered fully and completely and those days were behind me forever.

These are things I have never spoken of to anyone. Only my sister knows. My husband has had a smooth, normal life and has never experienced such emotional traumas. He is usually impatient with any autobiographical accounts and so I never discussed these details with him, except that he knew I had been ill.

When I returned home, cured after the many years spent in hospital, it seemed to be a miracle. I went to my maternal grandmother's house to meet her. My great-grandmother was still alive. My maternal grandmother, who had spent her life looking after 10 children, said to me: 'Don't mess up your life with marriage. What is there to look forward to in marriage? Be like Dr Padmavati [a well-known heart specialist]. See what a lot of good to society she does!' But my great-grandmother said to me, 'Marry if you want to marry and find the man you like. Marriage need not be either a compulsion or a taboo.'

EVOLVING A PHILOSOPHY OF LIFE

I loved to read from the time I was very young. Saturday used to be library day in the school. I would wait eagerly for it and finish the one book we were given the same day. Every summer vacation was spent reading. Both my grandfathers had their own libraries. I read all the English and American literary classics, read poetry, philosophy and popular science.

I also wrote some stories. Some were published and the rest are still in my attic.

Being by myself came naturally to me. Indeed, as a child I loved wandering off by myself and sitting quietly near a mountain or river bank. I did a lot of this solitary musing in Coimbatore, Nagpur and

Shimla. Other children of that age would automatically gravitate to a group of companions in vigorous physical play.

I remember an incident that happened when I was 5 years old. I was staying in Coimbatore with my mother and I had a great fascination for the Blue Mountains, which I could see from my house. I used to think I could just walk down and reach the mountain. I kept walking towards the mountains for several hours till I got lost. I remember seeing a turkey and following it. It was fortunate for me that my *mama*'s (mother's brother) friends saw me and brought me home.

In Shimla, while returning from school, I would sit on the stone steps that were surrounded with wild roses for a long time before coming home. I sometimes think that I have a strong memory for smell. I can almost smell the geraniums that grew in my maternal grandfather's house. It was a huge house with many trees and a lovely garden.

When I was ill, being bedridden, I had plenty of time to read. Some books were sent by father, some by my father's youngest brother. He wrote me many encouraging letters and introduced me to the great thinkers of our time—the Huxleys, Russell, Freud, Will Durant, Radhakrishnan and others. I read biographies of great people and loved reading about artists. I collected prints of great paintings. Toru Dutt, Emily Bronte and Amrita Shergil were my favourites. I read a lot of Tagore, too.

A cousin of mine sent me brushes, crayons and paints, and I did some landscapes. What fascinated me was the relationship of human beings to the universe and the extraordinary resilience of the human spirit. I firmly believe that we need what Julian Huxley called 'the sense of the sacred'.

In my teens, I wrote some poems, some of which were published.

My mother was very religious and believed in prayer. She also observed all the Hindu rituals. There was one ritual in our house that I loved. Every Friday was Lakshmi (the goddess of wealth) *puja*. The whole house was decorated with *rangoli* (lime powder decorations made by hand on the floor). When we returned from school, we could not eat anything, but waited for our father to return from work. Then we all sat together and sang *bhajans* (religious songs), and when the rituals were over and we had eaten *prasad* (blessed food offered during religious ceremonies), we ate our meal together. My father was religious too at that time and very particular about ritual purity. Once a year he observed the ritual of reading *Sundara Ramayana* (a religious text) and during those 10 days he fasted rigorously. After my mother's death, he made a complete break with religion and became an atheist. He had fasted and prayed to the gods for my mother's life and the gods had turned a deaf ear to all his pleas to save her. I missed those rituals, because they had brought me a sense of the sacred. Rituals in themselves, as a mechanical way to obtain favours from God are abhorrent to me, but rituals can also give a spiritual significance to everyday happenings. Rituals are a way of keeping the link between ourselves and the world around us, of making sacred and mysterious ordinary day-to-day life and events. I like our tradition of naming rivers that carry the waters of life and sustain us after goddesses—Ganga, Yamuna, Saraswati. Tagore also expresses a mysterious communion where the divine touches the earth.[2]

CATCHING UP ON LOST YEARS

I wanted to make good the lost years, but at first I did not quite know what I wanted to do. I met Kamala Nimkar on the advice of my doctor about voluntary socio-medical work. Mrs. Nimkar conducted occupational therapy classes in KEM Hospital, Bombay. The work did not interest me and I gave it up after two months as it did not stimulate my mind. I had enjoyed painting and drawing, and art had been a hobby and I had won some prizes in school. My father felt I should do what I wanted. He was very liberal that way. Later, however, looking back, I often felt he could have guided me a little more and sat with me to discuss things I was not sure of. I did voluntary social work for some time, working with the municipal corporation to help TB patients. Since I loved drawing and painting, I joined evening classes at the J.J. School of Art, but somehow I felt this could not be my lifetime vocation. I had realised art was only a hobby for me; what I wanted was a solid academic achievement.

I prepared on my own and sat as an external candidate for the intermediate examination with mathematics, economics and history from Nagpur University. This stimulated me tremendously and I enjoyed my studies, particularly mathematics. Since there was an unforeseen delay, I missed the date of admission in Bombay for B.A., so I went to Poona, where a friend of my father's had me admitted to S.P. College, though I would probably have liked Ferguson or Wadia better. My goal for the years ahead was to do solid academic work. I loved reading and study. My aim was to be a university teacher and a professional. I did well in the B.A. and held a merit scholarship. I remember that the atmosphere at home during this time was not a happy one. My father, a widower, missed my mother and, though very successful in his career, constantly complained about the inept housekeeping. There was constant conflict with his son-in-law, too. He retreated into his shell, unable to respond to his children's emotional needs. Our feelings went unnoticed. After all, he was a man. Whenever problems came up in the family, the usual sort of problems all families face, my father insulated himself in his shell and left us to cope with them and did not extend any sympathy to us. I learnt from this that men and women need to build emotional warmth, intimacy and closeness with their family members, their children, friends, colleagues and collaborators. It is usually women who create these networks. Men do not think that it is essential for them to do this, but for greater mutuality and reciprocity between men and women in the family and at the workplace it is necessary. For human relationships you need to be present for each other, to give each other priority, to set aside time and space in one's life. Men do not consider this to be important. They give their profession exclusive priority. This is lopsided. This is something I have missed even in my marriage.

I remember an incident which occurred on the eve of my M.A. examination. I had a quarrel with my father's sister who was staying with us. It all began with my brother telling me that she had refused to give him food. I asked my aunt, 'Why?' This resulted in a big quarrel, with my aunt flaring up and telling my father that either I leave the house or she. I took my brother to my mother's youngest sister, who was also in Delhi. Everyone was shocked, but I refused to go back till my father backed me up. The quarrelsome aunt packed up. After some years this aunt forgave me and we were friends. Subsequently, my father's youngest sister Vijaya came to stay with us. She really tried to belittle us. People generally got the idea that our aunt Vijaya worked so hard, which was not true. This was one thing about my father which we did not like. He was easily influenced by her. I often wonder if it is correct to assume that modern forces are breaking up the family. Families were most often fragmented.

After completing my M.A. (in economics) at the University of Delhi (1958), I planned to do my Ph.D., but somehow my heart was not in it. The atmosphere at home was tense most of the time due to various family conflicts. My younger brother was not doing well in school and everyone scolded him severely. I tried to defend him and there were serious quarrels. Also, at that time I had got emotionally involved with my future husband. I felt I was wasting my time and wanted to become independent. I was keen to get a job immediately. I was convinced women would not be pushed around as much as they were if they had professional competence and the means to be economically independent. So I set about taking a B.Ed. degree, which would entitle me to teach in a school. I received a merit scholarship for B.Ed., taught economics in Lady Irwin Higher Secondary School for two years, and enjoyed my work.

I was then invited to go to the USA on a scholarship to do an MSc. in education at the State University of New York (SUNY) at New Paltz. At that time the Central Institute of Education had an exchange programme with SUNY, under which they nominated me. I went to complete this course and returned to Bombay in 1964 and got married to Krishna Raj. He had joined the *Economic Weekly* soon after his M.A. My interaction with American students somehow strengthened my conviction that our culture had much to offer. I also read feminist literature for the first time in 1963, including Betty Friedan and Simone de Beauvoir. I had a beautiful friendship with a young undergraduate. We are still in touch with each other.

I met Krishna Raj when I was doing my M.A. We had a great deal in common and shared to some extent similar attitudes to life. Neither of us cared much about wealth and had the same all-absorbing interest in analysing and understanding what was happening in the world around us.

Strangely enough, my own family did not object to the marriage. It was almost as if they expected me to find my own partner. His family was very upset. In fact, Krishna Raj did not even inform them because he did not want to face a scene. His sister came to know of it by accident, and then wrote me a very sweet letter welcoming me into the family. We had a civil marriage and a small reception for friends. He went off to work at the paper immediately afterwards, which scandalised everyone.

By and large, my husband and I have the same temperament and interests, though naturally we are also different. He is very tolerant and has a certain definite philosophy regarding human relations. He is able to distance himself from people and does not let those whom he dislikes upset him. He is unfailingly courteous even to the people he does not like. He was always busy with his work and I had to shoulder the major share of the responsibility of the home, but his contribution was by no means marginal. He did try to spend time with the children, following their interests and making them feel loved and wanted. He supported me fully in my professional commitment. In fact, often, when I was ready to resign because of childcare problems, he insisted I should not give up.

Perhaps because I had lost my mother I tended to overcompensate, especially in the case of my daughter, whom I felt was more vulnerable. Leaving them in the care of servants during the day did produce a lot of anxiety and tension. When I had a severe servant crisis I sent my daughter (she was just over a year old) to my parents-in-law. She was there for six months. My father-in-law used to write me beautiful letters every week describing everything the child did so that I would not miss her. I had to bring the child back when my father-in-law became ill and had to go to Madras for treatment. He died two years later of cancer. He was a warm person and talked very freely to me. My mother-in-law, too, was a good person, but she was more reserved, probably because of the language barrier.

PROFESSIONAL, WIFE AND MOTHER

I had a couple of temporary teaching jobs till I got a position as a postgraduate teacher in economics at Kendriya Vidyalaya. I was there for five years and liked my job very much. The school, too, appreciated my efforts at creative teaching and I got a lot of support from my students.

Since our work demanded so much of our time, we solved the problem of making free time for both of us by having a full-time housekeeper on a generous wage, and treating her as a member of the household, but there were many problems, too. Each one left after two to three years, and we had to keep looking for replacements. Two things struck me: how class intruded into the relationship; and how, despite all my sympathy, help and involvement with the maids in a very personal way, they would favour the man of the household.

Methods, Strategies and Skills of Working

My interest in innovative teaching methodologies and curriculum development led me to take a job as a senior lecturer in education in

Gandhi Shikshan Bhavan, a teacher's training college of the University of Bombay (1971–75). However, I decided to give up this job when I felt that the hard work and wholehearted dedication I gave to the preparation of lectures and assignments did not call forth a similar response from teacher trainees. I resigned when I realised that it had become a dead end for me.

It was when I was looking around for a job that I heard that Neera Desai of SNDT Women's University was opening a Women's Research Unit. It sounded exciting and so I went to meet her and she invited me to join her. Naturally, there was not much money involved, and after working as a senior lecturer, many would consider it a comedown to work as a research assistant. However, I did not care. I found the work meaningful and that is all that mattered. It has been a joy to see how the research unit has grown from two tables in the sociology section to a full-fledged research centre in an independent building, with an excellent library and full-time staff. The credit should go to the SNDT University for its foresight and to the committed work of Neera Desai who started it, laid its foundations and attracted talent to build the place along with me.

Even as a teacher at Kendriya Vidyalaya and as a teacher-educator at Gandhi Shikshan Bhavan, I had been involved with research in curriculum, teaching methodologies and teacher education, and had published many papers. When I joined the research centre there was a difference; for the first time my yearning for an academic life and the deeply felt need to serve a cause coalesced. The setting up of women's studies in many universities is good as it takes the message to many, but it is also full of hazards, insofar as it is likely to be done without much preparation, insight or perspective. Mere study of 'Women' does not constitute women's studies, which is a way of seeing, a way of analysing and a way of feeling and acting with regard to women in society.

Building up the Women's Research Centre at SNDT University was a kind of a contribution to women's struggles, as documentation and research are also important to the cause of women's struggle for justice. Such knowledge must be shared with others, with the object of searching for solutions. Many rigid attitudes are due to ignorance and an inability to see a situation from other points of view. We need to help people to search for alternatives, to look at the world from a fresh point of view. Recently we had a visit from Dr Yash Pal of the University Grants Commission. We had arranged a special display of our efforts to promote women's studies. He looked at the display and at our documentation centre and said, 'How does all this help women?' One could well ask, is such a question ever put to scientists, to economists, to sociologists: 'What is the good of having documentation in your subject?' But this is a standard response to women's studies: 'What good will it do?' Could we ask the same question of any intellectual activity?

[Postscript: This narrative was told to Rita Montero in 1984. Twenty years have passed. I have been busy with women studies teaching and research; though not a front rank leader, I have been supportive of the women's movement and lent help in my own way. My children have grown up. My son completed his Ph.D. in engineering and has settled in the USA. My daughter is a software engineer and after working for a few years in the USA, has now settled down in Bangalore. After the children left home, my husband became more attentive to them and we had a closer relationship and shared many things. We spent holidays with our children. My husband's work pressure had eased, thanks to IT and the fact that the *Economic and Political Weekly* had stabilised. He spent more time at home and helped me with running the household. Sadly, this idyll was not to last. He passed away very suddenly last January (2004) and I have been left to carry on. My women friends have been my greatest support during this time.]

NOTES

1. Yajnavalkya was a sage of the early Vedic age who had two wives, Datayani and Maitreyi. When he wished to divide all he possessed between them before going to the forest, Datayani accepted what she was given but Maitreyi asked him to teach her all he knew. Yajnavalkya held the view that women cannot aspire to spiritual knowledge, that their domain was earthly things, but by her request Maitreyi challenged his view. She is considered to be one of the women scholars of the Vedic age who participated in religions discussions.
2. This following poem of mine describes the first hesitating steps of independent adulthood:

   To him that hath is given, they say
   There was a bird
   That wanted so to fly.
   It looked and looked, but could not find its wings.
   It saw the others soar.

Catching the gold from the sun.
Others winged and circled past.
Joyful, dipping in the wide blue.
This little one that could not fly.
Wept so bitterly.
'Tell me where I get my wings?'
The others laughed and flew away
Didn't you know, you little fool.
Wings come to those who fly.

7

The Times that are a-Changing *

Priti T. Desai

Is there something special about the lives of three ordinary women? Ordinary lives lived during the 20th century? There is nothing unusual or dramatic—most women have had parallel experiences. Women were born, raised and married off, and in turn raised a family—so the cycle of life continued. They coped with life. Some with a hauteur and self-respect like my *Aajiba* (maternal grandmother) but within the confines of the milieu they were born into. Some like my mother grew up in momentous times—two World Wars and their aftermath, in the colonial but resurgent India that followed Gandhi's call. Did the events outside affect her? Were there no seeds of rebellion? None. But she learnt to reflect, to think, to react. And me? I never thought that the way my life evolved, not fashioned by my own design, was different. Yet, being single and independent came naturally. Now, with hindsight, I can see how small steps and a slow pace led to change.

So here is our story of three women. We hailed from south Gujarat, Desais from the heartland where Anavil Brahmins live. My family and our forefathers belonged to the area that is spanned by the river Tapi on the northern side, the southern demarcation being Vapi. Though Brahmins, Anavils did not perform priestly duties and were a rustic lot. The landholders cultivated their land with bonded labour. With the pressure on land increasing and the advent of British rule, the younger generation looked for employment in the railways and postal services in the early decades of the 20th century and gradually moved to other professions and regions. The custom of dowry was

* Originally published in the *Indian Journal of Gender Studies*, Vol. 6, No. 2, 1999, pp. 241–59.

prevalent and still is. I must admit, daughters were unwelcome. Education was a means to economic betterment and to social status. The Gujarati dialect spoken by Anavils makes them easily identifiable, and its coarseness manifested in *galis* (swear words) and blunt retorts does not bespeak a milieu of culture and refinement. But my parents spoke a very refined Gujarati.

My Mother's Last Days

I still remember vividly the morning of 18 December 1996 when I felt that my mother and I were going our separate ways. A few tears fell as I sipped my morning tea and recalled how in January 1995 she had come home after a hip replacement operation. I thought I would transform her into a fighter, and we clashed many times as I reminded her that exercise was the only way to freedom of movement. Of course, at times I felt she had the right to choose, but somehow her inactivity infuriated me. I tried to get her nutritive intake back to normal when, after nearly three months, she remonstrated and said, 'Don't force me to drink soups, I have never liked it. Leave me to my kind of food.' It was only Zafar's poem, *'Na kisi ki ankh ka noor hoon, na kisi ke dil ka karaar hoon'*[1] that still drew her—it was my only way to reach her; the piety of hers that had earlier asked for Vishnu *sahasranamam*[2] had given way to the romantic in her.

In her last few months we sang songs from all the Indian languages—this was my very special link with Mummy as my sisters did not know them. My childhood memories resurfaced with her departing ones. It was a slow downhill journey made difficult by the loss of independence, anger at her vulnerability and the recurrent bitterness of the past that refused to let go its hold.

Her favourite song said it all:

Chuni chuni kankar mahal banaya,
Log kahe ghar mera re,
Na ghar mera, na ghar tera,
chidiya rain basera re.
(Carefully choosing each little stone, a palace is built; people say it is my home. The house is neither yours nor mine, it is merely a night shelter for the bird.)

Dementia, hallucinations and strange dreams—it was agonising to see Mummy slipping away. She has gone on a journey, never to return. This was no journey with baggage and companions, this was a lone trek into the wilderness of the unknown and infinite. 'Mummy, I have tears, this is just to tell you I loved you dearly yet failed to convey it through a lifetime. We as specks of dust may never meet. Yet as long as I live I will repeat "Mummy I loved you".' This is what I wrote in my diary two years ago.

She was anticipating death once she turned 73—her mother and sister had departed at that age. The last two decades of her life felt too long as they spelt loneliness. When I retired, she mumbled, 'I wish I had the stamina, we could have travelled together.' On my 60th birthday her blessing was, 'Hope you do not live too long to find your body disobeying you.'

All of her four daughters were working women, so the 8.30 A.M. to 6.00 P.M. span was dull, though to relieve it she had fitted in a schedule of *puja* (worship), rosary chants, newspaper and magazine reading, and live television coverage of cricket. Maybe this was not enough. She needed targets and goals for her crusading spirit to pursue. Her life was spent in ensuring her children's education, looking after a handicapped husband, or overseeing her youngest brother's incurable sickness and also his family. Once she had done her duty, she lost her will to fight her recalcitrant body. I should view her as a Hindu *nari* (woman), her childhood dominated by her father, and her youth and old age by her husband. Though a widow, Mummy was lucky not to be dependent on her children. Yet she had to be accommodating as three unmarried daughters lived with her.

PARVATI

Aajiba, My Maternal Grandmother

I still see my *Aajiba* in the front room of her house facing the street, sitting in the straight wooden chair, eagerly watching for the *tonga* (covered horse-drawn cart) to wind its way up the curved slope and head towards her home. Her daughter and grandchildren were coming from Bombay for the summer vacation. I would get down, run to her and plonk myself on her lap, and she would gently hug me. I had a special bond with her—I loved her, her old things, her cooking and her rather dependable assurance that if Mummy ill-treated me, she would scold her and be on my side! My childhood anchor away from home.

My mother viewed her as a rather old-fashioned woman who would chastise her children in the presence of others—an exhibition of her power and status, a stern, dominating matriarch. When *Aajiba* died, a rare letter from Mummy reached me in which she wrote: '*Ba* [mother] died 20 years after *Bapuji* [father]. She was self-willed and self-reliant. God kept her so till the very end.'

My Grandmother's Family

Aajiba had been named Rudiben by her parents. She was the daughter of Khandu Jeevan of Hanuman Bhagda, a port at the mouth of the river Auranga, the rows of brick houses and a few *havelis* (mansions) in the town signifying its affluence. The village temple enshrined a large idol of Hanuman, which distinguished it from another village named Bhagda. Khandu Jeevan was a prosperous man, a *lakhpati* (rich man) trading in timber, who owned land and mango orchards. From family stories, it appears that he was a traditional patriarch whose rural, agricultural background rooted him in the village. His home in Hanuman Bhagda was a sprawling palatial house with two storeys, chandeliers in the sitting room, and a huge shed at the back built for the cattle.

Aajiba was one of eight siblings (four boys and four girls), positioned in the middle and was called Jiji. One of her brothers had died very young, leaving a child widow, who was beautiful, and I recall having seen her with a shaven head and in a red sari, the widow's colour. The three brothers were in the family timber trade. *Aajiba*'s elder sister was widowed in early youth. She had returned with her two daughters to her father's house and lived there until she died. She, too, appeared stern, was immersed in *puja*s in the morning and emerged only at meal times. *Aajiba*'s strong sense of self-respect meant that in later years she rarely relied on her father's family, be it even for gifts of mangoes. The fact that her father had refused a loan to her husband to pursue legal studies was a setback—a patriarch's failure to support the daughter's aspirations. It ruled out metropolitan living in Bombay, which would have offered easy access to education for her daughters and also exposure to urban life.

Aaja, My Grandfather

Aajiba was married off at the age of 11 to Kasanji Dayalji Naik, and her name was changed to Parvati at the time of marriage. Kasanji's father hailed from the village Haria, but later moved to the town of Valsad. *Aaja* started his working life as a teacher in a small town, Gandevi, not very far from his native Valsad. His extraordinary flair for the English language, which he taught with dedication, so impressed R.C. Dutt, then the *Diwan* of Baroda,[3] that *Aaja* was invited to come to Baroda where he could be given a job that would use his potential. This did not happen as R.C. Dutt died soon after and my grandfather had no friends in high places. Instead, he moved to a government job in Nagpur and finally to Pusa in Bihar where he worked for the colonial government in the Agricultural Research Institute. After seeking premature retirement in 1933, he moved to Bareilly in the then United Provinces as an adviser to a newly established sugar factory.

Aaja was one to be reckoned with, for he was a university graduate, in government service, and inevitably had to bear the burden of repaying debts that his father had contracted, assist in paying dowries for his sisters and help out with other family expenditure. For *Aajiba*, whose writ ran in family matters, her husband was her breadwinner, confidante and companion. *Aaja*'s support to his parents and siblings was accepted as the norm, though the inequity of this burden was also noted. *Aaja*'s own educational background influenced his sons' careers—all were university graduates. The daughters were literate and he rued his posting in Pusa where he could not send them for secondary schooling and further education. Perhaps he sought to remedy this imbalance by choosing sons-in-law who had university degrees and a comfortable family background: families with a connection to the police force or the film industry, while widowers were ruled out. His extreme fondness for his firstborn, a daughter, was noticeable. Yet his patriarchal domination was later realised by his sons who had no personal choice in their careers—*Aaja* decided it all! The budget for the daughters' weddings necessitated a strict savings routine, which *Aajiba* adhered to. In the Naik family the purse strings seemed to be controlled by the patriarch, but the matriarch had a controlling voice in disbursements for household expenses, education of sons and so on.

From the little village of Hanuman Bhagda to Gandevi, Nagpur, the small settlement in Pusa and ultimately to Bareilly, *Aajiba* travelled from Gujarati-speaking areas to Marathi-speaking and then to the Hindi-speaking heartland of India. Her links with her native land were close in the early years. Hanuman Bhagda was hardly 4 miles from Valsad where her in-laws lived. *Aajiba* had 11 children, of whom eight survived her, the three youngest daughters having died in infancy during 1920–30. My mother was her fifth child. All her deliveries were at home with the assistance of a midwife. Thus, her life from the age of 20 to 44 seems to have been one of childbearing and rearing. *Aajiba* was literate in that she could sign her name, read Gujarati newspapers and the scriptures, but rarely wrote to her married children who lived in other towns.

Domestic Life

Household work, embroidery, knitting and tailoring were part of women's lives—they were prepared thus for marriage. The role of a mother was to train her daughters in these tasks. My grandmother and mother conformed to the traditional mores of orthodoxy in dress for girls—the *ghaghra* (ankle-length flared skirt) and *choli* (short blouse) in childhood, and after puberty saris were worn. *Aajiba*'s understanding of adolescence was rather limited, and I do not think even *Aaja* had thought of it or had any influence on her rigid, rustic mind. Once their periods started, there were greater restrictions on the movements of the girls and even conversation with teenage boys—their brother's friends—was not allowed. During menstruation it was customary for girls to observe an untouchable status for three days and to have a ritual bath on the fourth day. A close watch was kept on the dates of the monthly cycle of each girl on the lines of a police record! The girls were told to return home before sundown if they were out visiting neighbours and a vigil was kept if the girls chatted with a male house guest or even a visiting cousin. Surprisingly, for a woman who bore 11 children, *Aajiba* understood little about the need to give her daughters information about sex and reproduction. My mother said that she was so naïve in her adolescence that she believed that even a conversation could result in pregnancy.

As *Aajiba* lived in north India, she was extremely conservative in social matters. The girls had to be married off, though age at marriage progressed from 13 years for the first daughter to 18 years for the fourth one. The caste customs were rigidly adhered to—dowry, jewels, gifts of cash, clothes and food were given to daughters. The sons, in comparison, married after they graduated—aged 26 years or more. These, too, were arranged marriages in which social conformity ruled. Selecting sons-in-law proved tough for *Aaja* as he lived away from the clan and his native district of Surat. Hence, he relied on the opinion of relatives about family backgrounds of potential sons-in-law, but his strict condition that they should be university graduates meant that those with agricultural holdings—prized catches otherwise—and rural families did not find favour. After marriage his daughters lived in towns and cities, not in villages.

A DAY IN MY GRANDMOTHER'S LIFE

She was grey-haired—she had greyed early, in her 30s, and my mother attributed it to her hotheaded temperament. Though petite, she was strong—she performed many more arduous tasks at home than any of her daughters or daughters-in-law. It is amazing that *Aajiba*, who was used to having servants in Pusa and Bareilly, had only one woman to help her when she returned to live in Gujarat to fetch drinking water, sweep the house and scrub the kitchen vessels. After *Aaja* died in 1937, she lived in Valsad, alone in the vast house, choosing not to live with her sons.

My grandmother woke early in the morning, swept the *puja* room and kitchen, and lit the fire to heat water for her ablutions. After taking her bath, she transferred the sweet drinking water (fetched from the common neighbourhood well and duly filtered) into the *matkas* (pitchers) and moved on to cooking where the protocol was rigid. She wore a silk sari, and if it was too warm the blouse was discarded and the sari draped around her so that no part of her body was exposed. A sampling of everything cooked was laid aside in a plate to be offered to the cow, and once the cow had eaten, it was time for our lunch! She took her own portion in a plate and gave the rest out so that the family, sitting at a safe distance away from her, could partake of their lunch. After her meals, she would empty the stove of the ashes, having earlier sprinkled water, dousing the unburnt wood/coal and puting it in the backyard to dry to save it for the next day, and then clean the stove with a clay solution. She washed the cordoned-off space and then came out and changed her clothes. Her kitchen uniform was hung on a hook in the *puja* room and she donned a freshly washed cotton sari and blouse. After this she picked up the newspaper, settled in her special chair in the front room, read, communicated and commented on the news. Afterwards it was time for her siesta when we children had to be quiet, and after about an hour, she was up again and sewed or mended clothes on her sewing machine, which was her prized possession. After tea in the late afternoon, she gave instructions to her daughters to cook the evening meal—the younger generation did not observe any dress and safe distance protocol. She ate a simple dinner in the evening, usually *rotla* (bread), lentils and a cup of milk. She never had breakfast or an afternoon snack. The only exception was *prasad*—a token in the name of God—though never a full helping. When there was a big family meal, the person selected to assist her was required to have an early bath, wear the prescribed silk clothes and no one could touch her. Until I grew up I thought this was the rule in all Anavil households in the countryside, only to discover that orthodoxy prevailed in some, in others convenience overruled the old practices. After dinner she would sit outside on the *otla* (a raised platform outside the house) on which most men and women sat once darkness descended, compare notes across the lane or have a private chat with a friend.

Friends and Family

Aajiba's outings were limited. I rarely saw her visiting her close relatives or contemporaries unless it was necessary in the interest of social obligations. The occasion could be a funeral, a visit of condolence, a pre- or post-wedding visit or a special shopping expedition for clothes or kitchenware that required her expertise. Being the lady of the house, she was also in charge of the production of preserves. This responsibility included the supervision of the massive summer work of making pickles and *papads* (lentil wafers), and grinding special flours on the grinding wheel. The *papad* and pickle making in summer was an exercise in community cooperation. She dictated the social protocol of visits and also decided on the type of gifts to be given on occasions like birth, *janoi, simant*, weddings, deaths and *vastu*,[4] referring to what had been given earlier and the economic status of the receiver vis-à-vis her own. Her sons sent her money for her upkeep to supplement the small interest income she had (from her own savings and what little her husband had invested on her behalf). Her own jewellery she carefully divided into two categories—her *streedhan*[5] she got from her father, and the collection of jewels gifted to her by her husband. Out of her *streedhan* she gave jewels to her daughters at various times that were socially sanctioned: on the occasion of weddings, *simant* and to a grandchild at birth, while the other pieces were divided between her daughters-in-law at the time of her death.

Though I was the fifth granddaughter of my *Aajiba*—the firstborn of my mother—she had a special love for me. My fair skin may have been the reason, though she teased me a lot about my city ways. My clothes—my European-style dresses with short panties—set me apart from the local children. My short hair, bows and clips, use of talcum powder—all these drew comments from her. I was sensitive to criticism, but her fond hug, a seat on her lap or an occasional bath with gentle scrubs conveyed her affection. I still recall with pleasure the final bath that she gave me when I was 19 years old—my mother just did not have a talent for communicating with touch—for a purpose. She needed a private chat with me to convince me that I should marry when I turned 20 for I should be a graduate then. She had someone in mind and kept on asking me what was wrong with the boy, and found my ambiguous and non-committal answers rather difficult to comprehend. At that time I chose to wear, and still do, colours I associated with her—bright red, deep grey, maroon and off-white. The moment she saw me in any of these colours, she would be greatly agitated. She would say, 'These are widow's colours, you should not wear them,' and I was happy to retort that they belonged to my *Aajiba* whom I loved. Once *Aajiba* died, her old cooking saris came my way as my youngest aunt who had them could understand this strange bond. Just a decade ago, leaving for Canada to join her son, she left an old pouch of *Aajiba*'s with my mother to be handed over to me.

Aajiba lived alone except during the last four years of her life when, on account of her high blood pressure, it was decided that it was not sensible for her to live alone. She was an unusual woman with a highly developed sense of self-respect. To manipulate for power in the family or for gain was not her style, but her frank open nature was a disadvantage in some ways.

KUSUM

My Mother

Mummy had the makings of a modern woman, but her wings were clipped by matrimony at the age of 15. When she was a child, she was sent to school escorted by her elder brother, to whom she was close. Schooling ended when she finished the seventh standard. Conservative attitudes towards co-education and the need to restrict a growing girl's movements grounded her early.

Once she reached the age of 14, the search for a suitable boy began. She was married in 1927 into a family that professed to be progressive. A fixed amount as dowry was not openly demanded, but the various offerings added up to much more than what would have customarily been given. My father, who was 22 years old, had a brilliant academic career, having obtained a B.A. with first class. He had a job and was studying law.

Mummy vividly remembered her first glimpse of him at the wedding: a very dark, bespectacled man with a red shawl and too much oil in his hair, not at all her idea of a Prince Charming. Her two older brothers were handsome and dandy; in comparison her husband must have looked ugly. She used to tell me that if she had had the freedom, she would never have married him but would have run away to Paris. Well, at least she chose a romantic city for her fantasy, for reality was not inspiring.

For a pretty, petite girl, it must have been a deep disappointment. I do not think she was fully aware of what sexual intimacy involved. A teenager hardly capable of combing her ankle-length hair, she entered the household of her husband and was expected to have the maturity to adjust effortlessly to the new environment of a joint family. From the very small town of Pusa she came to Bombay, with its maze of buildings and little greenery. The first floor flat in which they lived was dark, dismal and claustrophobic. She lived there with her husband and in-laws, who included her brothers-in-law and their families. She missed the open vistas and fresh air of Pusa. She viewed her childhood in Pusa as idyllic. The flowers, fruits, trees, serpents and scorpions, the menacing winds and floods—of these she talked often, and we labelled it Mummy's long-playing record. However, the impact of metropolitan living widened her horizons with a variety of neighbours and school friends.

Soon she was enrolled in a girls' school nearby and her intelligence took up this challenge, for within two years she passed the Karve matriculation examination. She was then enrolled in a modern co-ed school to do the Bombay state matriculation exams but was prohibited from appearing for the examination. Her father-in-law happened to be an examiner, and he was not willing to forsake it because of the money it brought. It was her first major defeat in life. Mummy took it as a permanent defeat and an end to any scholastic achievement. The Bombay schools gave her the feel of a metropolitan society. But her long school years between 1927 and 1931 were marred by ill-health due to malaria.

The change in her status from daughter to wife meant little. My father was an awkward husband who should have been openly supportive of her vis-à-vis his family. There were subtle conflicts and silences. Silence became her way of coping with reality. In 1929 my father left for England, and the two years he was away was a dark period always recalled with extreme anger and hostility. When my father returned in 1931, he rented another flat next door and life brightened somewhat for my mother. The hateful mother-in-law died in 1933. During 1931–34 my father was sent on assignments to Madras and Lahore, and he took his wife along. These were their happiest years together. Returning to Bombay in 1934, they shifted to a cosmopolitan locality with large colonial bungalows. Compared to my grandmother, my mother had a comfortable lifestyle once my parents returned to Bombay. My father insisted on moving to a big two-bedroom ground floor flat in a quiet, cosmopolitan, upper-crust locality, which again was a sore point with Mummy who would have liked a flat on the upper floor, an idea vetoed by my paternal grandfather who lived with us. Here, we had a full-time help and a cook. Mummy's daily routine during the week was a reading session after lunch at 11 A.M., a little siesta and thereafter afternoon visits to friends and relations, returning home by 6 P.M. to coincide with my father's return from office. As the years rolled by and the family grew, the housekeeping routine was filled with the chores of childcare and cooking. Life was getting more expensive, and my father's philandering limited the household resources.

The Arrival of Four Daughters

We were six children, of whom five were girls and one a boy. Mummy lost a 7-month-old daughter. The childbearing period of my mother lasted for 14 years. Each childbirth was traumatic. Her third daughter was born with a cleft palate. My mother's commitment to this daughter was total and my father's family often remarked that such a girl would have been starved to death in the villages of Gujarat. Finally, in 1946, my only brother arrived after four daughters. She must have heaved a sigh of relief when the son arrived. Yet she conceived again and in her own way tried to abort but did not succeed. Her last child, yet another daughter arrived in 1948. With the birth of my youngest sister Bindu, whose name means 'full stop', our family was complete. Mummy often told me that had I been a boy she would never have had more children.

Unhappy Bondage in Marriage

In her marriage, my mother was emotionally distressed by my father's behaviour. She could not bear the strain of mental torture that her husband inflicted on her—he accused her of infidelity though it was he who was the errant unfaithful husband. This led her to attempt suicide once, but it did little to resolve the problem. We were lucky that Mummy survived, but her spontaneity and friendliness were affected. Her unhappy bondage in marriage led to periods of extreme stress. Her self-image suffered and her unhappy personal situation meant hurts nursed and inner bitterness deeply embedded in her psyche. This, however, did not show as her outward behaviour was correct and generous.

Accepting it as a woman's fate, she did not fight it but tried to cope in silence. It must be a hard battle for most women with similar experiences who choose silence rather than confrontation. Mummy's logic was that mental bruises were tolerable, after all she had not suffered physical torture. I said to her once that she had shown 'no guts to walk out'. She told me she could not leave—who would support her and for how long? She was not economically viable. Her realisation of this weakness and vulnerability, however, did not spur her to plan careers for her daughters. Her goal for them was marriage. Like all mothers in her milieu, she wanted brilliant and handsome sons-in-law. Sad that none appeared. Mummy must have felt rather rejected as a mother of unmarried daughters. Her only son chose a British bride, but this tradition-bound Hindu housewife accepted her with great grace.

A Major Setback

In 1956, when my father was 51, he suffered a stroke that paralysed the entire right side of his body. My mother was only 44 then and faced the grim reality of a hard and difficult life ahead. Papa's career ended with this setback. For this egotistical man, dependence on his wife must have been intolerable. He had been cavalier with money and now, with only one daughter with a postgraduate degree and four schoolgoing children, the future was not at all rosy. Once we were in crisis, the extended family living with us for many years distanced itself. Mummy battled on—she stood by her husband and saw to it that he had a comfortable life at home. She had not forgotten or forgiven the past, but her deep faith in the law of karma[6] enabled her to treat him with humane fairness.

She proved that she could manage the family's finances well. She encouraged her children to pursue the careers they wanted, for they set their goals themselves. She was not an ambitious mother. She gave us the space to live our lives. Her love for literature was catholic: both my parents spent a lot of money on books and, in fact, she found it hard to follow the social convention of collecting jewellery for daughters' marriages. In retrospect, I feel that books and education were our true inheritance. Music was dear to her heart and she started learning classical Indian music in Lahore. The presence of her father-in-law and his disapproval put an end to this passion on her return to Bombay. When I turned 12, she found a music teacher for me and I still cherish the invaluable inheritance of music. She had an extraordinary ability to communicate with others and those who entered her heart rarely left it. Her cool charm made her a friend to persons of every class and creed, and she had a genuine feeling for the family of humankind.

The sphere of sexuality was my mother's area of darkness. She failed miserably in helping me face this tricky but necessary crossing. My first menstruation was a nightmare I can never forget. Mummy observed menstruation taboos so blindly that she turned a normal physical fact into a humiliating experience. Her irrational orthodoxy ran so deep that she could not rid herself of pseudo-religiosity. Having grown up in a religious family, Mummy had an immense faith in rituals. This, too, was an area of disagreement with my agnostic father who had a secular outlook and did not care much for the practices of Hinduism. Her otherwise open mind was a closed one also in matters of food. No cuisine other than Gujarati was acceptable, and eating out was derided. She gave away the rich cakes that came for Christmas to the cleaning woman as she felt it was un-Brahminical to eat such products. The obstinacy of my parents and their lack of communication made open discussion impossible; leave aside matters religious and social, even food taboos were not discussed.

Mummy was both a survivor and victim—the rebel in her never sought a positive way to confront reality. Her 'no win' stance made her a loser. To survive, she made some compromises. She was mixed up. The rigidity of her upbringing and the deep imprint of ritual and social conformity were at loggerheads with the urban, cosmopolitan life she had to live. When compared to her peers, she was sophisticated and cultured in her language, her taste in clothes, her elan, her feel for music and drama and films. When she attempted something she tried to excel—her knitting skills were to be reckoned with.

Gandhian influences did percolate to her—*swadeshi* was her creed. It shaped her ethnic taste in clothes long before ethnicity became a fashionable elitist idea. Our house was visited by vendors from all over India—the Bengali *babu* (gentleman), the elderly Muslim patriarch from Chanderi, the Mehrotras from Lucknow, the *dharmavarams* and *kanjeevarams* from south India. For me, *salwar–kameez* outfits were stitched in Lahore and sent to Bombay by friends, *ghararas* were copied from Muslim friends. Mummy believed in Indian couture, native and elegant. She took us to Gandhiji's prayer meetings, bought tokens for khadi but did not play an active political role. She disliked power-seeking politicians; the only politician she admired was Gandhi. She never voted in any election, maintaining that the candidates did not meet her stringent standards of honesty, integrity and political morality. She questioned political moves like the prohibition with her firm belief that human behaviour cannot be regulated by law.

So the personal did not become political for her. Her sharp intelligence and organisational skills could have been channelised, but were never used for social causes except at the micro level of her family. Wedged between the harsh and gender-biased attitudes of her clan and her own ideas, I think she stood for individual freedom with a commitment to duties and responsibilities that gave dignity to a person.

Mummy had an amazing faith in God, her anchor during life's crises, especially when her husband was afflicted with paralysis. She prayed, fasted, donated money and got *pujas* performed. Her abiding faith was unshaken even during the last two years of her life when she was totally bedridden. The withering of her body made her miserable and her constant refrain was, 'When will He call me? When will He set me free?' I used to tell her that since I had no special talent to impress her dear friend God, I could not intercede. She should tell Him that He was not much of a friend if He could not be relied upon after a lifetime's allegiance. Immediately she would say, 'Why blame Him? It's my karma that demands this suffering.' On the afternoon of the day she died, she asked my sister Sita to recite the *slokas* that had been part of her *puja* ritual. She mumbled along with the words; that was the last time she spoke, for in the evening she silently slipped away in sleep.

PRITI

My Childhood

As my parents' first child, I was welcomed and loved, especially by my father, who spoilt me thoroughly. Childhood was a glorious time, for I was not disciplined by strict methods. I was subject to very few restrictions, tagged along with my parents, even for late-night visits to friends, ate what I liked and wore what I liked. Evenings at the beach on weekdays and excursions to the zoo, museum, port or gardens during the weekends were routine. My parents were my friends. Growing up with adults, I knew few children. The neighbours changed so often that any relationship with my peer group withered too soon. While visiting cousins in Bombay I met a male cousin who was so bossy that I prayed at the local temple that God should bless me with seven sisters! I told my parents so and hence when sister after sister followed, Mummy said, 'No wonder! You had asked for them.' When Sita, my sister who had a cleft palate and harelip was born, I adored her. When an aunt told me that I should agree to part with her, I refused saying that even if her looks were different, she was mine and no parting would be tolerated. A shy, reserved child, I found it difficult to mix with strangers, except a few to whom I took to very easily. Being the eldest and because my parents ruled that I had to be protective of my younger siblings, a caring relationship with them was ingrained.

As I grew up, my childhood happiness slowly evaporated. My paternal grandfather who lived with us went mad. It was confusing when someone who had been lovable suddenly began to behave strangely. 'The mad family into which I was married off', a phrase my mother had often used before, was now real. In 1942, when I was 8 years old, I had met an uncle in my father's village at a family wedding. He never spoke, dressed cleanly, read newspapers, but was considered mad. I now saw a different kind of madness. Grandfather became foul-mouthed, violent and uncontrollable, suddenly transformed from an immaculately dressed, active, book-reading, card-playing, cheroot-smoking patriarch who was the principal of a local school, to someone fearsome. He slowly recovered, but now he was jobless and morose. He went regularly to the library and on long walks, and would be my accomplice if I needed support in any prank.

Soon after he recovered, another event unhinged me. One night, I woke up to an anguished cry from my mother, for one of my sisters and I slept in my parents' room. Both of us were startled out of sleep and ran to her, whilst other family members rushed in from the other room. She had swallowed poison in an attempt to commit suicide. She was uncontrollable, she was slapped and her head bent down so that the iodine that she had drunk should be purged out. An antidote was quickly administered by an uncle who lived with us. He took control of the situation and this calmed her somewhat. We clung to her desperately as both of us could feel the terror and anxiety of the situation. Dawn rose and life went back to normal, but something within me had crumbled. Why did she do it? Silence ruled and later Mummy told me of her predicament. In those confused adolescent years I felt uneasiness and conflicting emotions about Papa, my favourite parent, and yet he had hurt my mother.

Strange that Mummy always compared me to her most hated object, her mother-in-law, and said that I was a malign reincarnation of her as I was born a year after her death! Nothing was right with me. She talked about the difficult time she had when I was born and I could never erase that memory. Even in the last year of her life when hallucinations, senility and pain made her suffer, she once said, 'Priti, last night was as agonising as the night you were being born.'

The shape of my head was wrong, my bust was too big, I menstruated too soon, my tongue lashed out—it was unforgivable for a girl to answer back. I had no social graces or artistic accomplishments. I grew up into a gawky, introverted teenager without skills and with just two close friends at school. I felt horrible and thought that everything was wrong with me. So I sought solace in reading. I learnt to love languages and poetry. Later, listening to Indian classical music became an addiction, though I refused to sing or play. I never had a word of praise from Mummy, and if someone complimented me, I was always reminded that it was ill-deserved. Though the mother and daughter did trust each other and shared many a secret (Mummy bought me my first lipstick), the bond kept us in constant conflict. As my studies at the university progressed, so did my initiation into the world of commerce and finance. Papa asked me to read some of his drafts to government ministries, representations on insurance, books on planning, nationalisation, corporate histories and so on. I found this challenging and when I argued with him, I felt that I too could think and express myself on subjects that mattered. I was never snubbed like I was on matters such as cooking or knitting. For womanly chores I had my rebellious face, and Mummy, who was my trainer, always wanted to cut me down to size. The two worlds were in stark contrast.

The Real World Outside

I finished my master's in economics with good marks and planned to study abroad, hoping it would enable me to develop a career. But that was not to be. Papa had the near fatal paralytic stroke, which meant an end to his active career. I was the eldest and felt that I had to stand by him. It took us a while to cope and sort out the frayed fabric of life. My dream of going to Cambridge for higher studies did not materialise. I started applying for jobs, only to find that most sectors did not employ women. I was told that since I was a woman I would not fit the job. I hated those bigwigs on the other side of the table; if they knew this they need not have called me for an interview! I had to get something on my own merit. It was difficult to understand that a godfather was a necessity in order to find a job.

My first job was a clerical position in the Bureau of Economics and Statistics, placed through the employment exchange, where the atmosphere was dismal. Luckily, I was selected as a lecturer in economics in Miranda House, a women's college affiliated to Delhi University, and left home.

Delhi awakened me in many ways. It matured me. I lived in the hostel, made friends with colleagues, discovered a new city and enjoyed teaching. The students were very fond of me, and from a shy and reserved girl, I became a confident woman. It also opened my eyes to the reality of higher education. I had idealised the teaching profession, but I received a jolt among intelligent and highly qualified women whose world was full of intrigues, snobbery and feudal values. Soon Papa received an offer from a reputed Swiss insurance company to act as an adviser. This would enable him to be active and have an interest in the field where he had worked with distinction. How was he going to do it? He had a handicap, his right hand did not function. He would require an able secretary. His close business friends who visited Delhi regularly told me that instead of being away from the family, I should return home and work with Papa. My parents did not pressurise me, but in a family where duty was emphasised, I felt it was my chance to be the son that I was not.

So another phase in my life began. I picked up shorthand and typing skills, which had a market, worked with Papa and honed my business skills. Working with Swiss personnel I gained insights into international business, but this too was a man's world. My role was that of a Man Friday. Career advancement was most unlikely. In my early 30s I had a freak accident that required surgery and a long rest. I realised that I needed to earn to pay for the inevitable expenses. To pay for this sickness I needed at one stage to do three part-time jobs—an eye-opening experience that made me look for a full-time job again. Thinking of migration, I got an immigration visa for Canada. At the same time, I landed a job in the immigration section of the Australian Consulate. I was told that it was a temporary position for six months; I could at least earn my passage to Canada, I thought, and joined. It was interesting to find a country that had kept itself white slowly allowing Asian professionals as immigrants. Whether it was extreme sensitivity or fear of an unknown country, I gave up the idea of migrating to Canada as the job at the Australian Consulate became permanent; the work environment was congenial, and my sincerity and work were appreciated. A change in the Australian government and a retrenchment policy led to the closure of the Australian Consulate. Once again it was the same old story of looking for a job, and now, in my 40s, it seemed tougher still. The lack of special skills was a constant refrain, but friends rallied round and I found work. I managed to become fluent in Marathi, got to know the younger generation of technocrats and MBAs, and so for the next two decades carried on working.

I survived through nearly four decades as a working woman. I discovered much more in the world. I learnt that widening the mind's horizons does not require graduation from famous universities. My interests widened. From economics and politics to arts, architecture, literature, music, theatre, crafts and textiles. I found limitless joy.

Life as a Single Woman

My parents' unhappy marriage disillusioned me. Moreover, being independent and having seen women being treated as chattel, it was impossible to marry traditionally. I would not have allowed my father to look for a husband, nor would he have done it. A few suggestions from friends did not meet my romantic ideals, for I believed that the man should propose marriage. Some did, but did not have the guts to ask me directly. It was done via emissaries, and in my youth I considered it cowardly. I did not realise that fragile male egos would rather not risk hearing 'no' for an answer. So, as I see it, real love never came my way. It is ironic that many of my male friends feel sad that I did not make a man happy! I am pleased at this compliment, but who knows, life's journey could have been thorny, too. While she lived, my *Aajiba* did not influence my ideas. Mummy decidedly did, and her anger at the way Anavils treated their wives and daughters was deeply imprinted on my mind.

When I was in the USA, I realised to my great surprise that to the Americans I was an oddity—they suspected that I must have a lover, a liaison or a lesbian fling. Could they not envisage a woman's life as rich and joyful without sexual relations? I had a very modern father, have innumerable friends whose affection I value, and I have lived my life my way.

My three younger sisters are single working women. We sisters lived with our parents as we were based in Bombay. We did not set up independent households as we did not feel the need. Being socially responsible and economically independent, we managed our income and budget individually, and we had total personal freedom. Being earning members, we contribute to the household's expenses. In fact, since 1972, we have been a household of women! Our brother and his family stay with us whenever necessary, but his is a nuclear family.

As Mummy's evaluation of Anavil men was extremely negative, she was not enthusiastic about a caste alliance. Moreover, she also knew that marriage without love was not our idea of happiness. She in her own way had laid the guidelines within which freedom of choice prevailed. Yet, as I reflect, I feel it was our upbringing that was responsible—we were independent-minded women who scared men brought up with traditional ideas. Maybe our expectations were unreal in the society in which we lived. Anyway, being financially independent and with a father who had brought us up with an identity of our own as well as confidence in ourselves, the insecurity of being unmarried did not haunt us.

The men who influenced me were many. Papa was my playmate as well as intellectual companion; the freedom that he allowed me was much more than what was experienced by my classmates and friends. My maternal uncles were quite chauvinistic, except for one who was a doctor. He was my favourite and taught me much. Whenever he was home, we had meals together and he would gently cajole me to try everything that was cooked, for as a child I only favoured potatoes! His love for Urdu poetry, *ghazals* and *qawwalis* also influenced me. He had worked in a small princely state in Madhya Pradesh, later moving on to Quetta and Chaman in Baluchistan, and finally to Okha in Gujarat. He used to relate his experiences to us, which were like enchanting stories of places far away. He influenced my life as I could talk frankly and openly with him. There was no tradition-bound awe. Despite having lived in small places, he had a universal vision, a sharp mind and was loved by every one in our houses, servants included.

Another relationship that I deeply valued was with my cousin (he was my father's brother's son) who had lived with us for nearly a decade. My senior by seven years, he was exceptional in his analytical skills, his understanding of world history and politics, despite the fact that his main interests were mathematics and theoretical physics. He was a rationalist and I discovered much of Freud and Marx under his guidance in my teenage years. Films were a passion with him, and I learnt to appreciate them with a critical eye. Yet, when my father suffered the paralytic stroke, he distanced himself from us, which I found difficult to condone. He must have had his reasons, but this change in a dependable cousin and friend was hard to understand. It was only when I met him in England, nearly 25 years later, that we renewed our bond. Similarly, my eldest cousin (Mummy's eldest sister's daughter) also influenced me—her appreciation of Mughal architecture, Gujarati poetry and her dependable love made a significant impact on me.

I find commonly held views about single people very unreal. The usual remarks are that a single person has no problems, no major responsibilities, is incapable of nurturing relationships and needs no privacy. Being married, being a spouse who has the reflected glory of a husband, seems to be the acceptable position for a woman, providing her an elevated social status. These attitudes have a wide prevalence, borne out by sayings like, 'Has one ever heard of an old woman dying who was unmarried!' On the other hand, I recall that in my mid-20s, I often heard some of my mother's friends saying that 'marriage is like iron *channas*, those who marry find it hard to eat, and those who don't keep yearning for it'. I can honestly say I have not yearned for a husband. If I had found a companion to share my life with, not just my body, I would not have resisted marriage. But to feel that I have been left on the shelf, or am in any way incomplete, is an admission of weakness. One is born alone, one dies alone. Why this conformity to a married status?

My Mother, Myself: A Reflection

When I turned 25, Mummy goaded me to do things on my own—be it a visit to the cinema, a late-night music concert or a drink with a friend in a bar. 'Don't be ashamed of anything you do' was my parents' advice to me. Be honest, Mummy always maintained; she could not tolerate lies. So I never told lies to Mummy. Yet deep within me remained the feeling that she hated and disliked me for a long time. I could not tell her so—in our culture that is something one never says to one's mother. But when I felt the galling chill, the frozen silences, were they imagined? The truth is that we never chose to confront each other honestly. Both of us remained immature and paid a price. Mummy chose an inner aloofness and cold contempt while being correct, while I chose to move away, bearing no ill will or grudge. Mummy and I delighted in exploring the horizons of the mind. But our paths were different. For Mummy rituals were deeply imprinted, texts parroted and occasionally discovered from the lectures she occasionally attended—these had divine sanctions. She was angry with the social and cultural mores she did not like, but she did not examine their inadequacies in a dispassionate and rational manner. She chose to ignore the rational way, which could have proved too unsettling for her. Mummy was a feminist who had quietly passed on the message that a woman had an identity and a will, and needed a space of her own. She was not a man-hater, but did not accept patriarchy. She rued the cowardice of her father who gave her the freedom to think but not to act. I wish Mummy had worked out a way of achieving, aiming, of giving substance to her intelligent mind, or being what she had in her.

NOTES

1. 'Neither am I the flame of someone's heart, nor am I the light of someone's eyes,' a poem by Bahadur Shah Zafar, the last Mughal emperor of India.
2. The holy chant of 100 names of Lord Vishnu.
3. One of the first Indian members of the Indian Civil Service, he later went on to become president of the Indian National Congress. After his retirement from the civil services, he became the *Diwan* of Baroda.
4. *Janoi* is a ceremony in which the sacred thread *janeu* is tied around the body of a male Brahmin child. *Simant* is held in the seventh month of pregnancy to bless the mother-to-be and the unborn child. *Vastu* is a house-warming ceremony.
5. Ornaments and cash given to a woman at the time of her marriage by her parents, her own property.
6. The Hindu philosophical belief that links one's present life with deeds performed in a past life.

8

Uneven Earth and Open Sky*

Saroja Kamakshi

Looking back, I find that the need to be in touch with creativity has been an impelling urge in my life. And I have searched for it, though not in a deliberate way, in many spaces—in my relationships, through my daughters, through responding to art. This is what has shaped me and what I think I have made of my life.

Through the years, my daughters, Priya and Malavika, and I have nurtured a relationship built on, most importantly, a sharing of artistic experience. Priya through her writing and Malavika through her dance.

At 68 I am creative collaborator and manager to Malavika, travelling with her in India and abroad as she presents her Bharata Natyam to diverse audiences. There is the performance experience—the backstage excitement and activity, the hush as the audience settles in expectantly. Later is the afterglow, with the applause and acclaim that the outside world confers on her. It is a heady feeling. But this is not all. There is the rehearsal experience in the intimate space of our inner courtyard, when Malavika and I share something we hold very close—the sense of the sacred in dance. And I am aware of different kinds of joy—moments of being in touch with something beyond and bigger than oneself and the exhilarating moments of success.

Ours is a household of women. Of three generations. During my interludes here, I savour the special quality of the spaces in which we live. Sitting on the swing facing the inner courtyard, I think of the varying rhythms of my life and how I arrived in this space I can call my very own. It is a space that grants me freedom. To be myself after two marriages and divorces. It is a creative dance space for Malavika who lives with me. An alternative space to create for Priya, who lives in Pune. A sheltering space to care for my mother in her old age.

Getting here has been difficult. I recall an incident that affected me deeply when I was about 6 years old. This was to be characteristic

* Originally published in the *Indian Journal of Gender Studies*, Vol. 6, No. 2, 1999, pp. 261–74.

of my parents' response to every crisis in my life. The terror of it remains in my memory. I was ill with dysentery. Seeing the doctor approach me with an injection needle, I started to scream and kick. It required two people—my grandmother and the doctor's assistant—to hold me down. My parents had fled to the garage and plugged their ears as they could not bear to see or hear their only child suffer pain. Their action was upheld as an example of 'unparelleled parental love'. It was only after nearly two decades that I questioned their attitude. But they were sure of their moral ground.

MY GRANDPARENTS

Until I was 12, I grew up in a joint household of grandparents, cousins, aunts, uncles, even distant relatives. It was a joint family with a difference since we lived in my maternal grandfather's house. During the British *Raj*, my grandfather had risen to be a superintending engineer and had been awarded the title of Rai Bahadur. He was married at the age of 22 to his 8-year-old cousin Lakshmi. His status assured them a life of ease and affluence. Lakshmi was a mother by the age of 13 and a grandmother by the age of 28. She was a matriarch whose presence was very much felt and whose position was unquestioned within the confines of the house. Grandmother was taught English by her husband. P.G. Wodehouse was a favourite author, whose books were avidly read and discussed along with radio news of World War II. Grandmother, with her strongly held views, actively participated in these discussions.

MY PARENTS

Meenakshi, my mother, was the third of four children. She was nicknamed Kabuli for she was a rebellious child even though she was afraid of her father. The family and a retinue of servants used to accompany my grandfather on his field tours. My mother and her younger brother, who adored her, enjoyed these trips immensely. Their childhood was carefree and comfortable. For most of the time they ran wild in the huge compounds of bungalows or in the camps. When they were taken out, the girls wore frocks, shoes and socks.

Marriage, however, changed all this. At 12, my mother was married to a 24-year-old lawyer, Pattabhiraman. My mother, a skinny tomboy, was dolled up for the occasion in a 9-yard sari and all her jewellery. Father wore diamond earrings and his long hair in a *kudumi*.[1] Father 'saw and approved'. Their horoscopes were matched. A grand wedding, lasting five full days, took place.

My father was a person drawn to the arts. He was short-tempered and because of this often misunderstood. My mother was intimidated by him. She hated what she considered his attempts to mould her into an obedient and submissive wife. And yet, when it came to family planning, unheard of in those days, and my upbringing, she had her way. One child, a girl, she decided was enough. On account of his temperament, *Appa* (father) was not successful as a lawyer. Moreover, he was a *veetu mappillai*, a son-in-law-in-residence who lived unhappily in the shadow of his father-in-law and brother-in-law. Coupled with the tensions and strains of an extended family, his feelings of isolation and inadequacy increased. So much so, that he lived in one room upstairs, had all his food brought to him by my mother and never spoke to any other family member. I remember feeling helpless and upset watching this as a child.

From being a carefree, strong-willed girl, *Amma* (mother) turned into an embittered woman, forever blaming the family for her situation and refusing to accept her own lack of will and assertiveness for her unhappiness. Later I realised that the moment anything went wrong, *Amma* gave up without the slightest effort; also, she never admitted to any mistake. And from this I learnt the importance of recognising one's mistakes and working hard against odds.

My father's sister was one of those colourful, gregarious characters. She was obliged to live with her in-laws, a most conservative joint family. Nevertheless, she found for herself creative solutions within the confines of tradition. She went on pilgrimages, visited holy men, and never missed marriages, birth or death ceremonies. Till the end she remained daring and spirited. Whenever my mother disapproved of me, I was compared to my aunt.

Childhood

I was born in 1931, delivered at home by an Anglo-Indian midwife. My father doted on me and gave me a lot of warmth and affection.

He called me his 'son-daughter' and never made me feel inadequate because I was a girl. Both my parents were proud of the fact that I stood first in my class throughout my years in school. We lived in a large and roomy house with many fruit trees, which I loved to climb, in the compound. When I could get away, the garden was my sanctuary where I would read my books of fairy tales. I recollect my childhood as being a lonely one although surrounded by people. It was a divided household, divided to a large extent on the basis of colour. A 'fair skin' as understood by us natives was most sought after. My aunt and her daughter were labelled 'dark'. This led to unpleasant comparisons with my mother and myself who, being somewhat lighter skinned, were considered 'fair'. This prejudice left my cousin with a deep inferiority complex. Even the grades the Scottish and Irish nuns at school gave me were attributed to my 'fair skin'.

Most of the time we children grew up in an atmosphere of distrust and suspicion fostered by the elders. The only time the air cleared was during festivals when participating in creative activities brought a feeling of togetherness. Maybe this is why, till today, I believe in the transforming power of art. Festivals were big occasions. In particular the *kolu*[2] display during the Navratri festival was very aesthetically done in our house and was the target of much envy. *Amma*, her sisters and my grandfather, now retired, created out of cardboard a whole miniature township with temple, theatre, school and houses, and also meticulously dressed dolls. The whole town was lit up with tiny electric bulbs. The women also embellished Ravi Varma[3] paintings with gold dust and precious stones. Or they painted. Or they embroidered in cross-stitch. Except on festival days, when, under grandmother's supervision, special sweets were made, the women did not go into the kitchen, which was adequately staffed with two Brahmin cooks. Ritual and tradition created the general ambience of a Brahmin household and, although we did not rigidly follow religious customs, the Friday *puja* (worship) was regularly performed. As regular as the *puja* was the weekly visit to the cinema house to watch the newest Hollywood releases. This was strictly for the adults. But they went separately—my parents one afternoon, my grandparents and visiting aunts on another. As I said, it was a house divided.

I remember there was always the sound of classical Karnatic music in the house on the radio or on records. My parents also attended live concerts. The one strong bond between my parents was an interest in music. Since *Appa*'s mother disapproved of violin lessons from a male teacher, *Appa*, over the years, collected many records so that *Amma* could learn through listening to the great Karnatic violin maestros. Evenings after school, I would find them on the terrace—*Amma* playing the violin, *Appa* criticising, appreciating, even attempting to sing! My negative attitude to the violin for many years thereafter was perhaps due to my feeling of being excluded from these music sessions. Yet the most moving recollection I have of *Amma* was when she played years later for a small audience at a private concert. I was so happy for her that I wept unashamedly in public! Nobody understood. Not even my mother.

Grandfather had bought the *Book of Knowledge* series, which, surprisingly, contained some fairy tales. *Appa* bought me my own copy of *Grimms' Fairy Tales*. I often escaped into this fantasy world inhabited by the flaxen-haired Goldilocks, Snow White, Prince Charming, witches and fairy godmothers. At the time it was exciting reading, but caused identity problems later.

At school, study meant learning 'by heart' as the Scottish and Irish nuns who taught us were themselves not well educated. Teaching mathematics to the higher classes was entrusted to a Brahmin. And I was often told to give the history and geography classes for my classmates. I must say I loved the experience.

MY MOTHER AND I

When I was a child, *Amma* was my role model. And I unconsciously tried to fulfil the expectations she had from me. In the 'divided' joint family in which we lived until I was 12, my loyalties were totally with my mother. Later, *Appa*, *Amma* and I moved into our new house gifted by my grandfather. I was then entering my adolescent years. My priorities in life changed.

I wanted to explore life and find my own voice. In our new home *Amma* had to manage the finances. *Appa* liked the good life. He enjoyed going on picnics and drives. He loved shopping and picking up lots of small, quite unnecessary things. He was irresponsible and self-indulgent although, as he used to point out, he had 'no vices'.

When the financial problems increased, there were ugly confrontations between them. But *Appa* always had his way because he used to storm out of the house angrily. I was caught in the crossfire, and being an only child made it much more difficult. While *Appa* never asked me to take sides, *Amma* would ask me to write long and bitter letters to *Appa* on her behalf. I hated doing this, but I felt I had to help her out. I was increasingly drawn by *Amma* into all her problems—financial, emotional and psychological. It resulted in a drift away from *Appa*. This led to feelings of frustration and anger in me.

'Not having enough money' became a lament in *Amma*'s life. It remained a lament because she never tried to work out solutions. The backdrop to our relationship was her theme song, 'I live only for you, for your happiness.' Later, when hurt, I started to question this, and she would say, 'How can I ever hurt you—even unintentionally? I love you.' Amma was overprotective towards me. All her fears were for me. And her fears kept growing—fear of the world outside, of open skies, of the tree in the courtyard crashing and falling on my head, fear of just about everything. Her fears burdened my life. Since she lived in fear for me, I could never approach her, not even in a crisis. *Amma*'s fears kept growing, and she kept insisting that her fears were related only to my well-being. *Amma*'s weaknesses meant that I accepted more and more responsibilities. On the threshold of my teens, I could not take my own problems to *Amma*. She gave me no support, so I started to look outside.

One fine day *Appa* brought home Harindranath Chattopadhyaya. It was our first personal encounter with a 'bohemian' character. Poet, actor, composer, Harindranath, or Baba as he was known, was colourful, irreverent and had a refreshing way of looking at things. Through him we met other artists, dancers and singers. There was a feeling of recklessness, of adventure, of breaking conventions, of great freedom. This lasted for a couple of years until *Appa*, on the advice of friends who got to know of Baba's permissive lifestyle, put an end to this association. But not before I got my great opportunity to play Ophelia opposite Baba's Hamlet—a brief and totally inconsequential appearance.

ROMANCE AND MARRIAGE

While in college, I longed for romance more than anything else. And there was Vasu, my best friend's cousin, tall, good-looking, sharp-witted. We met whenever we could, helped by friends, who, bribed with chocolates, provided alibis. We met in secret and went on long drives. Meanwhile, Vasu dropped out of college to join the Merchant Navy. This only made him a more romantic figure in my eyes. We swore undying love for each other. Our plans initially met with parental disapproval since we were not of the same community, although we were both Brahmins. Eventually, Vasu and I were married at Tirupati in 1953. In many ways his family was more conservative. And I had to be taught by elderly aunts the customs and manners of the Sri Vaishnava community to which Vasu belonged.

Soon after marriage, I sailed to the UK on a cargo ship with Vasu. He was third mate—way down in the hierarchy. The officers and their wives on board were people I could not relate to. Their backgrounds were very different. I missed music and books. But I was in love and that was all that mattered. To be on a ship, to 'keep watch' on the bridge on long nights was an enthralling experience. I was with the man I loved, looking at the sea and sky at night as the ship moved through them, watching him in the moonlight and starlight in his white uniform. Both of us were incredibly 'mushy' at this stage.

While Vasu sailed away to different ports, I stayed in London, a huge, bewildering city. To keep myself occupied, I joined a local polytechnic for a course in library science. Here I met Inez, a young Spanish widow and we became friends. Together, we laughed at the barbaric Anglo-Saxon 'natives' of London. It was Inez who introduced me to the pleasures of wine.

On Vasu's next visit to London I joined the ship and we now headed towards the icy North Sea. When I returned to London a few weeks later, I discovered to my utter joy that I was pregnant. When I came home to Madras I was five months with child. During my pregnancy, I began to study Sanskrit with Vasu's grandfather, an aesthete and a scholar. My encounter with the West had given me a great thirst to discover my own heritage, and I did a lot of reading on art and culture. Priya was born in 1955. She was a beautiful child and she filled me with delight. She gave a new meaning to my life. Priorities shifted and I could cope with changes in my marital relationship.

For a few years I was the lonely wife whose husband was out at sea. I persuaded Vasu to take up a shore job in Bombay as nautical surveyor. And for the first time, Vasu, Priya and I lived together. Very often my parents came and stayed with us. I was determined that Priya should not face the loneliness I knew of being an only child. And, in 1959, Malavika, my second daughter, was born. Domesticity and the responsibility of parenthood did not suit Vasu, although initially he tried to be the middle-class husband and father. Vasu and I were drifting apart. In 1961 Vasu went to London for further studies. I joined him there, leaving my children in the care of my parents. Six-year-old Priya felt a sense of abandonment.

GROWING APART IN MARRIAGE

In London Vasu and I shared a small apartment, almost strangers to each other. It was a time of deceit, marital infidelity and betrayal in a cold and alien country. There was nothing to stop me from returning to India and my children, but I was determined to experience life and whatever it had to offer at this stage, including a disintegrating marriage. I wanted to face and survive the darkness and my determination gave me strength. I was standing at the edge of an abyss. Yet there was another aspect to life in London that I was discovering. Alone, I often went to concerts, to the theatre, screenings of new wave films, to museums and art galleries. There was also the wonderful world of books that was open to me as I worked in a library, and I tasted Western literature. In these two years I learnt some hard lessons about life. But, most of all, I learnt to rely entirely on myself.

I returned alone to Madras and my children. I met Badrinath, an IAS officer who quoted poetry and philosophy and was interested in probing human relationships. As we drew closer, our relationship developed to the point when Badri proposed marriage. Vasu, who by now was involved with an Englishwoman, an ex-colleague of mine, agreed to a divorce. But after agonising for a few weeks, I decided against taking this major step. Priya and Malavika were 8 and 4 years old respectively, and I was afraid they would not accept Badri, and my relationship with them would be damaged. Eventually, Vasu and I settled down to a life of disharmony in Bombay. Badri and I went on to become good friends.

A few years later, Vasu had to go to sea again, this time as captain. The children and I were to travel with him with all the privileges reserved for the captain's family. The children were in a high state of excitement, looking forward to it. However, it suited Vasu better to leave us behind as his English friend was waiting for him in Australia. Priya was heartbroken and shattered. I felt a great sense of anger and outrage. This was the first of many betrayals my children had to face.

The bitterness continued. Vasu's relationship with his children was at best tenuous. My job at the *Times of India* financed my children's education at the Cathedral School. A good education, I felt, would help them think and explore for themselves. It was at the *Times of India* that I started contributing articles to their various publications. I enjoyed the writing, the bylines and the extra money.

MY DAUGHTERS

Malavika was 7 when I took her to *Guru* Kalyanasundaram of the Sri Rajarajeshwari Bharata Natya Kala Mandir. The *gurus* (masters) came from a highly respected *parampara* (tradition) of Tanjavur and I am eternally grateful to them for being in Bombay and for the very good training they imparted.

Priya was an immensely gifted but a difficult child. I encouraged her in whatever creative pursuit she was excited about—painting, poetry, nature studies or mass communication. I also put in time with Priya, helping her with homework. We spent some enjoyable hours making scrapbooks on nature studies or peoples of the world. Priya would do brilliantly in subjects she liked and just scrape through in others. Malavika's school graph, like her emotional one, was more even. As a mother trying to motivate her children, I found I had to adopt very different strategies for the two of them.

Malavika was hard-working, disciplined and very gifted. And she always stood out in dance class. I would rush home from work, drive her to class thrice a week and take her practice sessions at home. Neither Malavika nor I imagined at the time that the grand and enriching world of dance would one day be central to our lives. I am very grateful to Malavika for opening this world out to me. I spent long hours talking to Malavika about the immensity and the grandeur of dance and its enriching potential in one's life. Meanwhile, the dance classes were beginning to reveal to me the beauty of line and movement, the precision and grace of Bharata Natyam. Priya's paintings and poems uncovered another world of beauty. When time permitted, I attended music and dance concerts. I also took the children on weekends to Borivili National Park where we would point out to each other anything of wonder or beauty that struck us. My involvement with my children, watching their potential develop, sustained me and added depth and dimension to my life.

Financially, these were trying times. Priya's dresses were usually cut from my sarees. Our eating habits were basic—no Cokes, no cakes. The upholstery was fading and the paint peeling off the walls. Yet I found money for canvases, paints and dance classes. Vasu at this time was planning to start a business in Madras. Though he was away a great deal, he provided money for basic household expenses. But I had to cope with the problems of day-to-day living. And deal with the psychological and emotional problems of teenage daughters. And my work. And single parenting. By temperament, I am impatient and I have inherited my father's hot temper. This made things even more difficult. Marriage to Vasu had given me no security—neither financial nor emotional. I had always been alone.

When I was 40 I was hospitalised for six weeks with a heart attack. These were quiet, still days with nothing to do but watch the light move across the sea outside my window. For the first time I felt that there was, beside my driving energy and my insufferable impatience, a calmness within me. And with this came a great sense of freedom.

Arangetram

Within a year of coming home from hospital, I was planning and preparing for Malavika's *arangetram*, her first public appearance on stage. She was 12 years old. I worked tirelessly with very little help from the family. There was much to do—raising money through advertisements, getting the dance costumes and jewellery ready, printing souvenirs and invitations, long rehearsals and so on. When it finally happened on 6 March 1972, I couldn't believe it. I remember the curtain going up, the three *gurus* on stage with the *talams* (beats) and the first notes of the prayer song. It was a most beautiful and moving moment because it held the strength and continuity of this awesome inheritance of Bharata Natyam. Also, for me, it was a reaffirmation of the place of dance in Malavika's life and mine. Twenty-five years later, on the same day, we made a pilgrimage to Chidambaram. And Malavika offered her dance in homage within the sacred precincts of the temple in front of the deity.

My Second Marriage

It was through Priya that we got to know her classmate Sarojini's family—her younger brother Sunny and father K.P.P. Nambiar, an electronic wizard with a great vision of building 'India's greatest electronic industry' in his home state, Kerala. Nambiar was also a single parent, being separated from his British wife. Nambiar and I found we needed each other's advice and support—he in the running of his house and I in matters relating to car or tax payments. Towards the end of 1971, the Sarukkais and the Nambiars went on a holiday together to Kerala. It was obvious that things were going in a particular direction with Vasu's tacit approval. By December 1972 Vasu and I were divorced.

In contrast to Vasu, Nambiar involved me completely in his life. This gave a great boost to my self-confidence. I felt needed. Nambiar could be spontaneous and whacky, breaking into song and dance when the mood got him. As I was to admit later, he was also manipulative, self-centred and egoistic. But I initially turned a blind eye to these aspects of his personality. Nambiar and I were married in December 1972. We moved to staid and conservative Trivandrum. He became chairman and managing director of Keltron, the electronic goods company he helped found. The early years with him were happy and fulfilling, and I shared wholeheartedly in his plans for the future. But I had to keep my innermost thoughts and feelings to myself because, for him, I was important only as his wife, not as an individual. Yet there was the excitement of being involved in the building of Keltron. We talked and dreamt electronics together. There were, of course, the inevitable tensions in the family with his teenaged children. Years after Nambiar and I divorced, on the few occasions I have met his children, they have been warm and appreciative. And I have been responsive. It is a good feeling.

DANCE TAKES ON A NEW MEANING

Malavika had just completed school in 1974 and relocating her was a major and difficult decision. I would have loved to take her to Trivandrum, but it was not the right place for Bharata Natyam. So Malavika had no choice but to go to Madras and live with her father. By this time Vasu was completely involved with his secretary, who was only two or three years older than Priya. She later became his wife.

We were very fortunate to find the right *gurus* for Malavika in Madras. *Guru* Kalanidhi Narayanan had the distinction of being the first Brahmin girl to learn Bharata Natyam at a time when it was not considered respectable. After a lapse of many years—during which time Kalanidhi got married and raised a family—she had just returned to teaching dance. And we were really lucky to meet her. Kalanidhi opened up the wonderfully rich world of *abhinaya* (expression) to Malavika. It was the inner landscape of emotions that Malavika explored with her *guru*. I cherished the many hours I spent watching *guru* and student in class. I knew then that we had been guided correctly and were on the right path. In *nritta* (pure dance), *Guru* Rajaratnam introduced Malavika to the grace of the Vazhuvoor school.

This was an emotionally traumatic time for Malavika. Suddenly, she felt abandoned and alone in Madras. It was her involvement in dance that sustained her and gave her life meaning and purpose. This was the time when dance became an all-consuming passion for her. Malavika, away from me and Priya, lonely and rejected by her father, began to discover the inner harmony of dance. I visited Malavika as often as I could, about once in two months, and it was terrible to see her depressed. But watching her at her dance classes was a joy. University education and the daily routine of college had lost all relevance for her and she decided to discontinue her studies. I was the only one who supported her in this, and therefore found myself severely criticised by a degree-conscious society.

Priya got married in June 1975 to Suresh Chabria. My son-in-law, an intellectual and professor of political science, was very knowledgeable on cinema. He later became director of the National Film Archives in Pune and now teaches film studies at the Film and Television Institute of India. Priya was very involved with her new life in Bombay and with adjusting to living in a joint family and marriage. Initially, like all mothers, I was concerned. Also, convinced as I was of her creativity, I was impatient with her for not exploring her potential. And I showed this. Priya on her part felt I was bossy and judgemental. This was the period when we most distant from each other. Later, however, I could see that hers was a marriage of mutual respect and enrichment. And I am very happy for both of them.

Difficult Times in Trivandrum

From the Keralites I learnt the importance of thrift, the necessity of owning a house or property, and the need to be alert to opportunities. I had never been financially secure and my parents had always quarrelled over money as my father ran through my mother's inheritance rather irresponsibly. Vasu, too, had never been prudent. I had not asked for alimony as I was planning to remarry. In Trivandrum I found myself living in comfort, but without much money to call my own. I decided to work and to save money. I joined an advertising agency and over the years invested all my savings in a small flat and some land in Madras. I always kept my personal expenditure to a minimum. With the help of a loan, I was able to build a small house in Madras. This was the wisest action I ever took; later it proved to be a lifesaver.

Problems in my married life were beginning to surface. The darker side of my husband began to show. While building Keltron, he was regarded as a hero, almost worshipped by the people, mostly unemployed and eager for job opportunities. But sustaining and managing the enterprise created unforeseen problems for which he was sharply and sometimes unfairly criticised. He began to drink heavily and flew into rages, becoming nasty and abusive. I tried the usual wifely strategies to get him to stop drinking, but with little success. He now sought power. When I lived in Trivandrum, listening to music became very important to me on the long evenings when Nambiar was away on tour. I began to enjoy being alone and having the large spaces of my house to myself. I also started lessons in yoga. This has been one of the most rewarding inputs in my life—for the values it provides and for the deep quiet it encourages within oneself.

Meanwhile, unknown to me, Nambiar was chalking out his strategies for a new business venture and a new wife. Initially, I was disbelieving; then I tried to talk him out of his involvement and salvage our marriage, but it was useless. She was a wealthy young widow (about two or three years older than his daughter) who was obviously going to finance his business venture. I realised that Nambiar urgently wanted me out of his life. To hasten the process, he began physically assaulting me. I had read about battered women, but I could not believe this was happening to me. Things got worse. When scars began to show, my parents and children were anxious that I should leave Trivandrum. In 1984 Nambiar left on a foreign tour. He had already planned my departure from Trivandrum with the connivance of some persons whom I believed to be my friends too. I packed my belongings and left. Not knowing what the future held. Knowing that I could not live there any longer.

Prasad, a generous cousin, offered me the use of a small room in his rented flat. But for this offer I would have had nowhere to go. His family comprised an invalid wife and two mentally disabled young men. Thankful for a roof over our heads, Malavika and I moved in. My parents also lived with us as they had no financial resources of their own. It was a time of hardship and deprivation. From being a *memsahib* living in a large bungalow with air-conditioned rooms and having chauffeur-driven cars, I was now sleeping on the floor since I could not afford a bed. In this congested flat, Malavika had to practise on the rough floor of the terrace, as that was the only space available. This was the time I sold my jewellery. Like a blessing in the midst of all this, I learnt of a good yoga institute nearby and started attending classes and lectures. I found the philosophy of yoga engrossing and worked over four years on Vyasa's commentary on Patanjali's *Yoga Sutras* with an eminent Sanskrit scholar. For the first time I felt I was leading a life of my own with no questions asked. It was a pleasure to watch Malavika grow in her dance. Dance was the centre, the essential core of our existence. With more foreign tours and with many more performances in India, our finances gradually improved. Yet we continued to live frugally in our single-room tenement. We slowly built up our savings; I sold my small flat, Malavika bought a second-hand car and we moved into our very own house in 1990. My parents moved in with us. My father died in 1993. We now have a caretaker family who look after my mother and the house when Malavika and I are on tour.

Over the last 12 years Malavika has been choreographing, interpreting and extending the Bharata Natyam repertoire, innovating within the tradition. As creative collaborator, I spend many hours discussing the subtext, the philosophical import, and the 'making' of dance. It is these moments that one finds most rewarding spiritually. In day-to-day activities, I coordinate her programmes, attend to correspondence and manage the finances. Since we work as manager–artist, artistic director–dancer and mother–daughter, we find that the many roles often overlap. In our personal lives we do have sharp disagreements, but our basic values and work philosophy bring us together again.

Priya held a variety of jobs in Bombay, which included a fairly long stint in journalism. In the late 1980s she moved to Pune with her husband Suresh. Being away from the stimulation of life in Bombay, writing took on a new significance in her life and she began working on her first novel, *The Other Garden*. This was published in 1994 and was critically well received. She had at last found her creative medium and I felt a great sense of happiness. I have over the years watched how her writing self has added a deeper dimension to her life. Challenging boundaries and 'being dazzlingly imaginative' as a fellow writer said of her, Priya is eclectic and courageous in her writing. Her creative self journeys into poetry as well as conventional male genres—sci-fi, horror, mystery—as she wanders on uncharted paths that open up to her. And I am grateful to her for bringing into my world the transforming power of the word.

CONCLUSION

At 68 I am thankful for what life has given me with art, yoga and philosophy being an essential part of it. I have always held that a strong trusting relationship with even one other person reaffirms and renews faith in life. And I am fortunate to have found this with both my daughters. However, my relationship with my mother has not worked out. But confrontations are fewer and briefer, with both of us getting older.

I think it is important to remember the need to live life creatively. And to hold within oneself the sacredness of all life.

NOTES

1. Hair tied in a top knot by men.
2. A display of dolls put up for the Hindu festival of Navratri.
3. A reference to Raja Ravi Varma (1848–1906), best known for his depictions of themes from Indian mythology in the style of European academy painting.

9

Abode of Colour

Vijaya Mehta

Introduction

How does one set about presenting a factual narrative about oneself, one's mother and grandmother? Facts as you pursue them and store in your memory can never be divorced from a point of view, your attitude at the moment and above all the colour and texture of your feelings. How can one then be judgemental in analysing an individual, be it your own self, your mother or your grandmother. I shall give it a try nonetheless.

As I think about all of us—my grandmother, my mother and I—my thoughts are a jumble. Personal biodata get entwined with environmental details such as traditions, customs and the forces set in motion by the wheel of progress. My narrative, therefore, may oscillate between the personal and the environmental.

My Maternal Grandmother

My maternal grandmother's story is based on hearsay as told by elders in the family. She was married at the age of 10 to my grandfather, twice a widower of over 30. Both my grandparents belonged to the Chandraseneey Kayastha Prabhu caste. (The CKP's are still known for their good looks, their love of good living and a progressive attitude. In modern-day Maharashtra a large percentage of professional women belong to the CKP clan.)

My grandfather's family worked for the Gaikwads of Baroda for generations. Some of them were Sardars, others worked as directors of the Royal Treasury, some as personal accountants. My grandfather was the *Sarsubha*—chief collector during Sayajeerao Gaikwad's regime.

When my grandmother entered the house, many of her stepchildren were older than her. Yet they accepted her readily as their mother. Given the high incidence of mortality among women during childbirth, the families of that period were accustomed to accepting young brides with old husbands, and the stepchildren were conditioned to having young brides as their mother. My grandmother had three children of her own. The oldest was my mother, then a boy and the third one another daughter. While giving birth to my aunt—the third child—my grandmother died.

My grandfather's first wife's is a story worth recounting. She was 3 years old when she was married to my grandfather who was 9, and slept right through the wedding ceremony. Normally a young married daughter stayed with her parents till she reached puberty. But the 3-year-old bride had no parents—they had both died in a plague epidemic, so she went to her husband's house. She would often sit on a swing and sing traditional songs (*owi*) about parental love. Her mother-in-law would gather the child-bride in her arms and weep. She grew up in her in-laws' house as part of the family. In fact, it was the only home she knew.

At the time of my grandmother's death my mother was 12 years of age and had studied only up to the fourth grade in Marathi. According to custom, if there was a death in the family and if a boy or girl is to be married, you have to do it within a year. That is why my mother was married off within three months of her mother's death. It would appear that my grandfather was probably frail and could not marry again or depend on anyone else to look after the infant. There was no other option except for my mother to take her infant sister along with her to the Jaywant house where she got married.

My Paternal Grandmother

My mother was married into a very rich feudal household, the Jaywants of Bhiwandi, a suburb of Bombay. The family owned vast amounts of land and the house was huge with several members of the joint family and poor dependent relatives living in it. My father's mother had 21 children. From amongst them only four boys and two girls survived by the time I was born.

When my mother joined the Jaywant clan, my grandmother was already a widow, wrapped in a maroon sari, covering her shaven head. As a widow she spent most of her time in prayer. She would go on a three-month pilgrimage every year to Kashi with an entourage of 80 people—including coolies, servants and relatives. She led an austere life, never eating onions, garlic or pickles. But according to my mother, after she was 60 she would smuggle in *bhajias* and *mithais* (savoury and sweet snacks) through her barber who came every week to shave her head. Many questions would flood my mind when I heard anecdotes about my grandmothers. I would think, 'Poor women! How lucky that I am born now!'

THE JAYWANT HOUSEHOLD

My *Varkari* Uncle

I still remember our ancestral home in Bhiwandi and the strong smell of *abheer*[1] associated with it. It was used in all the religious rituals in the house and my uncle marked his forehead with it along with sandalwood paste. I remember vividly the Navratri festival, the decorations, the excitement and the noisy celebrations.[2] The bells in the prayer room rang loudly every morning, afternoon and evening like in the temples—maybe to keep the gods awake. The uncle younger than my father was a *varkari*.[3] He travelled to Pandharpur (a township nearly 150 miles from Bhiwandi) on foot every year, joining the procession of devotees. The Pandharpur *yatra* (pilgrimage) in Maharashtra continues even today.

He sang *kirtans* in our house till late hours every night. My uncle as the *kirtankar* would expound the philosophy behind the songs.[4] He would sometimes get into a trance-like state and dance, playing a string instrument (*ekatara*) with one hand and keeping rhythm with the other on symbols (*chipalya*) to the loud accompaniment of drums.

My *varkari* uncle was married but had renounced wordly pleasures. Wherever he went, he was always accompanied by his two disciples—one a barber by caste and the other a sweeper. He would mix food served to him and share it with his disciples. As youngsters we found the food mixture ritual revolting. It was only much later in 1950 when our ancestral home in Bhiwandi was converted into a temple to commemorate my uncle's memory that I realised what a large following he had who worshipped him and considered him to be the moving spirit behind the eradication of untouchability in Bhiwandi.

Black Magic and My Uncle's Wife

Whenever my *varkari* uncle's wife Kamala*kaki* came to visit us in our Bombay house for a couple of days the atmosphere would be overcast with fear. She indulged in black magic, everyone claimed. She was considered dangerous for children and for happily married couples. Small black cross-like marks would appear on our bed linen after she left. When my cousins and I grew up we tried to convince my mother that the black crosses were nothing but marks caused by washerman's marking ink.

By the time we were teenagers, Kamala*kaki* became our favourite aunt; she had a fantastic sense of humour despite a very unhappy marriage. It was rumoured that my *varkari* uncle used to beat her during the initial years of their marriage before he totally discarded her as his wife. She stayed on with the Jaywants, was accepted as a member of the family and looked after, but had no status in the household. She remained childless. Apparently, she faked a pregnancy once by tying strips of cloth around her belly increasing the layers every month till one of her sisters-in-law discovered her bluff in the sixth month.

Everyone was convinced that she practised black magic. When asked about her black magic by me or my cousins, she would burst out into peals of laughter—but never admitted that she did not practise it. Maybe she did to win over her husband who overnight renounced all worldly pleasures and spent time on *bhajans* and *kirtans*. Maybe she wanted to bear a child—who knows! She lived alone in a small room at the back of the house and died at an old age, with third-degree burns while cooking on a stove. My mother was with her in the hospital till the very end and said, 'See, she had a witch's death!'

The prosperity of the Bhiwandi household with its large joint family did not last long. According to my mother, one of the reasons for losing the fortune was my *varkari* uncle. He never earned a penny and indulged in philanthropic deeds that the family had to constantly support. One of his many disciples took a massive loan from a moneylender. My uncle agreed to be the guarantor. The disciple died and as guarantor my uncle had to repay the loan, and to raise the money the Jaywants had to sell a large amount of land.

Though my mother never mentioned it, none of the four Jaywant brothers (including my father, who was the eldest) looked after the property. They were brought up as a rich man's sons and did not think in terms of money and estate.

The major reason for the downfall of the Jaywant household was also the end of the serfdom era. The feudal system was fast collapsing when the 'land to the tiller' Bill was legally introduced. I remember Rama, our farmer, who had worked with the family for generations, who went to court and finally got ownership of the land he tilled. My mother was deeply hurt, but the wheel of change could not be stopped.

MY MOTHER

My mother was a petite woman, very fair with long silky hair. She was extraordinarily efficient and tidy. I never saw her 9-yard saree crushed or her long hair untidy. She was always in total command of whatever she did and received tremendous respect from her families on either side. Even her two stepbrothers, much older than she, consulted her on family matters.

When she entered the Jaywant household in 1908 at the age of 12 (probably born around 1896) with her 2-month old sister, she was the only *suhagan* (married woman whose husband is alive) in the large family. All the other women, her mother-in-law, two of her husband's sisters and two of his sisters-in-law were widows. They had all lost their husbands either in the plague epidemic or stricken by brief illnesses for which proper medicines and treatments were not yet discovered. The large feudal Jaywant joint family welcomed the new bride and her infant sister. The infant was brought up by the family, educated and later married at the age of 18 to a very bright law student.

At the age of 13, as the only *suhagan* of the house, my mother single-handedly managed a big traditional wedding of her younger brother-in-law and from then on remained the central focal point of authority in the Jaywant household.

She came to Bombay with my father. Her first son was born when she was 16, another son at 18 and a third, a girl (that is, me), arrived when she was almost 40. Father stayed on in Benares and died when I was 6 years old. My second brother died at the age of 27 with meningitis within two years of my father's demise. Though I was young, I still remember the turmoil and anguish my mother went through. My elder brother, *Bhai*, 22 years older than me, his quietly pleasant wife Vahini, whom he had married just before my second brother died, and my widowed mother became my parents.

My mother did not talk much about her childhood except her journeys with her father as a collector and some haunted houses she lived in. She hardly ever mentioned her mother's or father's death, but was always full of anecdotes about the Jaywant family.

She ran my brother's house and continued to do so as I grew up, even when my sister-in-law Vahini was 40 and had four children of her own. My mother received the pay packet every month from my brother, kept accounts, decided the menus and did the shopping. She was shaken when I insisted that she should allow Vahini to look after her own house. It was as if her reign on the domestic domain had ended.

I was her baby and the purpose of her life. After I got married she stayed with me often and spent a lot of time with my two sons, which was a great relief to me as I could return to my work within a fortnight of delivering the baby. She died at the age of 78. My mother was a very capable woman, the ultimate authority in her own world and had all the makings of a natural leader.

THE ETHOS OF THE PERIOD: 1910–35

With educated men getting job opportunities in cities like Bombay, the feudal joint family traditions started gradually to disappear. In large joint family households the women's domain was geographically segregated from the men's. They occupied the kitchen, *mazghar*, which was used as a dining room during meal times, the prayer room, the granary-cum-storeroom (*kothichi kholi*), the delivery room (*balantinichi kholi*) and, of course, the courtyard at the back with its *tulsi* plant. The men used the first floor and the front portion of the house. Constraints of space in urban apartments ended the *zenana–mardana* segregation since women and men had to share the same space.

Away from the large joint family, women in the cities had much more time on their hands and a rapport with the world outside Marathi society. Joint family relatives visited them often, but could not stay on in their small urban homes.

The progressive movement influenced men from the urban Marathi middle class and upper middle class. They were exposed to British education and administrative systems. Education for women, widow remarriages and child marriages were subjects often discussed. Women as equal partners in society was an intellectually accepted norm. The literature of this period reflects this trend amply, but very few families lived by this norm. Those who did were looked down upon and treated with suspicion. But the process of emancipation of women had already begun by 1910 in Maharashtra.

Social Changes

Gradually, over the years, women's issues and their solutions became a social movement. Women joined schools. Their husbands and fathers not only supported them, but pushed them towards education. The national movement created a definite niche for women's participation. It shook the feudal joint family structure further. As a society Maharashtrians realised that there were larger responsibilities they needed to shoulder besides their feudal households. Awareness of being citizens of India and participating in the freedom movement or hearing about it constantly stirred Maharashtrian men out of their feudal slumber.

During this period many women in Maharashtra started writing, became doctors, participated in social work and the freedom movement. In cities like Bombay, girls' schools were opened and Bombay University enrolled women for their graduation courses.

Early Childhood

My father, the oldest of four brothers, was educated. He moved to Bombay to work in the Customs department and support the family in Bhiwandi. My mother and two brothers accompanied him. I was born much later. As a child I remember our small three-room apartment always full of cousins, aunts and uncles, who visited us frequently and stayed on for months during vacations. An aunt, *Bai* (my father's elder brother's wife), widowed at the age of 13, lived with us. My mother treated her with great respect as her elder sister-in-law. Another old widow with a maroon sari covering her shaven head often visited us. We called her *Bapuchi-Mawshi* (*Bapu*'s aunt) and looked forward to her bedtime stories.

We lived on Lamington Road off Grant Road. Dadar then was considered a distant suburb. For me, as a young girl, Bandra and Santacruz were like foreign cities. Many like my father, who had lost their feudal empires, lived in *chawls*. There were middle-class *chawls* and working-class *chawls*. There were Brahmin *chawls* and Saraswat *chawls*. I remember living in one when my father was still alive.

There were three rooms—kitchen, sitting room and a bedroom. When relatives came to stay, which they often did, the women and children would sleep in the kitchen and the bedroom, and the men in the living room—all on bed rolls which were stacked in a corner during the day. We had a bathing place in the kitchen, but the toilets were in one corner of the common balcony that connected all the apartments.

The *chawl* had its own culture of community living. Children played in the common balcony and neighbours kept an eye on them. Any illness in the family and the neighbours did the running around, cooking food if required. A lot of literature has been written about the *chawl* culture.

Now it is no more. The younger generation has moved out to the suburbs, selling their *chawl* apartments to small traders. Most of the *chawls* now have little shops selling car spare parts or used as godowns for readymade clothes. The community living concept has disappeared.

My Father, Aunt and Uncle

My father was a well-paid officer in Customs and was also a member of the Theosophical Society. Later he became a full-time worker, gave up his job and left for Benaras to took after Annie Besant's office. When he left, I was yet to be born and both my brothers were in college. They reacted strongly to my father's decision to quit his job since they were forced to give up their studies and start earning to maintain the Bombay house. My father apparently told them that he had spent most of his life looking after others and it was time for him to do what he liked most. I must have been conceived while my father came to Bombay on his annual holidays. I do not remember much about him, but there are images that I can recall.

I remember attending his Theosophical Society meetings in Blavatsky Lodge in Bombay. They were conducted with a great sense of decorum, peace and orderlines in contrast to the Bhiwandi rituals full of noise, smoke, fragrance, loud singing and dance.

My father was fair, bald, tall and handsome, as my memory has stored him. I recall his touch as he carried me once in his arms to pacify me—I was maybe 4 years old. My mother had washed my hair with *ritha* nut and water and by mistake some of it had trickled into my eyes. My eyes burnt and were swollen. I howled and refused to open them. I remember his taking me in a Victoria (house-drawn carriage) to consult a doctor.

The second image of my father, very vivid in my memory, is of his sitting on a *patla* (low wooden seat) in the kitchen near an open shelf full of brass tins lined up in rows. My mother asked me to give her one of the tins. I reached for it, it slipped from my hand and fell on his bald head cutting his scalp a little. I was frightened when he died of diabetes—may be a year later—I thought the accident with the tin had caused it all.

My teenage years were spent with the Karniks, my mother's sister and her husband. My uncle was the bright young man who married the infant sister brought into the Jaywant household by my mother, raised and educated by them. Uncle, popularly known as V.B. (his initials), was a lawyer, a trade unionist, and highly revered for his commitment and intellect. The couple had great respect for what my parents and the Jaywants had done. My aunt regarded my mother and our family as her natal home.

Move to the Karnik Household

There was a lot of sadness in my family with two deaths in a short period—my father's and then my brother's. There was no one my age to play with, so from the age of 8 my aunt and V.B. took me over. They had two sons slightly older than me and I grew up with my cousins and their gang of friends—all boys. Everyone thought I was the Karnik's daughter. During my childhood, I never felt nor was I made to feel different in the gender context or as a fatherless child. Sharing family burdens was done naturally then with a great sense of ease.

I came into the Karnik household from a traditional background where religion meant rituals and superstitions and some belief in magic. My mother observed all religious ceremonies and rituals—Navratri, Gokulastami, Ganapati, Shravan, Nagapanchami and Sankranti. During Navratri the oil lamp in the prayer room had to last for 24 hours—if it went off even for a second, it was considered a bad omen. I remember my mother getting up at 2.00 A.M. to pour oil in it and make sure that it was burning throughout the night. Fear of God's wrath, loud prayers and ringing of bells were the sounds in the Jaywant house. V.B. Uncle's house was in great contrast to this. *Puja* was considered an irrational activity. He stopped my aunt from having even a single image of a deity. She made no effort to understand the reason behind his refusal to allow her to observe any religious activities, but instead came to our house to participate in all religious rituals.

The Radical Humanist Movement

V.B.'s house was also the Radical Humanist Party's office. Perhaps that is the reason why he did not allow a single image or picture of a deity to be hung on the walls or any religious rituals to be observed by his wife. I was far too young then to understand the philosophy of radical humanism. His intellectual friends would gather every evening and talk, and as a young girl I just loitered around. I knew M.N. Roy was their leader, that he had worked with Stalin and loved cats, and had a European wife Ellen.

I distinctly remember the evening on Chowpatty sands when V.B. explained in very simple terms the meaning of his movement to me—I must have been about 10 and was greatly impressed. The Radical Humanists considered human beings as the only living species endowed with reasoning and rationality. Human beings, therefore, owed it to life and their own societies to behave rationally. They questioned everything that was irrational, which included *pujas*, superstitions and the role of destiny. All these were, according to them, escape routes to make something or someone else responsible for your own well-being, your deeds and misdeeds. The Radical Humanists were not against religious philosophies, but opposed religious practices. Faith in itself was acceptable, but not if it came in the way of fulfilling your responsibilities as a rational human being. They maintained that your only support system could be you yourself—only then could you contribute to society and help build a nation. The Radical Humanist Party remained on the periphery of the Indian political scene, but when I look back, I realise how much I was influenced by its basic principles.

The Rashtra Seva Dal

After the Radical Humanist influence, joining Jayaprakash Narayan's volunteer corps, the Rashtra Seva Dal, at the age of 12 came as a natural evolution of my growth process. Jayaprakash and his associates believed in creating new citizens of India through the Seva Dal, who would think and act above religion, caste and class, and work towards building up a socialist democracy.

The Seva Dal operated more like a community activity. An open space would be selected and children of that area invited to come and play. The national flag would be hoisted and along with playing team games, patriotic songs were sung. A young person from the community would be selected as a *shakha pramukh*—leader in charge of every evening's play-session. Gradually the children were introduced to the concept of a caste-less and classless society, and the dignity of labour through projects that the kids participated in enthusiastically. I distinctly remember one such project. We were given the responsibility of clearing the central courtyard of a *chawl* (which is normally used as a garbage dump) and convert it into a playground for a *shakha*. We all marched into the *chawl*—20 of us aged 10 to 12, knocked on each house door, announced that we were starting our cleaning operation and attacked the garbage dump armed with brooms and dustbins. Many of the kids lived in that *chawl*; their parents followed us within minutes and a playground was created. We hoisted the national flag, sang patriotic songs and played games. As Rashtra Seva Dal *Sainiks* (volunteers) we felt proud that we had worked as a team, convinced the caste conscious elders about the dignity of labour and created yet another *shakha*. Like the Radical Humanists' principle, the teachings of the Rashtra Seva Dal stayed with me and helped me later in building up my theatre and film teams.

After I joined the Rashtra Seva Dal I outgrew and began to dislike the rituals in my mother's house. Some major confrontations resulted with my mother and my brother. For instance, the *prasad* after a *puja* was distributed to all the family members but never given to our domestic servant since he belonged to a lower caste. I refused to eat the *prasad* till the servant was given a share. My mother and brother were against this and did not know how to resolve the problem. God would be contaminated and angry. However, she gave a cautious warning—'Never ever tell anyone!' I wonder how God reacted to her secretive deal?

There are times when I miss not introducing those rituals to my children. I wish I had passed on something to them—maybe the cultural aspects without any superstitious implications—leaving it to them to decide how much to accept or reject.

ENVIRONMENT: 1935 ONWARDS

By 1935 the tide of progress and women's emancipation had already reached the Maharashtrian middle classes and my generation rode on it very smoothly.

Historically and traditionally, Maharashtra has always respected and recognised the strength of its women—Karve, Phule, Tilak, Pandita Ramabai, Ranade and many others carved out a definite niche for Maharashtrian women in society. The progressive movement and later the freedom movement further emancipated women in Maharashtra. I was born in this supportive environment.

The city of Bombay offered the best of two worlds. Opportunities were readily available and it was up to an individual to decide how far to reach out and take them. The pre- and post-independence era was charged with a sense of commitment to society both politically and socially. Socialist democracy was a phrase often used and practised.

Twists and Turns

My family's attempts to get me married in the usual 'arranged' mode failed miserably. I would burst into uncontrollable tears the moment a proposal came my way. It was not that I was against marriage—I very much liked the idea of being a bride—but perhaps was not emotionally prepared to be a wife.

While completing my master's degree in economics and politics, I drifted into intercollegiate theatre, which later on developed into a passion. It disturbed my mother and brother greatly; not because I had chosen to act, but because I had given up the prospect of a civil service career and the possibility of an excellent matrimonial alliance that was my brother's dream for me. Acting as a career had no stigmas or taboos attached in my family since my cousins Nalini Jaywant and Shobhana Samarth were already established filmstars.

My First Play

I was passionately involved in the Rashtra Seva Dal during my college days. In my final year in Wilson College, however, I felt the passion subsiding; may be because many of the Dal volunteers and our leaders had joined the Socialist Party. The Seva Dal was becoming more and more an extension as a youth wing of the party. I was restless and suddenly one day I realised that the Seva Dal had drained out of my system. I had a lot of spare energy and time on my hands and so I jumped into organising annual cultural functions in college and wandered into my first play. I rehearsed, put on make up, stepped onto the stage and stayed there for 40 long years! I have always found that major decisions in my life were taken suddenly, almost accidentally.

From college functions to winning intercollegiate competitions and then on to acting in the annual festivals organised by Mumbai Marathi Sahitya Sangha, my stage career grew rapidly and unobtrusively within a year. I was then 18.

Mumbai Marathi Sahitya Sangha and Dr A.N. Bhalerao

The Sahitya Sangha, a literary organisation, had a dynamic leader in Dr A.N. Bhalerao heading its cultural wing. Though a medical practitioner, he devoted his entire life to the revival of Marathi theatre, which had lost its audiences to the new entertainment medium of the cinema, forcing all theatre companies towards bankruptcy by 1935. To win back lost audiences, Dr Bhalerao, through the Sahitya Sangha, organised annual theatre festivals held outdoors in the Medical College Gymkhana, with a seating capacity of over 3,000. Marathi filmstars were invited—like Baburao Pendharkar, Durga Khote, Vanmala, Snehaprabha Pradhan, Rajan Jawle and Raja Gosavi—to participate along with renowned stalwarts of the Marathi theatre. His strategy worked and the festivals ran to packed houses.

Dr Bhalerao then became my mentor in Marathi theatre. The Sahitya Sangha productions gave me an opportunity to work the best talent in Marathi theatre and also created a bond with its artistic traditions, which became a very strong point of reference in my later experiments with theatre as an art form.

I must have been a good listener. I recollect my long chats with Marathi actors and directors, old enough to be my grandfathers, about their theatre experiences and discoveries. My first professional play was *Zunzarrao*, a Marathi rendering of *Othello*. I played Desdemona at the age of 18, and *Othello* was over 60—Nanasahed Phatak, a great actor known for his electrifying performances and booming voice. The other cast members were film and stage stars all over 50.

I received immediate recognition as the new discovery of Dr Bhalerao, but was never treated as a star in the Sahitya Sangha. I remained a 'theatre volunteer' in the Seva Dal tradition and remember arranging chairs in Sahitya Sangha's open-air auditorium and numbering the seats with a piece of chalk before going into my dressing room to get made up as Desdemona. Overnight media hype and stardom did not exist in those days—you worked in theatre because you loved it passionately.

I completed my master's degree in economics and politics while working at the Sahitya Sangha. My mother and brother were restless for my marriage and thought my chances of a good matrimonial alliance were fast deteriorating with my association with old Marathi actors, some of whom were rumoured to be drunkards with a wicked eye for young girls! Dr Bhalerao pacified my parents and assured them that he would personally keep an eye on me, which he did by arranging an escort to and from my house to the rehearsal hall every day and by attending rehearsals himself.

I was tempted to join films as offers poured in from producers. My cousin Shobhana Samarth, an established filmstar, was very keen that I join her actor's agency along with her daughter Nutan who had already been launched as a movie actress at the age of 14. I almost signed a contract, but instead met Ebrahim Alkazi, which changed the course of my professional journey.

Alkazi

Alkazi did theatre in English through his ensemble Theatre Group. He was trained in England at the Royal Academy of Dramatic Arts and invited me to join his group and offered to train me formally, but on one condition—I had to stop acting in Sahitya Sangha's traditional Marathi plays during my two-year training period. I joined Alkazi after assuring a distraught Dr Bhalerao that I would return after two years to Marathi theatre as a better equipped all-round theatre person. I consider Alkazi my guru in theatre. He introduced me to the American and European contemporary and cultural theatres, instilled an aesthetic perspective of theatre as an art and created a new awareness of an 'ensemble' concept.

On a more personal level, he led me out of my middle-class Marathi environment, taught me how to speak English and carry myself in dresses. It was tough initially. I concentrated more on the sound of the English words rather then the meanings; wearing dresses made me feel half naked since I had not worn any after I was 10. It was always a *ghagra–choli* (long skirt and blouse), and on reaching puberty a sari. I made many non-Marathi friends during my Theatre Group days.

Alkazi later moved to Delhi in the 1960s to head the National School of Drama, which he revolutionised. In fact his work and presence in Delhi created a new dynamic theatre movement in the capital city.

Marriage and My Mother-in-law Durga Khote

I returned to the Sahitya Sangha after my two years of training with Alkazi, brimming with new ideas, and was awarded a cultural scholarship by the Government of India. As a scholar I was attached to two guides—Adi Marzban for direction and Durga Khote for acting.

Adi Marzban guided me in launching my own experimental group at the Bharatiya Vidya Bhavan, and my association with Vijay Tendulkar, the playwright, started, which continued for 12 years. I was 21 when I directed my first play written by Tendulkar, which also was his first attempt at writing a full-length piece. I had two work spaces now—Sahitya Sangha for traditional play and Bharatiya Vidya Bhavan for my experimental work. My association with my acting guide Durga Khote proved to be a turning point in my personal life. Our teacher–student relationship soon developed into a very close bond. I met her son Harin and married him when I was 24. My mother and brother at last breathed a sigh of relief. My marriage was celebrated on the lawns of Durga*bai*'s apartment house. For my mother and brother it was the ultimate event of satisfaction and joy. Nearly 200 of my father and mother's family members joined the wedding celebrations for seven days, living in a specially rented house.

Durga Khote, my mother-in-law, affectionately and respectfully called *Bai*, was an iconic figure among Maharashtrian women, being the first educated women to join the film world in the late 1930s. Brought up in a Victorian tradition in the aristocratic Lad family, she was a fascinating embodiment of contradictions. She had very strong views about social etiquette, ethics and class structure. On the other hand, she displayed a natural warmth and an open generosity.

The Lad family (changed to Laud in a very British manner) was progressive to the core. Her father rode in his Rolls Royce, accompanied by his wife and three beautiful daughters, and attended all the premiere shows as a patron of the Marathi theatre, sitting in the first row of the playhouse—a revolutionary act in those days when female audiences sat segregated in a corner of the balcony on mats (not chairs) to watch Marathi plays. Many of the old actors I met recalled fondly how the Laud family's presence converted the premiere shows into glamorous events.

Bai was married into the Khote family—rich traders by profession. There is still a pavement at Chowpatty named after them. The Lauds and the Khotes were Saraswat Brahmins who, like the CKPs, were progressive, many of them having been educated in England. After *Bai*'s two sons Bakul and Harin were born, the Khote's lost their fortune overnight in a bad trade deal. Proud and independent, *Bai* refused to turn to her rich father for help. Instead, she managed her family in a small apartment by giving English tuitions and later joined films to support her two sons' education, ignoring the vicious humiliation inflicted on her by society, and went ahead to become one of the most revered actresses in Indian cinema.

Widowed at a very young age, she remained the only breadwinner of the family despite a remarriage, an uncomfortable alliance that lasted 14 years. She educated her two sons in the best Bombay school, sent the younger son abroad for further studies and lived in a large apartment in Gulistan on Cuffe Parade, one of the elite areas of Bombay.

When I married Harin, I entered Gulistan, beautifully maintained by *Bai*'s daughter-in-law and Bakul's wife Kristina, a Polish Canadian. As a Khote, I stepped out of my middle-class milieu and entered the highly Westernised and sophisticated Bombay society. My theatre work, however, became more defined in its middle-class character. A distancing from the middle-class lifestyle may have given me a better perspective of its culture and behaviour patterns.

Rangayan: A Theatre Movement

After I married Harin, I started my own ensemble, Rangayan (meaning an abode of all pervasive aesthetic experience; full of colourful emotions), which became a landmark in Marathi theatre during the 1960s. Rangayan introduced and popularised new concepts of playwriting, production, direction and acting. Vijay Tendulkar, Dr Shriram Lagoo and a host of other present-day leading actors and playwrights worked in Rangayan and considered it as their training school.

Rangayan encouraged new playwrights and also presented translations and adaptations of contemporary Western plays. As a laboratory of experimental work, it pledged itself to doing only a specific number of shows of each production instead of spending creative time on repeat shows, however successful the presentation was, so that as an ensemble we could move on to new experiments. The annual programme was planned a year in advance and presented on schedule. After several acclaimed productions, Rangayan closed down in 1972 due to bitter and painful clashes amongst the core group. Perhaps it was a necessary and unavoidable break. Any activity undertaken with passion and commitment undergoes the pangs of birth, a peak of achievement then an inevitable end. Rangayan's span of 12 years will always remain an important chapter in Marathi theatre history.

Bleak Years

Rangayan's closure shook my confidence and faith in my work. While I was recovering from the shock, my husband Harin died suddenly of a heart attack at the age of 36. The stroke hit him at 5.30 A.M. and he was no more two hours later. We were married for less than five years and I was widowed at 20 with two sons—Ravi, 3, and Devan, one and a half.

The human mind is an amazing thing. I distinctly remember my first reaction after the doctors at Breach Candy Hospital declared Harin's death. The first thought that flashed through my mind was: 'So what if Harin is dead! Thousands of people die every day. Today one of them happens to be your husband. What's so special about it!' The thought still amazes me—may be it was an intuitive defence mechanism. I did not grieve after Harin—I do not think I had the luxury to do so. I had to care for my two young sons and two devastated old women—my 70-year-old mother and a 60-year-old mother-in-law.

What a coincidence that *Bai* and I were both widowed overnight at a young age with two young sons. But that is where the similarity ends. *Bai* had to struggle to support the family, which I did not have to do. I had the full support of my loving family—my mother, brother and the Karniks. I was blessed with very progressive in-laws. They were all keen that I remarry and start life all over again. Harin and I lived in a company flat, which needed to be vacated. My moving into Gulistan, *Bai*'s house, was considered as an alternative, but only for a brief while. *Bai* and Bakul both felt that I needed to retain my independence. They helped me buy a flat in Ashoka Apartments on Nepean Sea Road, overlooking the sea.

It was lonely without Harin, and I turned to theatre within one month of his passing away. *Bai* supported me financially, but I was not comfortable with the arrangement and needed to earn enough to look after my family. To keep me company, my friend and Pandit Ravi Shankar's disciple Dr Penelope Estabrook moved in to share my apartment. My large living room was always busy with Ravi Shankar's *riyaz* (practice), private exhibitions of my sculptor friends, and music recitals by musician friends.

I was a partner in Durga Khote Productions, an advertising film production company, which *Bai* and Kristina ran jointly. *Bai* was very keen that I take on more responsibility of its day-to-day operations. I tried it for a couple of years, but chose ultimately to join mainstream theatre as freelance actress and director. I did not want the Khotes, however loving, to support me and my sons in my personal life as well as professionally.

Despite the artistic atmosphere surrounding me, I remained restless and lonely. The radical humanist message of facing life and coping with it alone was my strength and also a burden. During the three bleak years of my widowhood I discovered a truth about myself. However self-sufficient and independent I was, I needed the support of a man in my life. Without it I seemed to lose my strength and became gullible.

Ideal Man

I met Farrokh Mehta initially through Durga Khote Productions; he used to write scripts for their advertising films. Our relationship developed during an English play we did together. Farrokh was a divorcee. His first wife Rashne, now in London, is a very close friend and well-wisher of our family. He bonded extremely well with my two young sons. I knew he would be a good father, and married him in December 1965. Our daughter, Anahita, was born after two years.

Farrokh has been my great strength and support. His relationship with my mother-in-law *Bai* was fascinating. She considered him an adviser for all her investment, which he looked after with a lot of care. He repaid in full the loan the Khotes had given me to purchase my Ashoka flat, and also looked after my two boys. I remember his telling *Bai*: 'They are my sons now. If you want to contribute towards their education or holidays, please open a bank account and deposit the amount. They will use my car and if it is not available, take the public transport.' It sounded harsh at that time, but earned him *Bai*'s respect. As a filmstar, she always felt exploited financially by people close to her. In Farrokh she met a proud Parsi who refused to accept her monetary support. My sons retain the Khote name—Ravi Khote and Deven Khote as Harin's living memory. A practising Zoroastrian, Farrokh prays every morning and thanks Harin in his prayers for giving him two 'readymade sons'. *Bai*, in her published memoirs, has devoted a whole chapter to Farrokh and called it 'Thank you Farrokh'.

I have always received support from all quarters—my parents, my in-laws, my friends and my husband. I hope I can extend it similarly to my three children who are grown up now and are achievers in their chosen fields.

I played over 80 different women in my theatre career and directed nearly 60 of the productions myself Acting is a fascinating art. Every time you play a role, you are reborn—your environment, your soul, your behaviour, your face—all are different.

While role-playing I stumbled on a 'truth'. Acting involves approaching fictitious (sometimes based on real-life stories) women from within their own internal rhythms—the way they react, speak and move around in their environment. Looking at them objectively and analytically does not allow you to enter their skins. You have to search for their souls. In the process of discovering these women, I realised that no one woman or man ever labels one's own self. A vicious character does not say 'I am vicious'. There is a personal conviction and faith in each of his/her action and reaction. It is the character's behaviour in the social context that is perceived by outsiders as vicious.

Likewise, a character is never 'a poor little suffering girl' for the girl herself. I do not believe that my grandmother went through life feeling nothing but self-pity. Human beings are survivors, discovering comparisons to make life worthwhile. The definition of terms such as 'worthwhile' and 'social contribution' may change with the times, but the essence does not. Each one wants to feel wanted and useful. A constant struggle to fulfil that need is what life is all about.

In *Sandhya Chaya*, a Marathi play, I acted as Nani, an old woman whose life revolves round her two sons—one is away in the army, the other settled in the States. She leads a lonely existence with her husband, awaiting the sons' infrequent letters and rare visits. It was fascinating to experience and live the old couple's loneliness and discover how they brought meaning into their lives every day with trivial routines, seemingly senseless to an outside observer.

I understood my mother while playing Nani in *Sandhya Chaya*—her obsessive letter writing when I was away in England for three years, her aggressive overprotection of my 50-year-old brother, though he was happily married with a family of his own. We were her achievements and a constant source of concern. We were her emotional support system in life, which gave meaning to her existence.

In *Barrister* I played Mawshi, character, set in the early 1920s. I was forced to study a lot of literature about women of that period. Mawshi, a clean-shaven widow since the age of 14, manages her nephew's large house. The nephew does not talk to her. Yet she fills her day with strict routines, has her fantasies, listens to music and chats with the servants, taking a vicarious pleasure in listening to gossip and prescribing home remedies. Like my grandmother, Mawshi had starved herself of spicy and palatable food throughout her youth, and one day abandons it all and starts eating fried savouries and sweets. She cannot and will not allow her life to be termed meaningless and pathetic. She has discovered her own emotional compensations and balance in life.

Working on Laxmibai Tilak's '*Smriti Chitre*' was the ultimate eye-opener. A Brahmin woman who, disowned by her family and society because her husband had embraced Christianity around the turn of the century, reflects in her autobiography on the turmoils in her life. While facing great difficulties, torn between Hindu culture and the doctrine of Christianity, she follows her husband to Ahmednagar. She stays away from him for 10 years and eventually becomes a Christian. Somewhere on the way, she realises that all religions basically are the same, so why not accept Christianity? At least it would bridge the gap between her and her husband, whom she loves passionately. Encouraged and taught by her husband, Laxmibai starts composing poems. Her memory pictures her strengths and courage, her earthy wisdom and resilience, and above all her fantastic sense of humour. Playing the role of Laxmibai and writing a screenplay opened doors to a world unknown to me and reintroduced me to the strengths of my mother and of all the two grandmothers.

CONCLUDING REMARKS

My journey through life had rough times and irksome experiences, but, as I said earlier, it is now a faint blur. A few of them surface off and on as reminders.

I regretted being a woman on some occasions. Working in a man's world of theatre, I never could socialise at parties and cut deals. I remained an outsider, an easy target for theatre gossip, not being present to air my views during after-show get-togethers. However much I wanted to, I could not explore unknown localities and people after Harin's death. I learnt that a young widow is considered and treated as an available commodity. Society around her watches her. However much I wanted, I could not go out alone at night like my male friends from the theatre and film often did. There were times when I felt I could do with a little more sympathy and understanding from society instead of suspicion and gossip. As a woman, I had to be very good at my work to prove my merit and worth in a male-dominated field. Like all professional mothers, I had to work really hard to maintain a balance between my career and home. My family missed me a lot, but they understood that my career was very important for maintaining my own identity and sense of self-worth.

The women whose role I played in theatre became a part of my real world. Through them I discovered my mother and grandmothers. My friends from the West argued with me, saying that women of the early 20th century found compensations because they had no choices. Their criticism presupposes that, compared to us present-day women, my mother and grandmothers had fewer choices. With the forces of globalisation and progress, we do have more choices, but the strength, wisdom and endurance with which my mother and grandmothers coped with life make them perhaps stronger than us modern women. They were governed by their social norms and ethical codes of conduct as we are by ours. They found an identity, distinct and centred, something that we also strive for.

Does it mean, therefore, that the issue of gender discrimination did not exist or does not pose problems even today? Of course it does and did so in my mother's and grandmothers' times. But tackling the gender issue need not be based on generalisations and by labelling women and their meaningful lives as mere pathetic survivals.

NOTES

1. *Abheer* is a black powder with a strong aroma of camphor.
2. Navratri is a festival during the first nine nights of the lunar month Ashwin. Ashwin falls during September–October.
3. *Varkari* literally means a regular pilgrim. It refers to a devotee making pilgrimages to Pandharpur—the abode of Lord Vithoba—every year to be present on

the *Ekadasi* (eleventh day) of the lunar month Ashadh and/or Karthik. Ashadh falls during June–July, Karthik during October–November.

4. A *kirtan* is a narrative based on a religious myth from the Puranas or on an episode drawn from the epics. A *kirtankar* is a person who expounds the philosophy of *kirtans*.

10

Striking New Roots*

Sushil Narulla**

I was just 8 years old when the idea of Partition first took shape. It was in Lahore, in 1941, that Mohammed Ali Jinnah, as head of the Muslim League, declared Partition as his main political goal. Within seven years of this declaration, the Indian subcontinent was partitioned into India and Pakistan. My story covers both this period and its aftermath.

My maternal grandmother was born in the walled city of Bannu. A predominantly Hindu and Sikh population lived within its huge mud walls, and its several wooden gates were meticulously locked at night. The city was built in the reign of Maharaja Ranjit Singh and the Sikh presence in its population probably dates to his time. The population of the walled city was around 30,000, distributed over 3,000 households, each having between 10 and 15 members. A fifth of these households was Sikh, the community to which my grandmother belonged. The Hindus constituted the remainder. For all purposes these two communities behaved as one integrated group. No sharp divisions existed and there was a great bonding between them; often in the same household there were both Hindus and Sikhs. Not only was intermarriage sanctioned, but often women would take religious vows to raise a son as a Sikh.

Outside the walled city, the British maintained their presence in the cantonment of Bannu. The predominantly Muslim population here was mainly made up of Pathans, a distinct tribal group. They constituted virtually 95 per cent of the population, and the Hindus and Sikhs

* Originally published in the *Indian Journal of Gender Studies*, vol. 6, No. 2, 1999, pp. 275–90.
** This piece was written by Leela Gulati as narrated to her by the late Sushil Narulla.

formed the rest. The Pathans were mostly small peasants, with a sprinkling of landed aristocracy. These were *zamindars* (landowners), who lived in huge mud-walled estates called *dalaan*. The peasants lived in mud huts. Interestingly, even the roofs, which were supported by wooden rafters, were covered with mud.

The Muslim population was divided into the poorer Shias and the aristocratic Sunnis, quite the reverse of the situation on this side of the Indian subcontinent. In parts of the North-West Frontier region, where those populations were unevenly distributed, riots erupted from time to time.

Bannu, being a British cantonment, was relatively peaceful. The Pathans spoke either Pashtu or a dialect that was a mixture of Persian, Arabic, Punjabi and Urdu, known as Bannuwali. This dialect was largely spoken by the Hindus as well. Each district seemed to have evolved its own dialect, peculiar to that region. Dera Ismail Khan had a dialect of its own called Dera Ismaili and Multan had Multani. The minority Hindu and the Sikh communities of this region had adopted many of the social and cultural habits of the Pathans. The men wore *salwars* and the impressive head gear of the Pathans. Women observed *purdah*, although only a few women wore the white *burqa* outside the confines of their home, particularly when they had to go outside the walled city and into the Muslim areas.

The women of the Sikh and Hindu communities, whose dress, language and food habits were similar, led a life of seclusion, with little exposure to the world outside. They had very little social interaction with the Muslim population, probably because they had to be protected from determined Pathans, capable of abducting them at will. It was different for the men. They were socially and culturally well integrated with the Muslim population, and also had common economic and commercial interests.

Homosexuality was believed to be prevalent in this region. For instance, Pathan tea shops often employed teenage boys to attract customers. The Hindu population was apprehensive of the security of both their women and young male children, whether the myth of the marauding Pathan was established or not.

My Maternal Grandparents

My grandparents originally owned land. At the turn of the century, due to the vagaries and uncertainties of the agricultural way of life, it became necessary for my grandfather to move into trade. Over the years, having sold most of the large holdings, the family ran a small shop in the city. Part of their landed property was retained for a long time, until it was sold to finance the medical education of one of the sons abroad.

Of all the children born to my grandparents, only six survived, the three older children being boys and the three later ones being girls. My two older uncles joined the flourishing trade of my grandfather. This was common practice at the time and my grandfather saw no reason to be different. Although there were many schools of all denominations in Bannu, they did not have much formal schooling as my grandfather found it meaningless for them to struggle with books for no foreseeable purpose. However, my third uncle was determined to study and become a doctor, a wish he pursued by going to England. This, no doubt, gave the family great prestige though at a heavy price. They became virtually bankrupt in the process.

Handsome, charming and reckless, my uncle led a colourful and unconventional life. He was married early, long before he left for England. The marriage, arranged by the family in haste, proved disastrous. My uncle's wife was uneducated and remained so, while he moved on. She was also sickly, stricken with tuberculosis. A coldness had crept into their relationship even before he left for England. His sojourn in England for many years created an estrangement between them. His only child was placed in the care of my grandparents, who patiently bore the financial and emotional responsibilities for the care of his family when he was in England. They were relieved when my uncle wrote that he was returning after having obtained his degree.

The news of his impending return home was received with great jubilation. The family viewed it as a great accomplishment that would spell an end to their troubles. On his return they hoped for a more stable and prosperous future. The men of the family journeyed to distant Bombay to welcome him with great pomp and ceremony. Their joy was shortlived. Much to their dismay and disbelief, my uncle arrived with an English wife. Furious and shocked, my grandfather refused to accept her within the family and insisted she return. Immediate arrangements were made for her departure, which meant more expense and unpleasantness between my uncle and the family. However, that was only the beginning of my grandfather's problems.

My uncle joined the colonial health service. He soon became involved with the wife of his European employer and, as interracial love affairs were banned by law, the family paid a heavy price once again to fight legal battles to protect him. Soon after, his wife died. He never succumbed to the pressure to remarry because of his three young children, two girls and a boy. Though so highly qualified, he was, for some reason, singularly unlucky, moving from one crisis to another. He never was really successful, and the family had to bear the burden of his misadventures.

THE THREE DAUGHTERS

The Christian mission hospital and the mission school were located outside the walled city. Most childbirths took place in homes and occasionally privileged women were taken to the mission *zenana* (women's) hospital. My educated aunt was the first to avail of this facility and this is also where I was born. When the first of their three daughters was born, my grandparents named her Brihawan, which meant the fortunate girl with many brothers to protect her. The second daughter came to be known as Maina *masi* (maternal aunt) to us. The third daughter, born after a lapse of many years, was my mother Gaura Kaur.

Girls received only a primary education. Although there were Hindu, Sikh, Muslim and government high schools in Bannu, they were open only to boys and co-education was unheard of. There were separate primary schools for girls of all communities. Sikh girls went to the *gurudwara* (Sikh holy shrine) schools to enable them to read the Sikh holy book, the *Guru Granth Sahib*.

Girls were married early to men of their parents' choice. The practice of pre-puberty marriage did not exist among the Sikhs. My mother's eldest sister Maina *masi* was believed to have been a child-widow. Married at the age of 13 years, and widowed within a year, she returned home in a departure from tradition. Since she did not have any children, her husband's family had very little obligation towards her. Children ensure a girl's security in her husband's family; she is entitled to the ancestral property on the birth of a son. Among Sikhs, the Jat community alone practised widow remarriage. Hence, Maina *masi*, who was not a Jat, was not remarried. Her husband's parents were prepared to take care of her, but my grandfather was apprehensive that she would be reduced to the status of a domestic, an extra hand in the kitchen, and decided to bring her home.

Soon after her return home, another tragedy befell the family: her mother died in childbirth, leaving a young infant. At the age of 14 years, Maina *masi* had to assume her mother's role and take care of the joint household and her infant sister, who was my mother Gaura Kaur. Although confronted with the grim realities of widowhood, this was the beginning of Maina *masi*'s growing importance in the household. She played a crucial role in running the household and my grandfather's dependence on her grew.

Another tragedy struck the family soon after this. Maina *masi*'s older brother lost his wife, leaving a young boy. Her brother's subsequent remarriage to a much younger girl enhanced Maina *masi*'s emerging position of dominance in the family. Having lost her mother at birth, my mother had no memories of her mother and considered Maina *masi*, some 13 years older than her, as her mother.

MOVE TO AMRITSAR

Tribal Pathans, who were different from the Pathans who lived outside the walled city of Bannu, raided the city some time in the 1930s, just a few years before I was born. They broke down the gates, entered the city, and looted and burnt shops in the inner city. The insecurity it caused within the Hindu community was one of the reasons why my elder uncles moved to Amritsar. By now my eldest uncle had a large family of six sons and my grandfather thought it would be wise to expand the scope of the business by moving from the small remote town of Bannu to Amritsar. This turned out to be fortunate for the family during the Partition.

My mother attended the Sikh denomination school for only a few years, but could read the scriptures. She was married early into a family of small peasants living in Bannu. On her marriage, she was given a new name and a new identity, and was called Gulab Kaur for her radiant, rose-like complexion. *Gulab* in Persian means a rose. Nothing in her upbringing was to prepare her for her life in the years to come. Married, with the usual dowry of cattle, gold and other household articles called *vari*, to a man at least 15 years older, she was deceived by two sisters-in-law. In a departure from tradition, her husband's two younger brothers were married earlier as her husband had been unwilling to marry.

The story goes that he had seen my mother on her regular visits to the *gurudwara* and had expressed a desire to marry her. However, this brief romantic element did not seem to figure anywhere in their lives. On the very first night of the wedding, my mother, all of 15, went off to sleep, tired at the end of a gruelling and hectic day. Her husband took great offence and gave her a slap. She did not forget this incident and shared the humiliation later with her children.

My Father and the Joint Family

My father was, for all purposes, the patriarch of a joint household of 20 members. His own father who was a village *patwari* (accountant) was a weak, gentle and self-effacing man. He had to travel to nearby villages and very often was not in Bannu to take care of his land. Very early in life he had handed over all his responsibilities to his elder son, my father. Tyrannical and an uncompromising autocrat with strong dictatorial tendencies, he controlled his meek parents, his four brothers and three sisters with great firmness. Because of his temperament and authoritarian ways, my father was accorded a great deal of respect by all members of the family, partly out of fear. A small peasant owning 10 acres of ancestral land, he was also a *hakim* (apothecary).

My father was the first member of his family to convert to Sikhism. So, while his father and two of his four brothers did not subscribe to the usual dress and other codes required of a Sikh, my father was a staunch convert. After his conversion, all marriage alliances of family members were made only with Sikh families. The religious practices in the house were conducted in accordance with the Sikh tradition and, except for his third brother's children, all sons were raised as Sikhs.

Family Relationships

The relationship of the four brothers with my father was cold and distant. They avoided him, while continuing to obey and respect his word. Their emotional bond was with my mother and their parents. In this joint household, my mother made a life for herself and her 10 children, of whom nine survived. My father, hard, violent and unrelenting, often beat my mother for no fault of hers. His outburst often followed the visit of a female relative whom he disliked or if my mother handed over leftover food to the Muslim cleaning lady. We, as children, found his violence extremely painful and my brother often physically shielded her from my father's blows, by sitting on her lap or holding her tight. This helped, for my father loved his sons and stayed his hand.

Discord between the women and their husbands was common in the household. Ayaram, my first uncle, born after my father, and a father of three children himself, had stopped communicating with his wife Sundri though they lived in the same house for 40 years. It is believed that they fell out when he tried to help his friends who were implicated in the killing of a young Hindu boy. The police tried to involve my uncle as he was close to this group. The family spent enormous amounts of money hiring a distinguished legal expert to get him freed. Those few years were a total disaster, but the joint family performed its duty. Looking back, it would appear that both sides of my family were involved in legal battles of one kind or another, virtually reducing them to penury. My uncle was finally set free and he went back to his government job in the treasury. He, however, paid a price in terms of family relationships.

Father's relationship with his second brother Saheb Ram was less than cordial. Saheb Ram, a Hindu, was already married when my mother entered the household. His wife Brinder, who was later nicknamed Bindri, came from a prosperous contractor's family. My uncle Saheb Ram joined his father-in-law, a contractor, and was away for long stretches of time. Bindri's wealth and Saheb Ram's dependence on her family strengthened her position. She would often return to her parents' home. Coming from a Hindu family, she seemed to have reservations in following Sikh traditions in our largely Sikh household. When she named her eldest son Advait, eyebrows were raised within the family, as this was done in clear defiance of my father's wishes. Unlike Ayaram's children who were raised as Sikhs, Bindri's sons did not subscribe to Sikh traditions and customs. Her position was privileged, yet in my father's house she dutifully observed the rituals of the prayer room, including those of opening and closing the prayer book.

Into this house my mother decided to bring in my cousin Gurcharan, the daughter of her eldest sister, Brihawan. She lived in Delhi and her father was a veterinary doctor in government service. The girl was a matriculate. She came into the household as the bride of Jeevan Singh, the third brother of my father, who was well educated, having completed a course in law at Lucknow. Gurcharan's parents were happy to have an alliance from Bannu as all Bannu families felt that marriages worked out best for their children if they went back to their home town. Besides caste, religion and economic status, regional location was also important. A Sikh boy from elsewhere was not as good as a boy from Bannu.

But the educated Delhi girl was a misfit in the family. She was not used to household work and was strongly supported by her husband in this matter. She wanted to study privately as my uncle was away completing his law degree taking more time than usual to accomplish this. The joint family once again supported him as he was a very charming and affectionate person. But the family scene got more complicated after this marriage. Sending my aunt to college posed major difficulties for my mother. Hindu and Sikh women in Bannu lived in seclusion in the household and went out in *burqas*. The *tonga* (horse-drawn cart) was also covered to prevent exposure to the public. Even within the household women and younger daughters-in-law covered their faces in front of elder family members. The custom of seclusion had to be strictly observed, even by Gurcharan. My father was totally opposed to the idea of her higher education and whatever mistakes she committed were attributed to my mother. An incident I can still recall is that of the young couple going out for a movie and returning late at night at around 9 o'clock. My father who had heard about the outing, was standing on the rooftop, waiting for them to enter the house. When they set foot inside the house, he screamed at them and wanted to throw them out. Respectable women from respectable households did not wander around late at night, even in the company of their husbands!

Ranjit Singh, the youngest of the five brothers, was my grandfather's favourite. It was becoming increasingly important to acquire an education at the time, and Ranjit Singh passed the matriculation examination after which he completed a course in teachers' training. By the time he grew up, the family was going through the process of disintegration. His parents felt that, unlike his older brothers, he was denied his legitimate share of family property. Later, he completed a diploma in engineering and worked as an overseer outside the family enterprise.

The Female Domain

My mother found herself at the head of this household and had to organise domestic tasks without the help of maids and distribute the work among the female members, the sisters-in-law. They worked hard, long hours. There was a cow and a buffalo to be milked and taken care of, and the cowshed to be cleaned. The mud floors of the house had to be cleaned and plastered with cowdung. Washing and stitching of clothes and the daily routine of cooking and cleaning fell to the lot of the three women. There was a great deal of discord regarding the division of household chores in the domestic domain. My grandmother was given very little work out of consideration for her age and status. As the prayer room and religious practices in the house conformed to the Sikh practices, the women followed the ritual of opening and closing the Sikh holy book both in the morning and evening.

Given the tensions in the domestic sphere and in particular the kitchen, in addition to restrictions regarding mobility and freedom, the cramped lifestyle and differences of opinion with Jeevan Singh, the separation of the households seemed to be imminent. Once my uncle returned home after completing his education in law, he wanted to work as an independent lawyer and it was evident that the family would have to divide its assets. He asked for the partition of the landed property and the other brothers, except my father, were only too happy to join in. All along, it had been a question of who would bell the cat. In the meantime, Gurcharan had become a graduate and also obtained a bachelor's degree in education and had started working as the principal of a school. She was the most educated and independent female family member. Her influence opened up avenues for the other girls in the family to obtain higher education, including me. She, however, continued to observe the usual family norms with the deference expected of her.

THE BREAK-UP OF THE JOINT FAMILY (1940)

The joint family was divided into four separate households living close to each other. Jeevan Singh and Ayaram chose to live in the same compound in separate houses. My grandparents as well as all other unmarried family members lived with my father. Our newly-composed household now consisted of 14 members, including children. Our family remained a joint household. When Ranjit Singh married, my grandparents wanted to be with him. Grandmother helped his wife settle down and establish herself in her new home. After the division of the landed property, each male member of the family inherited

2 acres of land. It was during this time that one day my father was unusually nice to my mother, trying to engage her in conversation. We later discovered that he wanted her to part with her gold bangles to buy some land that was on sale at an attractive price. I wish my mother had kept her bangles, they would have come in handy when we migrated to India. Like many other unwilling players in the drama of the Partition, we had to leave behind our land, but we could have carried the gold.

THE RUMBLINGS OF PARTITION

It was around this time that the partition of the country into India and Pakistan was announced. Most of my mother's family had already made the transition to India. During the 1930s her two brothers had moved to Amritsar and with them, her father and widowed sister Maina *masi*. My mother's married sister Brihawan was in Delhi. At the time of the Partition, her third brother was in Lyallapur. He escorted his children back to India and left them in the care of his parents and widowed sister. His story is blurred. Some say he went back to Pakistan to recover his property. But years later, in 1990, his eldest daughter and my aunt Brihawan told us that out of sheer dejection he had committed suicide. This news was kept secret from all of us, particularly the children; thus, he was another casualty of Partition in our family.

In Bannu indecision and anxiety plagued the minds of the panicstricken Hindu population. My father refused to move, though many Hindu families had started migrating. His argument was that the Sikhs had lived in that part of the world even during the Mughal period. He saw no reason to leave his property and explore unknown lands. It was very difficult to persuade him and equally difficult to leave him behind. My mother did not enter into these deliberations, although she had strong connections in India. My lawyer uncle, Jeevan Singh, was uncomfortable about the delay, though not quite certain about the decision to leave. He had just established himself as a lawyer and had become president of the Bannu Bar Association after a bitter contest with his brother-in-law. He also had many good Muslim Pathan friends.

FLIGHT OF THE FAMILY

My uncle's indecision and uneasiness showed up in different ways. Looking back, it would appear that in his tremendous anxiety to protect his family, he came up with the ridiculous idea of sending his 9-year-old son Darshi to India with a Muslim friend who was travelling to Dera Ismail Khan. My uncle Ayaram was posted in the government treasury there. My uncle reasoned that it was a good plan because there were connecting flights to India. When the time to send Darshi approached, he developed cold feet. He came over to my father and requested that my brother Ujal also be sent along with Darshi.

My uncle persisted and managed to persuade my father to give his consent. The two Sikh boys, dressed as girls with long pigtails and black *burqas*, escorted by the Muslim friend, left by bus for Dera Ismail Khan on their way to their Indian destination. The journey was uneventful and they reached safely. Unfortunately, the man with whom my uncle Ayaram shared the house, a Hindu treasury contractor, was under surveillance. The occupants of the house were in great trouble. Ayaram was absolutely furious with his brother for having sent the children without consulting him. Of course, there was no question of any communication between people in those chaotic days. People did what they thought was best in order to protect themselves and their children.

Since the police watched both my uncle and his contractor friend, he could not even go to the airlines office to purchase their tickets as he might be accused of trying to flee with the treasury money. In the end, by pleading with the pilots of the aircraft who agreed to have them on board out of consideration for their young age, the boys managed to take a flight to India. They travelled on two separate days with only a bag and an address in their pockets. They got separated from each other and, only by sheer chance, reunited in Delhi and later joined us in Amritsar.

The situation started deteriorating rapidly and by 30 November 1947, within three months of Partition, it became clear that it was not possible to continue to live in Bannu. My uncle Jeevan Singh, even more restless following the departure of his son, decided to buy tickets for the entire family to travel to India. He managed to sell all his property for a good price with the help of his Pathan friends and left on the fateful journey to India. Only my father was still adamant enough to stay back.

A large number of Muslim friends had come to see my uncle off and while the family, consisting of three young women and eight young children, got into the train with all their baggage, my uncle continued to talk to his Muslim friends on the Bannu railway platform. He could not get into the compartment in time. The train left without him. We did not see him entering our compartment. We later heard that his friends had encircled him and prevented him from taking leave of his elder brother before boarding the train. Finally, they pushed him into the guard's compartment and got in themselves. The train had barely covered a couple of miles when they attacked him with a dagger and killed him with the very pistol my uncle had gifted them some time ago. The murderer was the same friend who had escorted the two boys of the family to safety in Dera Ismail Khan. They had thought that my uncle was carrying the cash received from selling his property. Fortunately, he had entrusted part of it to his wife Gurcharan. They threw out the dead body with dagger marks and a pistol shot on it. Bannu was a small place and the next morning my father, on his regular walk to the *gurudwara* at four in the morning, heard the shocking news. The body was handed over to him by the police and the cremation was done according to Sikh rites. My father dropped a postcard to his son in India, saying, 'Your mother and brothers have all left for India and your uncle has been murdered. I don't know what has happened to the rest of the family. I cannot tell you the shock and anguish that my brother must have gone through.'

Meanwhile, the family travelled on, unaware of what had transpired. When we reached our next stop, the Madi-Indus station, the ticket collector asked us for our tickets and on discovering that our tickets were not with us—our uncle had held on to them—mercilessly made us get off the train without our baggage in the cold winter evening. My mother had to assume responsibility for the group, and found herself in charge of two very young women, herself who was not much older. A crowd of Pathan men had surrounded us and one could overhear their plans to take away the women. Many women had been abducted and raped in those days of frenzy.

There was a military camp just across this railway station and a military officer crossed over to check on the crowd on the platform. My mother and aunts went up to him and pleaded in Pushtu and

English to help them. My aunt's English education probably helped, and we were taken to the military camp under his protection.

THE REFUGEE CAMP

We were eventually transferred from the military camp to a refugee camp, and it took the family a month to reach Amritsar. My mother's two brothers lived there, a new trading outpost started in the late 1930s. It was the only silver lining on our terribly depressing horizon. And it was here that my aunt learnt from a radio announcement that her husband was no more. Regarding her son, who had left home dressed as a girl, she had no news and was totally devastated. She only recovered when my father finally arrived a month later to confirm what had happened.

My brother located Darshi by sheer coincidence in Delhi, travelled to Amritsar to meet us and return the child to his mother. My mother's sister Brihawan, who was the mother of my slain uncle's widow, also came to know the news. The two families were absolutely furious with each other. Strangely enough, my mother had to bear the hostility, abuse and bitterness caused by this brutal murder. Her brothers and sisters went to the extent of accusing her of having engineered events to escape the fate of her sister-in-law. They also felt that she should have asked one of her teenaged boys to be with their uncle. They were inconsolable and all their anger was directed towards my innocent mother.

My father arrived a month later. Upon being consulted about the future of his brother's wife and two children, he refused to say anything and left the house. That was the final blow from which my aunt never quite recovered. She went away with her father to Bikaner, where she received complete protection, and help to find a job and raise her children. My father was by then a destitute, not knowing where his next meal would come from. Though she did not realise it at that time, my widowed aunt was much better off than us.

After her traumatic crossing, my mother had hoped to find solace and comfort with her brothers and sisters, but she found the environment hostile and decided not to stay with them any longer. We came away to Delhi to join my brother in the refugee accommodation arranged by the government—the Kingsway Camp. It was close to the place where Gandhiji held meetings in the evening.

THE KINGSWAY CAMP: HERALDING TRANSITION

We were unprepared for life in the refugee camp. The walls of our sheltered upbringing had given way to community living. We lived in tents alongside thousands of refugees, each with terrible stories to narrate. Times had changed. The joint family and patriarchy were the first casualties of the transition. Women's education and mobility was another positive consequence. In this turmoil, the edge between male dominance and female subservience had softened. Radical social change was occurring and we ourselves were not aware of the extent to which migration to India had changed us and how very liberating in a sense it was for us women, though it had come about in a traumatic manner and in a very short span of time. For once, it was impossible to observe *purdah* or attempt seclusion in the camp environment. I learnt to cycle to go to college. The question of marriage was shelved as there were so many other things that took precedence. Basically, the change created more space and empowered women in more ways than one.

My father, who had ruled the house with an iron hand, became a much mellowed man. With his home and lands taken away from him, he was totally dependent on his two sons in India, one working as a clerk and the other studying law. Most important for us, he no longer beat my mother on the slightest pretext. His anger, often expressed in throwing plates around and refusing to eat, totally disappeared. However, my mother continued to bow down to my father every morning and evening as she had done in Bannu from the day she had married him. She was respectful to him and never allowed us children to be rude to him in any way. He continued to be the symbolic head of the household. But my brothers, now employed, were in effect the ruling voices in the family.

There was chaos and confusion all around, but the rehabilitation of the refugees went on peacefully, with great dignity and care. Jobs and school admissions were arranged for refugee men and women for the asking. This instilled a ray of hope in the minds of millions of dislocated men and women.

My brother's earnings as a government employee sustained us, but we were too many. In the Delhi summer, the heat in the tents was unbearable. Pratap, my younger brother, fell ill with a very high temperature. We knew that the least we could do was to shift him to a place with a better roof. It looked as if this child was going to die if something was not done. An aunt's husband, living in a camp near us told us of a room built for stable boys that was vacant and unused. It was next to his and was locked. In our desperation we broke the lock and moved my sick brother in. In the evening the claimant of the room came with the police. All the men in the house disappeared leaving my mother to face the police. She, who had never spoken to an unknown man, came out furious and told the police in no uncertain terms that if something happened to her young son they would be held responsible. The police were humane as sympathy for the victims of Partition abounded, and my brother slowly recovered.

It turned out that we were in the outhouse of a place called Kitchener House, the residence of the commander-in-chief, occupied later on by India's first prime minister, Jawaharlal Nehru. We could see him riding by in the mornings. We stayed here only for a few months after which we were allotted a place at the Purana Qila.

One of the first tragedies our family faced as a result of the political upheaval was the loss of my grandfather. He was extremely upset over the brutal murder of his son Jeevan Singh. He went through a phase when he had nightmares of being stabbed and constantly spoke about his son, mourning his death. One day he requested a neighbour to give him a lift to the railway station and left without telling any of us. He went to his younger son Ranjit Singh. But he lived for less than a year after the Partition. The trauma had been too much for him. My 70-year-old grandmother was left alone. She had virtually lived all her life with him, having been married to him at the age of 8 years.

Move to Purana Qila

The Purana Qila is a massive fort (believed to have been constructed during the time of the Pandavas, the heroes of the *Mahabharata*) of great architectural elegance. We lived here for many years until 1964. We were three generations living in a four-room temporary barrack construction with asbestos roofing over our heads. It was unbearably hot in the summer and severely cold in the winter. However, we had good facilities for schooling and shopping, and access to water and electricity. Also, there was reasonable privacy. Here we lived—my grandparents, my parents and nine of us children. My mother was the only person responsible for the housekeeping, and she would not let me share the chores.

The intense orthodoxy of the early days had changed and I was allowed to study for five years. This was around 1952, when my brother wanted to go abroad and my mother was heartbroken at the thought of letting him go. Life was hard and she needed his emotional support. She insisted that I should be married before he left for England.

MY WEDDING

A hasty marriage was arranged for me with a young person whose parents were known to us in Bannu. My husband was the son of a school master and had a degree in law. I had barely finished a bachelor's degree in education and had begun my career as a teacher. It was sad that my first pay, instead of going to my family, who had worked so hard for me, went to my in-laws.

My mother was emotionally devastated when both her son and daughter left home. It was during the summer, when the heat was oppressive, that my mother decided to visit me as I was expecting a child. She came all the way and, in rigid adherence to custom, refused even a drink of water at my house. She went back in the heat. At the bus station her purse was stolen and she could not board the bus. She walked back in the mid-afternoon sun, reaching home totally dehydrated and with high blood pressure. Before any help could be summoned, she succumbed to a heart attack.

The loss of our mother was difficult to bear. Strong and brave, she had been our emotional anchor in our darkest years. She had changed and adapted to all the circumstances and demands placed on her. Our need for her was great and we mourned her loss. My brothers had no emotional attachment to their father and had been totally dependent on my mother who was always a picture of graciousness and affection. I tried to return home to cook and care for my eight brothers, but with my other responsibilities in contributing to a family that had little to offer me and depended on my earnings, it was not a permanent solution. We desperately sought a way out.

It occurred to the family members that it would be better if the household acquired had a female member to look after the family. I do not know whose idea it was, but the orphaned daughter of my uncle who was a doctor and who had died after Partition was chosen as the most appropriate person for the role. She had been raised by his sister Maina *masi*, and was shy and diffident. After my grandfather's death Maina *masi*'s position in the household weakened, she depended on her brothers and their families for support and was now destitute. It was probably her idea to put pressure on this young girl to marry my brother. Although he was an engineer, he was dark and suffered from an inferiority complex as my father did not like him and discriminated against him in favour of his other sons. Consequently, he always sulked, felt depressed and developed a melancholy personality. Laj, my cousin, and Bhajan, my brother, were cross cousins and such marriages had never been encouraged. But changed circumstances had brought about a change in our customs. They were unsuited to each other and the marriage did not last even for a day and the couple separated. It took nearly 15 years of persuasion from the family to get them to reconcile. The care of the family then fell to the lot of my grandmother.

MY GRANDMOTHER

Ammaji (grandmother) cooked delicious meals with her trembling hands and always worried about rats and bandicoots taking away the food. She slept in the centre of the room dressed in colourful clothes—bottle green *salwar* and matching *kurta*, and a pink chiffon *dupatta*—and all around her were pots and pans of different sizes with lids weighed down by heavy stones. She was also very scared because she always felt the younger boys stole money from her when she slept. She made the place a home and every morning in the summer would go from bed to bed and kiss all her nine grandchildren while they were asleep. The affection she could give was enormous and she was the picture of the perfect grandmother. Afraid of seeking help from her son, my father, she never dared ask for domestic help. When attempts were made to hire a maid, my father was so difficult that they refused to stay on. Grandmother took care of the house admirably in her old age. Her eyes would water and her hands shake, but she still lit the fire and cooked with a little help from her grandsons.

It was sad that eventually when the family moved to better housing—allotted on the basis of property claims—in improved economic circumstances, none of her sons or grandsons could accommodate her for one reason or the other. When her other sons deserted her, I felt my father could easily have helped her. An arrangement was made with the three daughters to look after her by turns. Finally, what remained was the bond between mother and daughters. There was no society to enforce norms. People did what suited them best.

THE SURVIVORS

Five of my brothers migrated abroad and changed their religious beliefs. They no longer believe in sporting the external symbols of Sikhism. Living abroad they look back at India with little nostalgia. They refuse to talk about the past and will do anything to get rid of their Indian identity if it would only leave them. Family relationships no longer matter, nuclear families and new ideas about family formation have come to occupy centre stage.

It was only when some of my brothers wanted to pass on their inherited property to me as I was not doing too well that old strong feelings against giving property to daughters came to the forefront. My father was opposed to the idea and, though I was his only daughter and I cared for him, he felt that property should be inherited only by sons. We had crossed the great divide between Bannu and New Delhi together, standing shoulder to shoulder, facing every new day sustained with new hope. We had grown, changed, adapted. We had been equals in our hopes and despair. We had crossed new frontiers, but in the end it seemed our prejudices remained unchanged. For my brothers, men, was reserved a higher destiny and I resigned myself with the thought that the more things seem to change the more they remain the same.

MY CHILDREN

Of my four children, my two daughters studied to be teachers and are married. In tragic circumstances in the 1950s, my elder son who was then a toddler, was run over by the neighbour's car as he was reversing. My second son made a career in hotel management, and last year he decided to move to England, a move I did not discourage although it did not have my wholehearted support.

Although my marriage was a failure, I had hoped my girls would make a success of theirs. It was not to be. My eldest daughter Preeti was married to a truck owner and settled in Gwalior. Out of my small pension I contributed towards the education of my granddaughters as their father was unsuccessful in his enterprise. As a child of Partition, I often think of my old grandmother, generous in the dusk of her years, of my brave mother, selfless to the end, and my young widowed aunt who single-handedly brought up her children. It is these women and so many unsung heroines like them who never let the inhibitions and seclusion in an earlier life deter them from building a new life for themselves and their children, amid the confusions and contradictions that followed the Partition. We owe them a debt of gratitude.

[Postscript: We are indeed sad to report that before this profile could be completed, Sushil died in February 1998. When she was finally and reluctantly admitted to hospital to be treated for kidney failure, it was too late. She died within a week, the neglect of her last years having finally taken its toll.]

11

Matriliny within Patriliny

Jasodhara Bagchi

I

I really would like to thank Leela and Arlie for making me do this piece of self-confrontation that does not come easily to a person such as myself. I have always been so interested in other people that it gave me a wonderful excuse not to look too intently at myself. The trouble with what they asked me to do was not merely to write about my mother and grandmother, but to relate them to myself. It is very difficult. I realised in putting it all down that the lens of memory is a self-preservative one, so that the negative and the painful get conveniently erased and we are left with what makes it easier to build bridges with the future. I will mention two additional complicating aspects of the matter in the case of this essay. I was composing it while vigorously researching motherhood in the Cambridge University Library, and basking in the company of my daughter who was writing a thesis in Cambridge, and, therefore, experiencing a long absence from home. It made me very susceptible while thinking of the way I related to my mother and grandmother. Some of this sensation at the pit of my guts has rubbed off as I write. I do not know that I would have written this way had the circumstances been different. So I begin this narration, deeply conscious that I am caught mid-stream, without Virginia Woolf's virtuosity in handling the stream of consciousness technique.

It is just over 28 years since I lost my mother. The years have done nothing to the intensity of the bonding except make it more selective. Though I had left my parents' house when I got married, circumstance compelled my husband Amiya, my elder daughter Tista and myself to move back to their house. In 1969 my father died very suddenly and my mother was too ill to be left alone. That was the time when a four-generational female bonding came into play, for which none of us was really prepared. My narrative will have to go back and forth between the home into which I was born and the one in which I was 'born again'.

II

Trying to calculate the time span that the three generations of the female line in our family would cover, I realised that it would amount to a span of about 110 years. Socio-historically speaking, the first half of this 100 years spanned a period of the most rapid pace in the growth of middle-class consciousness in Bengal. What had once been characterised as the nationalist 'resolution' of the women's question is now seen as the terrain of multiple contestations. Women entered the arena of mainstream political struggle, while being deferential to the family, underplaying 'difference', while women writers continued to engage with the world at large, questioning at every step, the so-called protective stance taken up by the patriarchal family. Nabaneeta's mother Radharani Devi's was one of the voices one heard in these debates.

My mother and grandmother were women who did not take up these public interventionist positions. But they were extremely articulate and self-aware women who were sensitive to the fault lines, with just that degree of assertiveness that created distinctive spaces for them within their families, however different these were from one another. One was the eldest daughter-in-law of a huge *zamindar* family that had amassed wealth in business and later in industry; the other was the eldest daughter-in-law of a middling family, but wife of an important professor of Botany in Presidency College, Calcutta. There was something about their respective self-fashioning that went on largely within the four walls of domesticity that rubbed off on me when I was trying to create a space for Women's Studies in Jadavpur University.

In trying to sift the ingredients with which these two very different women negotiated their respective sites, certain commonalities do emerge. The first was a determined, rational effort to organise the domestic economy, not in the passive instinctual kind of way that is often ascribed to the exclusionary Enlightenment agenda of Western hegemonic discourse. It was, rather, in clear opposition to this, an effort to merge the ratiocinative with the intensely affective, both operating within the context of the family. What I am trying to signal to is that though very well organised, there was an overflowing affective quality about them that anyone who had come in contact with them still recall with vividness. Fun, humour and personal warmth are qualities that have lingered not only with me but my daughters and many other friends and relatives.

I hope I will be excused if, at this point, I pause a little over why it is not at all useful to capture these lives and mine within the customary binary of tradition/modernity. The signs I read in this inter-generational account are newer ways of relating to one's inner legacies through the challenges opening up for their everyday lives by the colonial organisation of society. Both my grandmother and mother were, in their own ways, intensely aware of Western social mores, but a well-honed process of selectivity was also set into motion not to let their own spaces be usurped by something alien that might act like an antibody. Looking back with the hindsight generated by my feminist research, I would say that both my mother and grandmother were 'new women' of their generations. I will try to capture the subtle process of the negotiations of the social terrain that this involved, to which I had access by fits and starts. Deeply imbued with the sense of propriety and lifestyle that contact with the West entailed, it meant very different kinds of negotiation for each of them to keep their sense of integrity alive. My mother, for instance, who was permitted to perform on a public stage, Rabindranath Tagore's *Mayar Khela*, being directed by the poet's niece Sarala Debi Chowdhurani under the personal supervision of the poet himself, had to resort to subterfuges to prevent male fans from calling on her at home because their visits might be construed as amorous.

The blend of rational universalism and the feelings-based particularity that has motivated me in my conduct, both private and public, I owe predominantly to these women.

In these days, riven as we are with oscillations between universalism and difference, do we relate to each other across cultures with more meaning if we speak through our matriliny? Since most of us do not come from strictly defined matrilineal kinship systems, it would add to our interest to see how a sense of matriliny may be prized out of a web located within patriliny, regulated by norms that are patriarchal. Do the patterns and relationships signal towards trajectories that have compelled us to gather here and communicate as communities of women, imaginary or otherwise?

To adapt two lines from a song by Rabindranath Tagore, I get better acquainted with myself when I see myself through my mother and grandmother. It is a process, moreover, that is still unfolding, even though it is now 28 years since the last of them died. What is extremely relevant is that I am the mother (proud is too mild a word to describe my status!) of two daughters, and the memory of my mentors going back to two generations enriches my present experience in an inexplicable way.

As I have already indicated above, a self-conscious looking back has made me face the startling realisation that both my mother and grandmother call out to being identified as 'new women'. Bengal, as one of the sites of the British colonial presence, went through a very complex process of class formation, which engendered the society in certain very fundamental ways. So far, very rich research by feminist scholars, both men and women, have provided us with insights into the complexity of the process. Reaping the harvest of these insights, I stake the claim just made on behalf of my mother and grandmother. This does not preclude the fact that my grandmother had hardly any formal schooling worth mentioning and that my mother went to a convent school. By juxtaposing them I am not proposing to lump together two very rich human beings whose sensitive nuanced existence deserve careful differentiation.

But in both their lived lives, for instance, I see a commitment to thinking things through before planning the day. Each in her own way was averse to chaos and anarchy, with a concomitant faith in 'culture'. As a member of the younger generation, I often found this exasperating and constrictive, and tried to subvert it. But now when I am not being regulated by it, I have learnt to identify myself with some of it and be deeply appreciative of what I could not. On the domestic management side what it amounted to was a careful allocation of resources, thrift without meanness, that negotiated space for others. Both women had to steer through the complex course of patrilocality, and thinking about their different lives I am brought face to face with the displacement this might entail. I shall try and map out the differentiated terrains that the initial displacement might have thrown up for each of us. However, while doing this, I must make a fulsome acknowledgement of one of the major sources of bonding that cemented us—that is, the world of expressivity that opened up through music. Singing alone or in unison, songs composed by poets and composers who blended the old and new, meant women like us could build up a world of our own without crossing over to the public world of performance. This is one area where I have vivid memory of not only three but four generations communicating directly and with intensity.

My Grandmother, Malatibala Gupta (née Sen): 1894–1970

The eldest child of her father's second wife, my grandmother was an elegant, poised and beautiful woman. This is not to suggest that her life was without turmoil and upheavals. What was impressive was how little she permitted it to fluster her external poise.

At the same time, she did not don the proud aloofness that beautiful women in well-to-do families among the Bengali elite often cultivated. The expressive-affective warmth of her personality she inherited from her father, an employee in the excise department of the colonial state. My grandmother's father, Indubhushan Sen, combined contradictory pulls in the making of his personality. Orphaned at an early age, he was brought up in the household of Sir K.G. Gupta, known for his Westernised Brahmo 'modernity'. He was also closely related to the remarkable Brahmo preacher Bhai Girish Sen, known for his translation of the *Koran* into Bengali. While partaking of this open liberal cultural atmosphere, Indubhushan took a great deal of care to retain his independent way of life, which was more that of a traditional Hindu than of a reformed Brahmo. Thus, he carved out an independent career for himself as soon as he could. But he was careful to maintain contact with and make himself available to his Brahmo elders and benefactors whenever they needed him. This appears to have left an indelible mark on the personality of his daughter, who displayed symptoms of this reformed Brahmo culture without ever being part of it.

One of the casualties of the refusal of my mother's grandfather to conform to the Westernised social mores of the Brahmos was the education of my grandmother and her younger sister. The obsession with the marriage of girls at the onset of puberty meant that they were taken out of school and married off in their early teens. It was her next sister Priyabala, a remarkable self-taught intellectual despite her early marriage, who mourned the loss of schooling of herself and that of her elder sister. This is vividly portrayed in her memoir

Smritimanjusha (A Treasure Chest of Memories) that has been published by the School of Women's Studies, Jadavpur University. Paradoxically, therefore, though born in the Vaidya community in East Bengal (the one that produced Vina Mazumdar), these two sisters were taken out of school and married early to satisfy their father's need to eschew the Brahmo patterns of reform. Priyabala went on to make up for this in her heroic endeavour to promote girls' education by starting schools in the village where she was married, and equipping herself with an educational diploma given by Tagore's institution, Visva-Bharati, by correspondence.

From the father, as I have already said, the sisters acquired the art of expressive conversation. He was a *raconteur* who attracted the villagers to come and listen to his stories. I got a taste of this secondhand in the wonderful storytelling powers of my grandmother. I would make her repeat again and again the description of the days of the Durga *puja* that was celebrated with great pomp in the *zamindari* household in the village. My mouth still waters as I recall her narration of the drums announcing the commencement of the first day of the Durga *puja*, when at the crack of dawn the children would wrench themselves from sleep and rush out without waiting to put any clothes on! I somehow feel gratified that I did manage to attend one of these grand occasions when I was about 8. The Partition coming soon after meant that it could never be repeated. We children would never see Rampiyari the elephant attached to the grand household again: Rampiyari who had impressed me as a child with her gentleness, and with what I thought were tears in her eyes when we left the village at the end of the autumnal *puja* festivities and all the fun that went with it! While for us it meant being deprived of a few exotic visits, I have often wondered what kind of a wrench it must have meant for people like my grandmother to be cut off form the rootedness of the village home. Her sister Priyabala, who had built up her whole world in the East Bengal village even after it had become East Pakistan, has recorded her desolate sense of loss once she had to give it all up and make a home in the alien surroundings of West Bengal several years after the Partition.

To come back to my grandmother and her sisters: the aspect of their lifestyle I look back upon with the closest sense of identification was music, which was the most prominent of the expressive bondings I could sense. While the daughters inherited from their father wonderful singing voices, it was the youngest, Renuka Dasgupta, who took Bengali listeners by storm with her one song 'Jodi Gokulachandra Braje Na Elo' that is still remembered by generations even after a passage of more than eight decades. She shot into fame and became virtually a household name. As a feminist, I now understand the acute shyness from which she suffered and her extreme aversion to publicity. Announcements of some of her early recordings had to refer to her as an 'amateur' to avoid the term 'professional', a near-synonym for a 'prostitute'.

For a personality like my grandmother, talents such as she may have had had to be hidden under the bushel of domesticity. It might have been her beauty that ensured her marriage into this rich *zamindar* family who ran an 'agency house' in Calcutta, owned several factories and became the pioneering cycle industry in Bengal, India Cycle. The brother next to my grandfather was the prominent Congress leader J.C. Gupta, looked upon with respect by the Muslim community in undivided Bengal, and whose blind lawyer son became an MP of the CPI (M) for a number of years. My grandmother was the eldest daughter-in-law of this celebrated Gupta family with its elaborate *zamindari* household in the East Bengal village home and the lavish urban lifestyle in the heart of the posh residential areas in Calcutta going back to the 1920s. When I was born, my mother's natal home literally fitted the traditional description of *hathishale hathi ebang ghorashale ghora* (elephants in the elephant stable and horses in horse stable), except in the place of horses one has to read about five cars standing in a row.

The legacy of her father came in handy for my grandmother. I never saw this enormous wealth affect her equanimity. She remained the same smiling unflappable personality in her prosperity as well in the financial adversity that befell her unit of the family towards the end of her life. Not having had to suffer the physical displacement that many East Bengal families suffered during the Partition of Bengal, she was nevertheless uprooted from her luxurious home due to reversals in her son's business career and had to live the last years of her life as a tenant, curiously enough, in the house that had been built by Vina*di*'s father in south Calcutta. I remember how in her old age she missed not the wealth but the warmth and human intimacy of the vast network of kinship she had come to adopt as her own as the adolescent bride. Yet there were bitter memories to struggle with, when the joint property and wealth evaporated through ugly family squabbles. As the only daughter-in-law of the house to be widowed in her early 40s, there was an aura of sadness mingled with her graceful and pleasant demeanour.

My grandfather died of tuberculosis that could not be cured despite several years spent in the West. He died 12 days before I was born. When my widowed grandmother came to my mother's bedside to look at me, her first grandchild, my mother, as she told me years later, hid her face in the pillows because she could not bear to see her beautiful and young mother in the white apparel of a widow. Throughout my conscious memory she played the role of the only grandparent I had known (my father's mother, a remarkable woman, by all accounts, died when I was barely 5 months old), and she did so with overflowing affection and remarkable judgement. You may think me biased because she complimented me on my choice of a husband as she felt that her daughter, my mother, in her generosity of disposition, might not have chosen as well as I had done. So, you see, she was a good sport!

It was clear that my grandmother was a woman with a great deal of inner resources. Even as a child I could feel that her traditionalism avoided the fixity of orthodoxy. The personalised piety that later drew me to do research on the religion of humanity that came to Bengal in the second half of the 19th century was something I had sensed in her spiritual life. Her wonderful singing voice, for instance, had no institutional outlet, but was used for communing with her personal God. This is where the Brahmo component in her early upbringing would enter. For her, prayers would be captured not through the Sanskritic hymn-singing of orthodox Hindu of ritual, but lyrics of poet composers like Tagore, Atulprasad Sen or Rajanikanta Sen. The music in this genre would intensify the affective-expressive quality of the words. If I were to identify any inheritance from my matriliny, it would be this genre of singing.

My grandmother maintained a smiling poise through prosperity as well as adversity. Without speaking any English, she had accompanied her younger daughter and her little boy (now grown into a famous philosopher of science and technology) to London, when she had gone to set up home with her doctor husband. My aunt waxed eloquent on how well she took all this alien environment in her stride.

The inner strength of her personality came out in one episode that I have cherished all my life. Ever since I was born, she had lived the life of an upper-caste Hindu Bengali widow, dressed in white with a separate vegetarian kitchen with a Brahmin cook. While her beauty in white and the aroma of the exquisite vegetarian cuisine, which she either cooked herself or supervised, were inspiring, what was empowering for me in my late teens was the stregth of her rationality when she could be persuaded by the doctor father of her daughter-in-law to give up the orthodox eating practice in order to protect her body, frail with diabetes. One wonders how much soul searching she had to do in confronting the *samskara* of her widowhood after practising it for nearly 20 years. It also taught me that reason was not always exclusionary and constricting. It could open up spaces as much as it might close.

My Mother, Nilima Sen Gupta (Tom): 1910–77

As the eldest child of the famous Gupta family, she was given the male pet name Tom. Though there was nothing tomboyish about her physically, in her mindset she was one. All her life having fought against the cruel ritual practice of deprivation to which widows are subjected in upper-caste Hindu families, when it came to her own turn, I was elated to find that she lived up to her professed convictions. Widowed suddenly in her 59th year, she spared me many anxieties by declaring that she would give up the symbols of marriage, that is, her *sindoor* (red vermillion on the parting of the hair and on the forehead) and her *loha* (iron bangle), but not what she was born to. She, therefore, neither adopted the borderless white sari that forms the widow's dress code in Bengal nor its vegetarian diet. What I am trying to indicate is that without any of the external trappings of a 'liberated' woman, she was singularly free within of the conventional hang-ups of a traditional virtuous woman.

She displayed this independence of spirit on many occasions. During the brief stint of honorary social work she engaged in, organising a day centre for students who did not have space to study at home, she did not hesitate to challenge bureaucratic inertia and delay. Bills got paid and kitchen sinks got installed with a speed unheard of in a government-sponsored institution. When warned against possible risks, she said that she did not earn a penny out of it and acted in the best interests of the institution she was asked to build, and that she was prepared to face the consequences. Many a time I have had occasion to think back on this episode in my mother's life when I organised the School of Women's Studies from scratch in Jadavpur University.

Responsiveness to friends, regardless of age, creed and class (caste not being a visible presence in elite life in Bengal) bonded me to my mother in a palpable way. Friendship constituted almost a conscious creed for my mother—she knew how to enter into it heart and soul. All my life I have been showered with affection by her friends and she knew how to extend it to mine. Nabaneeta will bear me out in this, and my mother, in turn cherished the love she had from Nabaneeta's mother, both an older and more celebrated woman. Like Mrs. Dalloway, my mother loved to create spaces where people could come together. One of the last such occasions was shortly before her death, when she brought all her friends together with little badges announcing the dates from which she had known them. The oldest friend was the youngest aunt, the celebrated singer, born in the same year and something of a look-alike. Her badge, therefore, said 1910. I might as well mention here that in my mother's family line there has been a delightful aunt–niece dyad that got broken as I was an only child. Friendship also brought with it a commitment and the courage of her convictions. When a very close friend's marriage broke up, while everyone else was politely looking the other way my mother did not hesitate to go up to her estranged husband, who was a nephew by marriage, and declare that she was heartbroken even at the risk of knowing that such an expression of concern was not likely to be appreciated.

My grandmother was a saint to her children, my mother was not. Our relationship, though deeply bonded, saw moments of exasperation on both our parts, but we never lost faith in one another. Despite an air of Victorian morality, that made her, for instance, write down worthy sayings of the day in our drawing room that I found a bit ridiculous after a point, she was at heart a catholic person, able to identify with persons and situations that were totally unlike her own. Friends who had transgressed conventional middle-class norms would confide in her and would get a lot of active assistance from her. Though not particularly Left-minded, herself she had several friends even in her own generation who were. Among the friends she was most proud of was Sudha Roy, the well-known labour leader, who taught mathematics in Kamala Girls' School and spent the remaining hours of the day and morning organising workers in the Metiabruz area in Calcutta. This was again in evidence when she was old and frail, when she threw open our house to Muslim guests from East Pakistan when the Pakistani army struck in 1971. Not only were they people we knew well, or eminent economist friends of Amiya my husband, but strangers, such as an elderly lady, her daughter and little grandchild who were accommodated without a murmur.

The convent-educated eldest child of the wealthy Gupta family, my mother created a new life for herself as the wife of an academic who had just begun his professional career, with her usual zest. My father had returned with his doctorate in botany from the University of Heidelberg and joined Presidency College when he married my mother. My mother adopted the life of an academic's wife with a progressive class subjectivity that brought a certain elegance that she had imbibed largely from her mother. From her she had learned the art of managing scant resources, making a little go a long way. I often tend to forget how much she prized economic independence. Inheriting a wonderful singing voice, she had been taught at home by maestros like Sailajaranjan Májumdar and Ramesh Banerjee. She could play the *esraj* (I still have her broken *esraj*) and the flute. All this, however, belonged to the leisured privilege of the wealth of her natal home. In our more obviously middle-class family, she used her talent to take up a part-time job as a music teacher in Kamala Girls' School, a local school that has attained some renown. The salary was a pittance, but she exercised her limited economic freedom with considerable pride and self-consciousness. She chose careful, mostly useful presents on each of the family weddings out of the savings from her meagre income. The sense of autonomy she exercised, in however limited a way, made her the first bourgeois feminist I had seen at close quarters. Wife of an eminent botanist of her generation, she was clear about her own domain. 'My kitchen is my laboratory,' she declared to the architect who was planning the house they were building in the late 1950s. So it remains one of the most spacious and well-lit rooms of the house we still live in. My involvement with women's studies happened many years after her death. I often thought of my new understanding of its theoretical base through the lens of her perception. I missed her greatly and felt a sense of closeness that I wish I could share with her

In the growing busy schedule of my father's career when he attained an all-India stature, he had to spend long stretches away from home. I was their only child and I was away in Oxford for a stretch of three years (these were before the present jet-setting days, when we spent 17 days on the boat, coming and going each way!) and then three more years as a Ph.D. student when my husband went back to teach in Cambridge. The adventurous spirit with which she spent those stretches of loneliness was born of her inner resources. Her sense of humour lit up the humdrum and the everyday, and drew people close to her. Next was her ability to empathise with people from very diverse backgrounds that made her a very good listener. I now realise that she was a 'counsellor' long before the days of institutional counselling.

She was an instinctive socialist who could make problems of working women her own. Her secularism was also spontaneous. All her life she enjoyed the company of Muslim and Christian friends.

My mother had never been to England. However, we used to tease her about the Anglophilia displayed in her laying the table with meticulous care, and her manners that we sometimes found quaint and Victorian. But her independence of judgement was fully in evidence when she chose my school. She did not opt for Loreto Convent, but chose a school founded by Mrs. Sarala Ray who had named it after her friend Gopal Krishna Gokhale. A mixture of Brahmo and moderate nationalism, Mrs. Ray wanted to attain the best of the East and the best of the West. What it did provide for us was a pan-Indian atmosphere that attracted students from all parts of the world. The secular cosmopolitanism of the school prepared us for being the lucky and confident generation that I think we were. My mother was a woman of judgement.

As I have already said, my mother's life meshed with mine in ways that were rather unusual because we had to move in with her under unusual circumstances. My father, who was too proud to admit physical illness, was captured by the 'sneaking thief men call death', just outside the gates of the Science College of Calcutta University as he was going in to take the practical of the MSc. examination in Botany. Breaking the news of this massive shock to my mother, who was already frail with cardiac asthma, we realised she could not live alone. We had just returned from Cambridge after my Ph.D. with my 4-year-old daughter Tista; my husband was finishing his last bit of teaching for the University of Cambridge. The rite of passage that this homecoming was going to be turned out to be much more far-reaching than we had anticipated. Tista entered into the domestic setting in which I was born. Tuli was born into it. My husband Amiya had to heroically adjust to an alien space. What I instinctively admired, but had a theoretical grasp over later, was that he crossed the hurdle of patrilocality without patriarchal protestations. My mother, with all her feminist inclinations, doted on him. He still complains that the day she died he lost his only solid ally in the household filled with women. What was amazing was that my father-in-law, a thoroughly rooted orthodox Brahmin, virtually unexposed to Western education, immediately saw the human need. My own life has enough evidence that good sense need not always look white, male and middle class.

Returning home after having left it at marriage usually has painful connotations in our culture—it could mean widowhood or, worse still, desertion. In our case there was a bonding of loss that marked it, my mother's extremely precarious health and the trauma of my father's death. I was totally unprepared for this, but it made me grow up in unexpected ways. Now in my mother's house there were three female generations—my daughter Tista aged 4 and a bit, my mother emaciated from her rotund bubbly self through sickness, and myself. The roles had all got intermingled. Caring and nurturing roles got interchanged—my mother was both my mother and child, my mother was both a grandmother and a mother to Tista, because I was out to work. Tista, who was always a very finished human being, became a caring, nurturing support to my mother. If Amiya had not been busy writing his book on the political economy of underdevelopment and helping me to sort out the maze of my father's papers to pay the estate duty, he might have felt left out. But then he has always been unthreatened by women.

For one year of this existence my grandmother was there like a rock beside her grieving eldest child. Once, while she was staying with us, Tista discovered her dentures in the bathroom, and was repelled by the sight. She figured out that it would be visible every time my grandmother came to stay the night with us. The next time she came for a day, Tista asked with her discerning innocence, 'How long will you stay?' My grandmother was quick on the uptake. With a twinkle in her eye she said, 'I am considering staying for a fortnight', and she hugely enjoyed the expression on her great-grandchild's face.

If I were to itemise the main ingredients of the bonding of these generations, I would have no hesitation in saying—music, cooking and a sense of humour. For the older generations there was also a deep sense of the spiritual and an intelligent commitment to housekeeping as part of their everyday existence. As a mode of practice I rejected both, but my feminism has helped me to perceive the continuity in all this, and has enabled me to acknowledge these as positive legacies, however problematically I might have related to these at the time. The spiritual calm that my grandmother displayed, despite her own deep grief, that one year she stood by my mother remained a pillar of strength. She did not live beyond a year after my father's death. The eldest son-in-law, who was only six years her junior, was still someone she could not let go of that easily.

In the house, full of memories of my childhood and adolescence, some blissfully happy and some painful, I became an adult responsible person coping with things I had never had to deal with before. I was deeply devoted to my handsome strong scientist father—it was daunting to try and take his place in the house, looking after all the legal complications with the help of my husband. Four memories of love sustained me, especially in these years. They are my aunt, my mother's youngest sister, who was a cross between an aunt and a sister; my mother's youngest aunt, who was my mentor in the kind of singing I do; my youngest uncle, one of the most modest and talented cameramen in the film industry in Bengal; and, finally, Kal*idi*, my nurse from the village, who came back for some of my mother's last years. Except for my uncle, all the other figures are gone from my life—but I feel replenished by their memory.

If this reads too much like a schoolgirl romance, I have to emphasise that we do belong to the lucky generation in the history of modern Indian society. Far from being a midnight's child, I was a thinking, feeling girl of 10 when India became independent. The Partition grazed but did not batter the family. Presidency College opened its gates to women and we received the best possible education, culminating in a state scholarship to Oxford. On my return, after a stint as lecturer in a very good women's college, I was even taken in at Jadavpur University. Not only was it close enough for me to walk, I became part of the department that we could build up into a premier English department in the country. I also underwent the agony and the ecstasy of building up an interdisciplinary School of Women's Studies. Elders like Neera*ben* and Vina*di*, friends like Himani, Susie, Leela and Maithreyi, and several others got us started, and here I am cherishing and being cherished by the memory of the two women who, in hindsight, have formed me to be what I am.

12

Three Generations of Women*

Mary Roy

My Mother

She is still alive and 90 years old. I live in the same little town as she does, but I have not seen her for 10 years. My sharpest memory of her is when I was a 4-year-old child and she was a young and beautiful woman. Standing in the living room dressed in white, with blood flowing from the wounds on her head. Scars inflicted by her Imperial entomologist husband wielding the Imperial curtain rods with which he beat his wife. Why did he beat her? For no reason at all. He was a wife-beater by nature. He did not drink, he did not smoke, but he womanised in a frenzied manner. At the age of 7, I can remember his excitement as he stalked new prey.

I remember, too, that Mother's white clothes drenched in blood were carefully stacked away. They were given to her brother (my uncle) who was director of the International Labour Organization (ILO) in Geneva. My uncle took the clothes to a firm of lawyers, M/s. King and Partridge, who even today play an intrinsic part in my life. In those days, they were asked to draw up a case for divorce. My father was incensed and for years after would refer to me as Mrs. Partridge and to my sister as Mrs. King.

The uncle died, my grandfather (Mother's father) died and the beatings continued with monotonous regularity, and no one in Mother's family remained to act as an occasional check. All of us would be soundly thrashed and driven out of the house whenever Father was in

* Originally published in the *Indian Journal of Gender Studies*, Vol. 6, No. 2, 1999, pp. 203–19.

a bad mood. 'Us' means Mother, elder sister, two brothers and myself, the youngest.

AND HOW THE BEATINGS STOPPED

My eldest brother George completed his B.A. (Hons.) from Madras Christian College in 1951. He was offered a tutorship at Rs 200 per month. This was a turning point in his life as he was now financially independent and physically strong. One day, a lecturer friend of his came to our house in Kottayam to visit him. George was as usual humiliated by Father in the presence of his friend. He saw the friend off at the bus stand and returned to the house to find that Father had turned his wrath on me (now 16 years old) and Mother. Mother sat weeping on a chair, her hair dishevelled after her beating. Father had snatched away my hairbrush as a prelude to beating me. George held both of Father's hands and calmly said, 'No! Never again! Never again are you going to beat your wife or any of your children.'

Father could not believe what his ears had heard! He obeyed. Instead of beating his wife, he pushed her off the chair on which she was sitting and beat the chair to smithereens. I have had this chair repaired and I keep it in my office. Father streaked out of the front gate of the house on to the road and out of our lives. He never came home again.

We would not have missed him at all except for the fact that in the eyes of our community we would never again find acceptance. My oldest sister had been married the previous year, with all the trappings an arranged marriage demanded. George had a job. My second brother John had an engineering degree. I had just done my school final exams. I was very vulnerable and could draw no strength from my mother who had been beaten and abused into subjugation. Fortunately, we had a house to live in, paddy from our fields and coconuts from our coconut trees. These were brought to us by my father's tenants. Father lived in Ooty and in Bangalore, collecting a massive wardrobe of suits, spectacles, watches and cuff links. I never saw him again.

MORE ABOUT MOTHER

In 1927, when she was 17 years old, Mother was married to the 35-year-old Imperial entomologist. She was considered very beautiful, tall and fair. Unfortunately, when she got married, two of her older sisters were still unmarried. This was an unforgivable crime, and all her seven sisters never forgave her for it—although, obviously, she was not to be blamed.

Mother was talented—she could sing and play tennis. She was good as a violinist and a pianist. While in Geneva, she took violin lessons from a famous teacher. She was a brilliant woman. She had taught herself to cut and stitch on a machine, and could sew wonderfully well. She was also an excellent cook. She knew her traditional onions. She had done short cooking courses in Paris, Geneva and London. She was a great teller of stories. Today, at the age of 90, she recollects how she was asked to play mixed doubles tennis with Lord Linlithgow, then Viceroy of India. She tells how she saw Isadora Duncan being lowered in a glass bubble at the Moulin Rouge in Paris.[1] She studied in finishing schools in London and Geneva. In spite of the tragedy that was her life, she taught her four children much—stories and songs, recitation and public speaking.

For the first four years of my life, Father had abandoned us while he lived abroad. We four children and Mother lived in Aymanam with Mother's father. For the next eight years we lived with Father in Delhi. Suddenly we were returned to Grandfather's house for no apparent reason. Then Father returned. He bought a cottage in Ooty and took me out of boarding school in Madras. I joined the sophisticated Nazareth Convent School in Ooty where I was a day scholar. My mother, father and I lived in Ooty. My sister and brothers were at college in Madras. I was 12 years old and studying at this wonderful school. I don't think I was particularly happy there, but at that time it was supposed to be *the* school since it did not admit Indian children. I was granted admission because of my father's status. I had similarly been admitted to the Convent of Jesus and Mary in Delhi, which in those days had very few Indian students.

We were new to Ooty. It was then a very small place, not crowded and touristy as you see it today. We had a little cottage down in the valley. One night—a cold, cold night in winter—there was a row between my father and mother. It was midnight by the time the row matured into a roaring storm. Father's uncontrollable anger was directed against Mother. He beat her and thrashed her, and finally opened the front door and pushed her out into the night. I was desperate. I had been watching the fight from an inner window. I knew I could not stay in the house with my father in his present mood. And what about Mother? With her poor eyesight she would not be able to see a thing in the strange outdoors. By now it had started raining. As I found one of the doors open, I ran out to my mother. In Ooty we had no friends.

I still remember walking in the cold night's rain. The neighbours must have been in bed and their windows closed against the freezing winter cold. Nobody would have heard us even if we had screamed. Of course, we would never scream. We were too ladylike. We were going to suffer in silence in the bitter cold! We hadn't time to take our coats or shoes. I remember saying: 'I must get my gumboots!' and again: 'I can't walk without gumboots!' and in utter despair: 'It's raining and it's bitterly cold! I must get my gumboots!'

Mother replied, 'Look, if you go there, he is going to catch you, you will be in there and I out here. So let us not think about your boots. We must think of a place to get shelter from the cold and rain.'

But I was adamant about my gumboots. I walked back home leaving Mother sitting outside in the bitter cold, on a little hillock. I went back and knocked at the door. Father opened the door, gave me my boots, and then pulled me inside and locked me up in the bathroom. I was terrified. I managed to climb out of the bathroom ventilator and go back to Mother. It was freezing. The only lights we could see were on the top of the hill. We knew it was the General Post Office. So we trudged up the road shivering. There were a few people inside. One of the peons went up to the apartment of the Post Master General and told him that there was a strange woman and her daughter down in the post office. The kind Post Master came down and took us upstairs to his apartment and gave us dressing gowns to change into. He asked my mother whom he should inform. She gave Grandfather's address. A telegram was sent. We stayed in his house till somebody from Grandfather's house came to collect us. We went back to Kerala. I was put back in the same school in Madras that I had attended earlier.

Life at Grandfather's was peaceful. He was a very kind man. We were very happy living with him. But he had nine children and I do not recollect how many grandchildren! It could not have been easy for a man to take on his married daughter and her four children. Still, my grandfather did it. I do not think I will ever forget the stigma that was attached to living in a maternal grandparent's house after being rejected by our own father.

My Father

He made the best of what the Christian Missionary Society (CMS) had to offer Indian Christians in the early years of this century. He travelled with church scholarships to America, Japan and England. He later joined the Agricultural Institute in Pusa as the Imperial entomologist. The institute moved to Delhi after the great Bihar earthquake. Everybody loved him except his own family. He was handsome and charming to everyone else. He had *always* hated his wife. With hindsight, I often think that she had asked for trouble by the way she exalted her own family and ran down his family. We heard only her version of family history, and grew up thinking that only Pathil was aristocratic.[2]

As if marriage to an abomination of a husband was not enough, Mother developed conical cornea and became nearly blind. At the age of 60 years she had a cornea transplant operation that gave her some degree of vision. I can imagine how lonely and frustrated she must have been in Pusa and in Delhi. There was no escape from her tormentor and the four small children clinging to her.

My Life in the University—And What Next?

I joined Queen Mary's College in Madras for my B.A. degree in something or the other. I honestly cannot remember what subjects I studied. I never had any textbooks, I never did any exams. College was great fun. It certainly could not be described as a 'temple of learning'. It was more a 'waiting room', marriage being the next step. In those days a three-year course ended with a single exam. So, at the end of three years, one got hold of a couple of books, read all day and night, and then appeared for the final examination. I got through with a gorgeous third class for everything. After this it registered, very clearly, that studies would get me nowhere. Anyway, I was discouraged from entering any profession.

I must admit that I myself was devoid of any ambition. I knew vaguely that nobody would 'get me married'. My father had walked out on the family once and for all. My mother, who had spent a major part of her married life being beaten and having babies in between, could not be bothered with making any decisions about me. I remember clearly that my academic grades, when they were good, elicited no praise from her. She did not care even if grades were poor and reports were not shown to her.

During my three years in college, I was a horrible problem. Most of my teachers offered to mark me present on the condition I left the classroom. It was a sort of pact. A few students and I formed a gang. Others thought us uproariously funny. Since I was not in the market as far as marriage was concerned, this seemed to be a 'fun' alternative. After college I was in a twilight zone, with no possibility of a career or marriage. With a B.A. degree, the only job opening was teaching. I was determined I would not do this. There was no money at home to apply for the graduation certificate. Therefore, there was no possibility of attending the convocation, wearing a tissue saree and the graduate's gown and cap. Nor would I record the occasion with a photograph that would be hung on the wall next to that of my sister.

So what did I do next? Nothing! I just sat at my home in Kottayam.

My mother was also at home. Almost a widow, but not quite. We both sat at home and did nothing. Even today I writhe when I recollect those times. I was 20 years old—supposedly the best years in one's life. I could have learned to cook. I could have learned to sew. I could have learned languages. I could have done an M.A. degree. But what did we do? We sat around in abject misery. There was no money to buy food. We lived on the little paddy that my father's tenant gave us. For curry there was green spinach that grew in the compound. Both of us lacked the courage and even the desire to work ourselves out of this horrendous lethargy that engulfed us.

I knew that I must struggle and extricate myself from this wretched situation. But to do what? Who would ever give me a job? What were my qualifications? Who would give me money to study further? Would it not be money wasted? Of course, there was the sneaking hope that my father would turn up and arrange a traditional marriage. Meanwhile, there were two occasions when marriage was broached. I clearly recollect the shame of being 'looked over' when everyone knew that not only was no dowry available, but neither was there a respectable family background! We suffered from middle-class morality of the most pathetic variety. My brothers were not going to 'get me married'. I don't blame them. They did not believe in dowry. There was no property anyway. They wanted me to work. But how do you get a girl to work, a girl who had been taught only this middle-class nonsense about her B.A. degree and nothing else? My degree meant nothing.

George had just returned from England. He was working in a company in Calcutta. I went to live with him for a while. This was the most miserable period in my life. It was more miserable than being at home. I took a typing and shorthand course with the idea of getting a job at the end of it. The others in the typing school were all Anglo-Indians and though they had not got their B.A. degrees, they were a damn sight better than I was. They all went on to become very good secretaries. I did not actually finish the course. I was a lousy secretary. I never could take dictation and I could not type. I kept correcting my boss' language. I was just not cut out for that sort of mindless job. But what else was there to do?

I was about 22 years old then. That was the time when my brother kept introducing me to friends as the 'millstone around my neck'. He exemplifies the stereotype of the Indian male chauvinist pig—desperately hiding his stripes and spots under an education gained in St. Columba's and St. Stephen's, Delhi, and Balliol College, Oxford, as a Rhodes scholar. We have clashed about the inheritance left by our father. We have clashed on a matter of principles. He pretends it is many other things.

I look back and wonder why I did not decide to do something about putting my life in order. I had a bachelor's degree. I was very well read, as reading was a solace in which I had drowned myself during the university years, and the one year of *nothing*. In fact, I can remember that at the age of 11 years I had read *Gone With the Wind* and *Rebecca* and every other book that my sister and brother brought home. They were six and seven years older than I respectively, and both were voracious readers.

I still fail to understand my inertia. 'The times' are an explanation. In the 1950s women who worked were either doctors, nurses or teachers. I was certainly not fit for these careers or for any other. I know I lacked sadly in self-esteem. One year in the little town of Kottayam had not helped develop any. I can remember going out to see the doctor in a rickshaw. In those days rickshaws had a cloth with which one could cover oneself against the rain and sun. I can remember that the first thing I always did was to pull up the cloth so that the world could not see me.

My mother was of no help at all. I now feel that her one-point programme was to save herself. Long ago, when I was a student in Delhi, I can remember getting my academic report for the year. I stood first in class six. My friends looked at me with awe. I went home and showed my mother my grades. The only response was a deep sigh. It spoke volumes. It said that class grades would not save me. It said that I was damned. I never ever spoke to her again about my academic performance in school or college. I only remember that my grades made a sharp slide downwards—to the very bottom—to the place where there was no hope. To the place where educated women with no dowries hid their shame.

Marriage, Babies and Then Separation

With my doubtful knowledge of typing and shorthand, I started work as a secretary in the office pool at Metal Box Company in Calcutta. I drove the boss I was assigned to berserk. I was really an awful typist and nobody could dictate shorthand notes to me.

Fortunately, along came Rajib Roy (or was it unfortunately?) who asked me to marry him. He had a very good job in a jute mill and much money to throw around. This impressed me. At that time, what mattered most was that he could provide an escape from the hell that was life in my own family. So I said yes to his proposal though I loved him not. My family was generally enthusiastic about this opportunity to get rid of me—and that too with a wedding that was reported on two full pages of *Femina*.[3] And, of course, no dowry.

I did not realise that Roy was drunk most of the time. He was drunk the day before we got married. He was drunk on the day we got married. But who cared! This was an opulent period of my life. I had money, servants and cars. I lived like a *maharani* (queen) in the jute factory where he worked and on the tea estates in Assam where he got a job after he was kicked out of the jute mill. We had about 18 to 30 servants at different points of time. I enjoyed it all while it lasted.

My husband was a good man though he was what he was—an alcoholic. He did not try to show himself to be otherwise. We were not made for each other. It was my fault that I had married him, and though I never had to face any traumatic experiences, marriage was just a very negative period of my life. I knew I had to leave him before I got caught in a situation from which I could not escape. He could not hold any job with his drinking habit. I had to go away before it was too late, before I was too old to start something on my own. So I took my two children and left. I was 30 years old. My son was 5, my daughter 3. I hold nothing against my husband. I do not keep in touch with him now, nor he with me. I knew he would not. I knew he was not bothered about the children. I am happy that we did not have any contact. I do not know where he is now or what he is doing.

He keeps getting married and divorced. Legally, he's still married to me. I have not followed the number of marriages or divorces he has been through. It does not affect me. Many people have asked me to comment on the Muslim Women (Protection of Rights on Divorce) Act.[4] What difference is there between a Muslim man who may *legally* have four wives at any given time and a Christian? The man can marry as many times as he wishes. If my husband has several wives, it does not particularly concern me. I am not interested enough to go through the blah-blah of courts and spend money to declare him bigamous. I am not interested in a divorce either.

TWO BABIES, NO HUSBAND, NO JOB AND A NEW LIFE

Things looked terrible. I knew I would never be welcomed at home. I established myself in a little cottage that my father had owned in Ooty and that nobody seemed to care much about. Father was dead. He had died without leaving a will. This, I realise, was the final act of vengeance he perpetrated. Today, 35 years after his death, his heirs are locked in a nasty never-ending legal quarrel about his intestate property. He has certainly had the last laugh!

For me, with my two little children, this was altogether a new experience in my life. In spite of the fact that very often we had no food for the next day, I was now facing a challenge. I was determined to fight to the bitter end to give my children the love, the life and the education I had been denied. This was a new 'me'. I salvaged my self-esteem. I decided to go back to the university and do a degree in education that would qualify me for a job in a school. This would be the ideal solution for a single parent with two small children. I would get holidays when they got holidays. My working time would be the same as theirs. No more did I regard a teacher's job with contempt.

However, I quickly learned that a teacher's life in a school was, generally speaking, a mean existence—especially if it was a residential school. I also learnt that the best way to use my education degree was to start a private kindergarten. Once this was established, I moved on to higher classes. Up to class five at first, and then up to class 10 and then up to class 12. Hey presto! A veritable miracle! Corpus

Christi High School has existed now for 35 years. It is easily the best school in Kerala and renowned as an excellent school all over India. The pupils from here are in diverse countries of the world. They have done very well in undergraduate courses and in the best professional colleges in India. Each one of them has been a success story, many of them astonishing their old teachers (us) of the potential we have unleashed. We are particularly proud of our girl students who have used the self-confidence garnered in this little campus to take on extraordinary challenges.

What is most important is that I am happy, I am economically independent and I have an important place in this society. I still cannot explain how all this came about. A miracle, no less!

THE STRIKING DOWN OF THE TRAVANCORE CHRISTIAN SUCCESSION ACT

By 1984, when I was about 50 years old, I was ready to take on my family and the Syrian Christian community.[5] The reason was an insult suffered 25 years ago. My mother and brother arrived in Ooty with several *goondas* (goons) and ordered me to vacate my father's cottage in which I had been living with my children. It was then that I first heard about the Travancore Christian Succession Act, which denied daughters any share in intestate property. I refused to leave the cottage. There was nowhere to go. On a salary of Rs 350, there was no question of renting rooms in Ooty. So it would have to be a court action. The court would have to be the Supreme Court. The action would have to be a plea for my constitutional right to equality. I was confident of securing justice from the Government of Kerala and the Union of India. I knew I had a good case. In 1984 I challenged the Travancore Christian Succession Act, which declared that when a man died intestate (that is, without leaving a will) his widow would receive a mere life estate in one-third of his estate, and the daughter shall receive a quarter of the share of a son or Rs 5,000, *whichever is less*. I took the matter to court to establish a principle. By now I had more money than my brothers. Fortunately, I did not have to depend on them or my mother for my livelihood. When I needed help, everyone laughed at me. No lawyer would accept my brief. So, 25 years later, when I was economically independent, and therefore unconcerned about 'what people would say', I travelled to Delhi and found a lawyer who filed a public interest litigation suit in the Supreme Court. And so, in 1984, I challenged the Travancore Christian Succession Act as violative of my constitutional right to equality under Articles 14 and 15 of the Constitution.

The Supreme Court struck down the Act in February 1986. The church, the legislature and the press declared then and declare today that the judgement would cause calamities that would hurl Kerala into hellish turmoil; that a spate of litigation would swamp the law courts; that the affluent Syrian Christian community would face economic distress. All transactions involving Syrian Christians, like the sale of property and bank security, would become invalid. It was also feared that an estimated 30,000 nuns who were not given dowry and therefore wedded to the church, would now demand their share in their father's property.

It must be noted that the Supreme Court laid down the general law to be followed in the case of intestate succession. It did not *specifically* deal with my case. In 1989 I filed a case in the Kottayam District Court for a one-sixth share in my father's intestate property. The court ruled *against* me and declared I had no right in this property for two reasons: (*a*) no partition could be valid while the mother's life estate existed, that partition would be in order only after her death; and (*b*) I had been gifted a house in Udhagamandalam (Ooty) by my mother, my two brothers and my sister. The court held that this was in lieu of my one-sixth share in my father's property.

The court did not take into account that these gift deeds were written at various times between 1964 and 1966, and therefore were pure and simple gifts. The gift documents were made out by M/s. King and Partridge, a respected firm of lawyers with offices all over India. And at the time these gifts were made the Travancore Christian Succession Act was in force. It did not visualise any share for any woman in a family. The judge violated his own ruling in (*a*) by pronouncing a verdict on my share. See (*b*) above.

I have appealed against this judgement in the Kerala High Court. It is now five years since my appeals were filed. After five years the case is not yet ready for hearing because of some minor technical error, that is, my sister living in Madras (and one of the parties to the case) had not signed the receipt of summons. You can imagine how many years it is going to take before the matter reaches the Supreme Court. If I get a judgement in my favour (that is, that I have a share in my father's property), I will have to once again file in the district court of Kottayam and petition them to identify my share of the property by meets and bounds, and a commission will have to be appointed for this. If the property is still not handed over to me, I will have to beseech the criminal court to forcibly attach the property through a court *imam*. All this will take a cool 25 years. I can afford to treat the matter as a joke. What of other women who have no house of their own and no income?

And let me, in a few words, tell you what I am made to suffer as a woman who has stepped beyond the limits of decorum. My school had decided to perform the rock opera *Jesus Christ Superstar* by Tim Rice and Andrew Lloyd Webber for its Annual School Dạy. The whole town rose as one to protest against the whittling down of male prerogatives—the community, the district collector,[6] the priests, the Marxists (who wished to please the Christians) and my family—in order to lead the chorus. It ended with a ban imposed on the performance by the district collector. I challenged the ban in the Supreme Court. The Court, in an interim order, said that the school could do one more performance. Listening to the chanting outside the school by various Christian priests and bishops and rubber barons, Christian charity was gloriously in evidence:

Break her legs!
Tie her with chains like an elephant!
Blood will flow down this road!
We shall shatter the school buildings!

—The Flip Side of the Supreme Court Judgement

Any social legislation must necessarily be accompanied by a certain degree of destabilisation of the status quo. Till 1986 the official worth of a Syrian Christian woman was one quarter that of a Syrian Christian man, or to be more specific, exactly Rs 5,000. No one protested on her behalf for 70 long years.

The church, the government and the courts are guilty of the deafening silence they chose to maintain in the years before 1986. Now that the Supreme Court has ushered in justice, they claim that the 'community is in peril'. In fact, the community has never enjoyed such prosperity as it does now. The Christian Forum for Women's Rights is determined that it will not allow any amendment to dilute justice.

Chief Justice Bhagwati and Justice Pathak who delivered the judgement of the Supreme Court made it clear that they were well aware of the problems that the retrospective nature of their judgement would raise. Nevertheless, they chose the alternative of striking down the Travancore Christian Succession Act from 1957 (and thus creating a retrospective period). It would cause less destabilisation within a small community than would have been the case had they resorted to a gender justice judgement based on the constitutional rights of women. This would have had repercussions all over India.

The intestate property of my father, the late P.V. Isaac, was estimated at Rs 10 million in 1984 in the petition presented to the Supreme Court. A Syrian Christian officer in the Wealth Tax Department used this valuation to slap a demand for Rs 700,000 on me as tax on my one-sixth share in the intestate property, which they claimed was in my possession since the date of the Supreme Court judgement, that is, 1986. I was asked to pay Rs 350,000 immediately, with another like amount of Rs 350,000 as penalty for default. This was stayed only with the intervention of the then finance minister Manmohan Singh and the secretary of the Central Board of Direct Taxation.

The same property was valued as worth Rs 1,500 only by his widow at the time of the death of my father in order to evade death duties. The district court used the Rs 1,500 valuation of the *same property* to declare that I had received a cottage in Ooty valued at Rs 15,000 as a gift, which was 10 times the total value of the intestate property. Therefore, I had already received more than my rightful share in my father's estate. Thus, two distinct valuations are used by the community, the media, the courts and the government taxation department as two big sticks with which to beat Mary Roy as and when the occasion demands! Unfortunately, in spite of being soundly thrashed, Mary Roy will not go away! Nor will the Supreme Court judgement be mutilated in anyway.

SINGLE-MOTHER PARENTING

I muse upon the relationship between myself and my children. A single parent who has had to raise her children through tortuous conditions, plagued by chronic asthma, acute financial distress and, what was even more hurtful, the rejection by family, friends and society. A divorced woman was a joke—never, ever do I recollect a word or gesture of sympathy or concern. The only friend I had was another divorcee similarly struggling with her job and her three children. But she, fortunately, had a supportive natal family.

I remember an occasion when we met other members of our Keralite society at a social function. Mrs. Johnson (the local dentist's wife) explained us to the gathering in a loud whisper: 'Used women who have been chewed like *paan* [betel leaf] and then spat out by their husbands.'

Much later, I realised that my children were aware of these social nuances. When they grew up, far from expressing any concern (and never ever any gratitude), they actually blamed their mother for their plight. My daughter's logic is: 'Forget about what you did for me when I was a kid. You wanted to give me food and clothes and education. I never asked for these things. So what should I be grateful for? Once I was 18 I asked for nothing and got nothing.'

I hate to remind her of the times when she had asked for money with a promise to repay. A promise that was never kept till her money miracle happened last year. Now she sends me unsolicited cheques. I do not need them. I give them away. But, of course, I am delighted!

Are touching and sentimental stories of 'everlasting love and thankfulness' reserved for families where there are *mothers* and *fathers* forming strong bonded units? People who cannot be hurt by society or by their families or by their children?

Indian society is peculiar. When a woman's husband dies everyone mourns with her—for a little while. And then she proceeds on her lonely journey for which she is totally unprepared. When a women is divorced by her husband, no one mourns with her. She is despised and she starts on her lonely journey scorned by family, friends and society. When her son dies, everyone mourns with her for a while. When a child storms out of her life, she can confide in no one and finds solace nowhere. She mourns in silent anguish. The first time I wept for my lost son was at the funeral of his friend. A boy who had died in an accident. Like my son, he was 25 years old. *His* mother comforted me. No one else had ever done so.

I remember walking to the Breeks School in Ooty where I was employed as a teacher. I held on to a lamp post till a racking cough subsided, till I retrieved enough breath to walk up to the next post. And then the drama was repeated. Worse still, I urinated in the marketplace because I could not control my bladder because of my cough and shattering attacks of asthma. And when I got home, I would just about make it to my bed. Overcome by nausea, I would vomit. And the vomit would be on the ground below my bed because I could not walk up to the toilet. I threw my best warm blanket over the vomit, to prevent my little ones from being afraid.

But, of course, they knew. All of 5 years and 3 years, they would huddle on the verandah outside my bedroom, entry to which was forbidden, and ask: 'Mama! Are you dead?'

Parenting is a heavenly here and now experience. But a single mother must know the rules. Drink to the last drop the bitter-sweet contentment it offers. The river flows in one direction only, always away from the present.

And pray to your God that the experience is never reversed, to leave you in a position of total dependence in the last years of your life.

MY DAUGHTER AND ME

Arundhati (my daughter) was aware at an early age that she was not exactly a delectable marriage proposition within the Syrian Christian community and would have to train herself as a professional in order to live life according to her own dictates. She learnt her lessons quickly and demanded independence from me on her 18th birthday. She raised her red flag of revolt and declared that she would not accept any further funds from me. She was in the third year of her five-year course in the School of Planning and Architecture at Delhi. I was distressed, but I knew the child. I knew, too, that marriage was the next item on her independence agenda. I knew the young man she intended to marry and generally approved of him, but not of the timing. I set out *my agenda.* She was welcome to put her plans into action. But I would never again pay her hostel and college fees. I did suggest that two years later, with a degree in hand, would be a far more appropriate time to declare independence. Arundhati was adamant and so we parted company for several years. Obviously, this was no more than a runaway wedding, with the groom and the bride quite confident that they could look after themselves.

My son got the same treatment when he declared his intention to marry, and his independence, both blessed by brother George.

No, I was not a harsh mother. I was a woman who had been hurt so often that I knew I would be hurt once again if I used the soft option, and so would they. Much has been made of my 'hard heart' and the fact that I turned away from both my children. I am very proud of what I did because it needed a tremendous depth of courage.

Both my children agree today that we have all come out of the independence era with flying colours. Our relationships are much stronger because we respect each other.

The God of Small Things is a chronicle of what Arundhati and her brother suffered as children in a house where their mother and her two children were not wanted. I quote the following passage from the book. One cannot tell the story better than the Booker prize winner!

Extract I

> The day that Chacko prevented Father from beating her (and Father had murdered his chair instead), Mother packed her wifely luggage and committed it to Chacko's care. From then onwards he became the repository of all her womanly feelings. Her Man. Her only Love.
>
> She was aware of his libertine relationships with the women in the factory, but had ceased to be hurt by them. When Baby Kochamma brought up the subject, Mother became tense and tight-lipped. 'He can't help having a Man's Needs,' she said primly.
>
> Surprisingly, Baby Kochamma accepted this explanation, and the enigmatic, secretly thrilling notion of Men's Needs gained implicit sanction in the Ayemenem House. Neither Mother nor Baby Kochamma saw any contradiction between Chacko's Marxist mind and feudal libido. They only worried about the Naxalites, who had been known to force men from Good Families to marry servant girls whom they had made pregnant.
>
> Mother had a separate entrance built for Chacko's room, which was at the eastern end of the house, so that the objects of his 'Needs' wouldn't have to go traipsing through the house. She secretly slipped them money to keep them happy. They took it because they needed it. They had young children and old parents. Or husbands who spent all their earnings in toddy bars. The arrangement suited Mother because, in her mind, a fee clarified things. Disjuncted sex from love. Needs from Feelings. (pp. 168–69)

Extract 2

> This was the bedroom into which Ammu would first be locked and then lock herself. Whose door Chacko would batter down.

'Get out of my house before I break every bone in your body!'

My house, *my* pineapples, *my* pickle.

After that for years Rahel would dream this dream: a fat man, faceless, kneeling beside a woman's corpse. Hacking its hair off. Breaking every bone in its body. Snapping even the little ones. The fingers. The ear bones cracked like twigs. Snapsnap the softsound of breaking bones. A pianist killing the piano keys. Even the black ones. And Rahel loved them both. The player and the piano.

The killer and the corpse.

As the door was slowly battered down, to control the trembling of her hands, Ammu would hem the ends of Rahel's ribbons that didn't need hemming.

'Promise me you'll always love each other,' she'd say, as she drew her children to her.

'Promise,' Estha and Rahel would say.

Twin millstones and their mother. Numb millstones. What they had done would return to empty them. But that would be later.

At the time, there would only be incoherence. As though meaning had slunk out of things and left them fragmented. Disconnected. The glint of Ammu's needle. The colour of a ribbon. The weave of the cross-stitch counterpane. A door slowly breaking. Isolated things that didn't mean anything. As though the intelligence that decodes life's hidden patterns—that connects reflections to images, glints to light, weaves to fabrics, needles to thread, walls to rooms, love to fear to anger to remorse—was suddenly lost.

'Pack your things and go, 'Chacko would say, stepping over the debris. Looming over them. A chrome door handle in his hand. Suddenly strangely calm. Surprised at his own strength. His bigness. His bullying power. The enormity of his own terrible grief.

Red the colour of splintered doorwood.

Ammu, quiet outside, shaking inside, wouldn't look up from her unnecessary hemming. The tin of coloured ribbons would lie open on her lap, in the room where she had lost her Locusts stand I. (pp. 225–26)

[N.B.:
Instead of Ammu read Mary Roy;
instead of Chacko read George;
instead of Rahel read Arundhati; and
instead of Estha read Lalit (my son).]

And yet other quotes from an interview given by Arundhati Roy:[7]

Q. You've had a complicated relationship with your mother—been something of a rebel—thrown out of home when you were very young. Has the book evened things out between your mother and you?

A. Things were evened out between us a long time ago. My book is dedicated to her. But it's true. It was a difficult book for her to read—not least because of the constant journeying between memory and fiction. But what I think is most difficult for her is the realisation that her troubles—her grief and anger at the world were transmitted through her to us—however hard she tried to protect us from it.

Also I think when she first read the book she probably searched it for signs of herself, identified herself with Ammu. But actually, Ammu as a character, were I to be brutally frank, is much more what I might have been, had I been in my mother's situation. She takes all the opposite turns from the ones Mary Roy took. My mother has been very, very responsible. Yes, she's fought battles, challenged the existing order, but she's done that with great responsibility.

She's very upright. Morally upright. She's a very respected person. Whereas I'm not. I don't qualify as moral, at least not in the conventional definition of morality. I've been accused of all sorts of things—some true, some not—but then I've never claimed to be a fine human being. I'm quite happy to have a character certificate that says 'Does not bear good moral character'.

Q. You mentioned that there seems to be a fear of a basic kind of freedom within yourself.

A. There must be something about me that gives this impression. I. don't know what it is. Perhaps it's because I'm sort of living out a feminist goal. I am a woman who has choices. Who chooses, who decides, and then takes responsibility for the decisions whatever they are. So maybe they get an impression of somebody who has escaped. Evaded the net. Someone who doesn't suffer enough.

But it hasn't come easily. It didn't just fall into my lap. When I was 18, I chose freedom over the safety of a home, good clothes and Johnson's Baby Lotion. But I did that when I was 18. I'm 37 now. I'm not a young rebel any more. I'm just reaping the benefits of having been one. I'm as free a woman as any that I know. The fortunate thing was that I didn't need to be married or oppressed or beaten to decide that I wanted independence at all costs. Perhaps this is because I had an extraordinary mother and an extraordinary uncle. My mother and he don't speak to each other—but he, though he doesn't realise it, is in some ways responsible for my ways of seeing. I remember something that happened—I must have been 4 or 5 years old—it was my birthday. I was getting a lot of the usual free advice from people—'study hard, come first in class'—my uncle called me to his room and showed me a ghastly bauble. My greedy heart coveted it immediately. He asked me if I wanted it. Of course, I did. He said, 'I'll give it to you if you fail.' That made a deep impression. Failure suddenly became something interesting. Worth examining. Perhaps even worth striving for. Certainly not something to be scared of. I'll always love him for that bit of wisdom. For giving me the courage to take risks.

Finally allow me to quote from her dedication to me in *The God of Small Things:*

For Mary Roy who grew me up
Who taught me to say 'excuse me' before
interrupting her in public.
Who loved me enough to let me go.
For LKC, who, like me, survived.

NOTES

1. An American ballerina who reached the peak of her popularity between the two World Wars. She also introduced many creative innovations into the classical dance form.
2. The family name of the author's mother.
3. A popular women's magazine.
4. The enactment of this legislation in 1986 followed a Supreme Court judgement that recognised a Muslim woman's (Shah Bano) right to maintenance on divorce from her husband under Section 125 of the Indian Penal Code (IPC). This judgement created a furore among the conservative sections of Muslim society, and bowing to pressure from them, the government removed Muslim women from the purview of Section 125 of the IPC and enacted separate legislation for them.
5. The Syrian Christians of Kerala are the descendants of the converts of St. Thomas who came to Kerala in A.D. 57. One of the oldest Christian communities

in the world, the name 'Syrian Christian' is a bit of a misnomer, signifying association to a mythic Middle East from which successive waves of Syrian Christians came to India.
6. Administrative head of the district.
7. The interview, conducted by Urvashi Butalia, appeared in the magazine *Outlook*.

REFERENCE

Roy, Arundhati. 1997. *The God of Small Things*. New Delhi: India Ink.

Afterword: The Colonised Coloniser

Arlie Hochschild

Woven into each moving narrative in this book is the paradox of the colonised coloniser. In *The Colonizer and the Colonized* the Tunisian author Albert Memmi reflects on the ways in which the colonised can internalise the values of colonialism, become its local lieutenants who enforce its rules, embrace its idea of honour, and even uphold its code of silence. The coloniser gets the colonised to do the psychological dirty work of colonising—to disdain, for example, the 'lazy natives'. However, the lieutenants also want to rescue other colonised people, for they have themselves suffered as victims of colonialism. Memmi focuses on this pattern of indirect rule as it impacts a general citizenry, and not on personal bonds within a family. For the most part, he also talks about men and not women. But the authors here describe a parallel paradox which issues from patriarchy and strikes far closer to home.

In patriarchy, grandfathers, fathers and sons rule over grandmothers, mothers and daughters. In the face of this powerful inequity, as these narratives show, privileges of caste and class are of no help. Indeed, throughout all the trials of feudalism, colonialism, Partition and early nation-building, it has often fallen to women in India to uphold patriarchy in two ways—by embracing customs which link the belittlement of women with 'family honour', and by abiding by what Leela Gulati calls a 'culture of silence'. This is not a minor, mannerly avoidance of certain topics. Here, then, it is internalisation and a matter of keeping real pain to oneself. Forced to leave school and marry an older man, 12-year-old Saras, in Gulati's narrative, found herself miserably stranded between an angry mother hastening to marry her off and aloof in-laws unwilling to welcome her. From neither did Saras receive enough love or resources to live on. But her new husband 'had no inkling'. Those who saw Saras' dilemma had no sympathy, it seems, and those with sympathy she didn't tell. For women of earlier generations, Saras' silence was not unusual, for it was thought dishonourable for a woman to complain; it was her lot to suffer. In this way, she was, paradoxically, forced into an authorship of her own suffering. What a pity that Saras didn't sit down to tea—in the manner of Michael Cunningham's novel, *The Hours*, in which Virginia Woolf's characters from different eras meet and talk—with Arundhati Roy. Roy, described in Mary Roy's narrative, would most likely have offered Saras her definition of a feminist: a woman who 'doesn't suffer enough'.

In a very different way, this culture of silence has made its way into social science and the arts. Nabaneeta Dev Sen describes how her mother, the well-known author Radharani, wrote lively poems echoing the voices of the kitchen, the bedroom, the girls' hostel, the young bride, the widowed aunt. For 12 years no one associated these poems with Radharani's name because she published them under a pseudonym, Aparajita Devi. Meanwhile, under her own name, Radharani published a series of tepid, unisex poems which avoided referring to women's real experiences. When at last Radharani admitted her authorship of the lively 'Aparajita poems', she disparaged them, saying she'd written them simply to illustrate how 'men think women write'. She imagined, we can guess, that the everyday lives of the women depicted would seem trivial, silly, unserious. And perhaps she thought that this devaluation of ordinary women's lives, their talk, their concerns, would rub off and devalue the writer of the devalued lives. In fact, Radharani was breaking a taboo, and that being risky, Radharani has Aparajita 'do it for her'. But authenticity had the last word; Aparajita's lively poems of everyday life, poems which broke through the culture of silence, were wildly popular and far outlasted the abstract, official and silenced poems to which Radharani had freely linked her name.

This volume follows in the footsteps of Aparajita, and other volumes of women's narrative. What distinguishes this from other such books is not simply the extraordinary achievements of the authors and the rich variety of communities from which the authors are drawn, but a great paradox which forms an arc over the lives described in this book.

This paradox is brought to light by the subversive assignment given these authors—to describe relations between grandmothers, mothers and daughters, even while they all grew up in households exclusively honouring links between grandfathers, fathers and sons. The further back in time, the deeper and more hidden the paradox, the closer to the present, the closer to the surface and more apparent.

The paradox is this. Mothers born early in the century were both the prison wardens of patriarchy and co-conspirators helping the prisoners to escape. A mother who dutifully upheld her family's honour had to enforce rules she knew all too well hurt her daughter. Thus she faces the unhappy choice between being good (by being the dutiful upholder of family honour) and being kind (sparing her daughter from hurtful practices). Nabaneeta Dev Sen describes how harshly Narayani (her grandmother) treated Radharani (her mother) after the latter became a 13-year-old widow.

> Narayani took off all her jewellery, chopped off her thick long locks, enforcing a widow's close crop, made her wear the borderless white cloth and forced her to wrap in widow's *chador* (long cloth) around herself. From now on she was to eat a proper widow's diet, *havishyanna*, only once a day. Radharani was to eat for the rest of her life what is usually eaten only by those practising austerity during the formal mourning period after a death. And what did Radharani eat on the fasting days, like the *ekadasi*? She ate nothing and she drank nothing. What if she cheated while taking her bath and quietly gulped down a few drops of bath water on a hot summer's day? To stop that, she was always accompanied into the bathroom by an invigilator, like a sister or a maid who would keep a careful eye on her penance (p. 27).

Narayani was not being cruel, Dev Sen tells us. As a devout Hindu, she felt she was preparing her daughter for the next life. In precisely what spirit did she impose these restrictions? Did she lovingly remove the glass of water, gently explain her reasons, or did she briskly whisk it away with a harsh rebuke? We may never know. Either way, the customs themselves make military training seem like a piece of cake.

Other practices included restricting girls' schooling and marrying them off as children. (In Vijaya Mehta's story, her grandfather's first wife who married him at the age of three fell asleep at the wedding.) Often the children were married to much older men as second wives, so that as young adults they became widows and faced some version of Radharani's ordeal. It often fell to the lieutenants of patriarchy—mothers, mothers-in-law and aunts—to enforce the restrictions. Mothers, thus, had to partly detach themselves from the daughters they hurt, to disidentify with them.

At the same time, mothers also strongly identified with their daughters as fellow victims of cruel rules. Thus, many mothers also—and in most cases more—strongly communicated messages of collusion: 'These rules are rigged against us. I know how you feel. I couldn't escape. But you can. Go lead the life I would have wanted.'

Some mothers fell to one side of the paradox, embracing the role of prison warden of feudalism—Gulati's embittered Seetha, for example, harshly passes on the hardships she suffered. Maithreyi Krishna Raj tells of a mother-in-law who denied her mother food and rest and when she felt ill accused her of malingering, once dragging her mother by the hair to a room she then locked because her mother said she had a fever. Priti Desai felt her mother projected onto her the image of a mother-in-law who had been cruel to her and was unloving. Saroja Kamakshi speaks of a relation with her mother that 'hasn't worked out'.

Other mothers—and many of the same mothers—also fell to the other side of the paradox, as co-conspirators planning the great escape. They split the ambivalence by embracing one hurtful custom but rejecting another. Or they alternated between stances. Or they muted the punishment of their daughters (stance of helper) or muted their sympathy with their daughter (stance of the warden). Priti Desai, however, speaks for many when she also describes her mother as a 'feminist who ... quietly passed on the message that a woman had an identity, a will and needed a space of her own'. Still others—like the severely battered mother of Mary Roy—reversed roles, being themselves the prisoner in a despotic marriage, and calling on her young daughter for help.

For their part, daughters differ widely in their response to their mothers' treatment of them. Some daughters were made wary, having been denigrated or arbitrarily blamed by their mothers, sometimes for the imagined sins of women in previous generations. Other daughters felt grateful for their mothers' steadfast support. And many aspects of these relations between daughter and mother were, of course, tied to circumstances well beyond patriarchy. But over all, the authors in this book seem remarkably attuned to ambiguities. Indeed, one wonders if the sensitivity of the daughters isn't honed by their exposure to the complexities of maternal love.

However, whichever side of the paradox comes to prevail, when the chips are down, surprisingly elderly mothers are often left to the care of their grown daughters. In Sushil Narulla's story of a Sikh family in the time of Partition, she tells of mothers and grandmothers who lovingly cared for sons and grandsons, but in their final years received care from their daughters and granddaughters. Narulla describes her grandmother Ammaji who lit the fire and cooked delicious meals with trembling hands, and would, in summers, go from bed to bed kissing all her nine grandchildren while they slept. But when the family moved to better housing, none of her sons or grandsons took her in. Instead her three daughters took turns looking after her. Finally, what remained was the bond between mother and daughters. Priti Desai poignantly describes nursing her aged mother as she drifted into death—a mother about whom she says, 'deep within me remained the feeling that she hated and disliked me for a long time' (p. 163).

Fathers did not face the same paradox with their sons that mothers faced with their daughters. Upholding the family's honour did not, for the fathers, fundamentally conflict with a father's love for and identification with his son. Perhaps fathers also faced the paradox differently with their daughters. For fathers, family honour was also pitted against what we now see as human kindness. But often, as the stories suggest, fathers didn't see it that way. A good number of grandfathers were described as tyrannical; the paternal grandfather of Hema Sundaram threw food in her grandmother's face because she served it too late. Perhaps most of the fathers in these narratives were neither especially cruel, nor were they great champions of women. Like Zarina Bhatty's father, they opposed their daughters' college education and human development. On the whole, the men felt patriarchy served them well, and a culture of silence often prevented them from sensing the real pain it caused.

Traditional Indian mothers and daughters shared this paradox with their counterparts elsewhere. The Chinese women who bound the feet of their daughters so they would not be called 'big foot' and disparaged as unmarriageable were locked into a similar paradox. African mothers who advocated the practice and female relatives who often performed clictorectomies on young girls to make them marriageable, faced the same dilemma. So, today, do American mothers who cajole their daughters into size 6 dresses, holding out to them a version of womanhood that is itself a hostage of capitalism.[1] In each case, women were enlisted as lieutenants to carry out edicts of which they were not themselves the ultimate authors. But as victims of the same system, the mothers could also guide their daughters to the trapdoor out of the system—through learning, work, and a revolution in ideas.

One basic point these narratives show us is that patriarchy is not simply a set of external rules governing property, name, or proper behaviour as if all these were detached from the inner, emotional lives of women. We might imagine that parental love is a matter so basic to human relationships that social tyrannies only form a thin patina on top of it. But these memories tell a different story. From them, we get the sense that patriarchy is composed of rules which link power, custom and honour. And the grip of patriarchy comes from the way these alter notions of love. Sometimes patriarchy eliminates a family member's attitude to women, as when Dev Sen says of her grandmother that she 'hated girl children in general, doted on boys and had blind spots and favourites'. Other times patriarchy doesn't seem to eliminate love as much as drain it of respect. For example, Dev Sen tells of an uncle who adored and was adored by his mother, but whose voluminous history of the family said not a word about her. All these complexities, then, are a part of what Jasodhara Bagchi so aptly calls women's 'inner legacy'.

These narratives carry another message as well. Basic to patriarchy is the idea that women are a burden on men, dependent and weak. As Hema Sundaram comments in her narrative of a Mylapore Brahmin family: 'Comparing girls with boys, how much responsibility girls are—oh how to find them bridegrooms, how to settle them. Boys after all will take care of themselves, once they are qualified.' But actually these narratives tell a different story.

For one thing, it was men who depended on women to feed the household, to clean the house, to raise all the children, to tend to medical emergencies, keep up relations with other kin, tend to religious rituals. Some 11-year-old new brides ran entire households, not their older husbands. So who was a burden on whom? To be sure, the system was rigged so that a parent lost money when a daughter married and gained money when a son did. Still, this financial arrangement can blind us to how dependent men were—and are—on women. In the American South it was often said that slaves became dependent on their masters, but how much more true it is that masters depended on slaves.

Similarly, we can ask: How could it be that women in these narratives are seen as weak? A woman had to be a tower of strength to endure the conditions of her 'dependence'. Many of the grandmothers were indeed powerful stoics. Radharani had to be strong to withstand her ordeal as a child widow. Women were strong; what they lacked was power. But strength without power is still strength. Thinking of her grandmother from the Chandraseneey Kayastha Prabhu caste, Vijaya Mehta reflects, 'strength, wisdom and endurance with which my mother and grandmothers coped with life made them perhaps stronger than us, the modern women' (p. 201).

In the course of three generations, the world within which women expressed this strength was shifting. Vijaya Mehta speaks, as other authors do, of women's 'status in the household'. That was a term which made sense in an era of large households. Today such households are shrinking in size, and the status within them is dwindling in importance. Correspondingly, a woman's status in the workplace has come to matter more. In addition, as Sushil Narulla's story shows, Partition broke households into many pieces. When the need and opportunity arose, a sheltered wife blossomed into a highly competent negotiator in her refugee camp.

But stoical strength alone, even in a new context, would not get women where they are today, without the heroism of those women who opened the prison door from the inside. Vina Mazumdar tells the moving story of her aunt, *Pishima*, who, unlettered herself, insisted that Vina's mother be allowed to take lessons from her *dewar* (husband's younger brother), even though it was strictly forbidden. The family was furious. This was a dishonour and a disgrace. But *Pishima* was ardent and she won. In fact, *Pishima* pressed for every girl in the family and wider community to go to school. As Mazumdar relates, one by one all the neighbours with daughters of school age agreed to send them to a new school, as '*Pishima*, a wet towel atop her head against the heat, daily collected and escorted 20 or more girls to and from school'. So forcefully did *Pishima* 'din this into the heads of my older cousins and my sister', said Vina Mazumdar, that she felt she heard echoes of *Pishima* in her mother's support for her to study, in 1947, at Oxford University. How many *Pishimas* and Radharanis are behind us all? May we know their stories, and link our spiritual genealogies to them. For they, like other women who need to be thanked, could deflect, rather than pass down, the troubles they have known.

NOTE

1. Indeed, one might even say that in the absence of some culture of resistance, modern advice books take on the role of mother in preparing American girls to

survive emotionally under capitalism. See Hochschild 2003. In addition, transnational flows of women from many countries of the South to countries of the North suggest another way in which mothers both help their daughters escape the imprint of patriarchal global capitalism and also pass it on (see Ehrenreich and Hochschild 2003).

REFERENCES

Ehrenreich, Barbara and Arlie Hochschild, eds. 2003. *Global Woman: Nannies, Maids, and Sex Workers in the New Economy*. New York: Metropolitan Books.

Hochschild, Arlie. 1973. *The Unexpected Community*. Englewood Cliffs, NJ: Prentice-Hall.

———. 2003. *The Commercialization of Intimate Life: Notes from Home and Work*. Los Angeles and Berkeley: University of California Press.

Memmi, Albert, 1991 [1965]. *The Colonizer and the Colonized*. Boston: Beacon Press. Originally published by Orion Press, New York.

Sennett, Richard and Jonathan Cobb. 1993. *The Hidden Injuries of Class*. New York: Norton.

Select Bibliography

Adelman, Marcy (ed.). 1996. *Lesbian Passages: True Stories Told by Women over 40.* Alyson Publications.

Ainley, Rosa. 1995. *Death of a Mother: Daughters' Stories*. New York: New York University Press.

Allenbaugh, Kay. 2001. *Chocolate for a Teen's Heart: Unforgettable Stories for Young Women About Love, Hope, and Happiness*. Simon & Schuster Trade Paperbacks.

Bachle, Rosemary Eckroat and Cathy Keating. 2001. *Women's War Memoirs*. Lightning Source.

Ballard, George. 1985 [1752]. *Memoirs of Several Ladies of Great Britain Who Have Been Celebrated for Their Writings or Skill in the Learned Languages, Arts, and Sciences*. Detroit: Wayne State University Press.

Bardhan, Kalpana (ed.). 1990. *Of Women, Outcastes, Peasants, and Rebels: A Selection of Bengali Short Stories*. Berkeley: University of California Press.

Bell, Beverly and Edwidge Danticat. 2001. *Walking on Fir: Haitian Women's Stories of Survival and Resistance*. Ithaca: Cornell University Press.

Binodini Dasi. *My Story and My Life as an Actress* (edited and translated from the Bengali by Rimli Bhattacharya, 1998). New Delhi: Kali for Women.

Bulbeck, Chilla. 2001. *Living Feminism: The Impact of the Women's Movement on Three Generations of Australian Women (Reshaping Australian Institutions)*. Cambridge: Cambridge University Press.

Butalia, Urvashi and Ritu Menon (eds). 1992. *In Other Words: New Writing by Indian Women*. New Delhi: Kali for Women.

Cahill, Susan (ed.). 1993. *Growing Up Female: Stories by Women Writers from the American Mosaic*. New York: Mentor Books.

Cassidy, Carol (ed.). 1999. *Girls in America: Their Stories, Their Words*. New York: TV Books Inc.

Castillo-Speed, Lillian (ed.). 1995. *Latina: Women's Voices from the Borderlands*. New York: Simon and Schuster.

Committee on Women's Studies in Asia (ed.). 1995 *Changing Lives: Life Stories of Asian Pioneers in Women's Studies*. New York: Feminist Press.

Conway, Jill K. (ed.). 1999. *In Her Own Words: Women's Memoirs from Australia, New Zealand, Canada and the United States*. New York: Vintage Books.

_________ (ed.). 1997. *Written by Herself, Vol II: Women's Memoirs from Four Continents*. New York: Vintage Books.

Conway, Jill K. (ed.). 1996. *Written by Herself: Women's Memoirs from Britain, Africa, Asia, and the United States*. New York: Vintage Books.

________ (ed.). 1992. *Written by Herself: Autobiographies of American Women: An Anthology*. New York: Vintage Books.

Das, J.P. and Arlene Zide (eds). 1992. *Under a Silent Sun: Oriya Women in Translation*. Stosius Inc./Advent Books Division.

Elder, Lindsey (ed.). 1996. *Early Embraces: True Stories of Women Describing Their First Lesbian Experience*. Alyson Publications.

Faull, Katherina M. (ed.). 1997. *Moravian Women's Memoirs: Their Related Lives, 1750–1820 (Women and Gender in North American Religions)*. New York: Syracuse University Press.

Figes, Kate (ed.). 2000. *The Penguin Book of International Women's Stories*. New York: Penguin Books.

Friedl, Erika. 1989. *The Women of Deh Koh: Lives in an Iranian Village*. Washington: Smithsonian Institution Press.

Glenn, Evelyn Nakano. 1988. *Issei, Nisei, War Bride: Three Generations of Japanese American Women in Domestic Service*. Philadelphia: Temple University Press.

Gore, Ariel and Bee Lavender (eds). 2001. *Breeder: Real-Life Stories from the New Generation of Mothers*. Seattle: Seal Press

Gorkin, Michael and Rafiqua Othman. 1996. *Three mothers, Three Daughters: Palestinian Women's Stories*. Berkeley: University of California Press.

Gorkin, Michael, Marta Pineda, and Gloria Leal. 2000. *From Grandmother to Granddaughter: Salvadoran Women's Stories*. Berkeley: University of California Press.

Green, John and Farzin Yazdanfar (eds). 1993. *A Walnut Sapling on Masih's Grave and Other Stories by Iranian Women*. Portsmouth, NH: Heinemann.

Hasselstrom, Linda, Gaydell Collier and Nancy Curtis (eds). 1997. *Leaning into the Wind: Women Write from the Heart of the West*. Boston: Houghton Mifflin.

Henderson, Peta. 1994. *Rising Up: Life Stories of Belizean Women*. Canada: Sister Vision Press.

Holland, Mary Gardner (ed.). 1998. *Our Army Nurses: Stories from Women in Civil War*. Roseville, MN: Edinborough Press.

Holmes, Sarah and Jennifer Tust (eds). 2002. *Testimonies: Lesbian Coming-Out Stories*. Alyson Publications.

Holmstrom, Lakshmi. 1997. *The Inner Courtyard: Stories by Indian Women*. Calcutta: Rupa & Company.

Hom, Sharon K. (ed.). 1998. *Chinese Women Traversing Diaspora: Memoirs, Essays, and Poetry*. New York: Garland Publishing.

Howard, Keith (ed.). 1995. *True Stories of the Korean Comfort Women: Testimonies Compiled by the Korean Council for Women Drafted for Military Sexual Slavery by Japan and the Research Association on the Women Drafted for Military Sexual Slavery by Japan*. London: Cassell.

Hudson, Roger, 2000. *The Grand Quarrel: Women's Memoirs of the English Civil War*. Alan Sutton Publishing, Ltd.

James, George Payne Rainsford. *Memoirs of Celebrated Women*.

Jordan, Teresa and James R. Hepworth (eds). 1995. *The Stories that Shape Us: Contemporary Women Write about the West: An Anthology*. New York: Norton.

Kalaw-Tirol, Lorna (ed.). 2000. *From America to Africa: Voices of Filipino Women Overseas*. FAI Resource Management Inc.

Katz, Jane (ed.). 1995. *Messengers of the Wind: Native American Women Tell Their Life Stories*. New York: Ballantine Books.

Khorrami, Mohammad Mehdi and Shouleh Vatanabadi (eds). 2000. *A Feast in the Mirror: Stories by Contemporary Iranian Women*. Boulder, CO: Lynne Rienner Publishers.

Krause, Corinne Azen. 1991. *Grandmothers, Mothers, and Daughters: Oral Histories of Three Generations of Ethnic American Women*. Boston: Twayne Publishers.

Krishnankutty, Gita (ed.). 1998. *Cast Me Out If You Will: Stories and Memoirs*. New York: Feminist Press.

Larkin, Joan. 1999. *A Woman Like That: Lesbian and Bisexual Writers Tell Their Coming Out Stories*. New York: Avon Books.

Laskas, Jeanne Marie. 1999. *We Remember: Women Born at the Turn of the Century Tell the Stories of Their Lives in Words and Pictures*. New York: Hearst Books.

Lewis, Frnaklin and Farzin Yazdanfar. 1996. *In a Voice of Their Own: A Collection of Stories by Iranian Women Written Since the Revolution of 1979*. Costa Mesa, CA: Mazda Publishers.

Liswood, Laura A. 1996. *Women World Leaders: Fifteen Great Politicians Tell Their Stories*. London: Pandora.

Marcus, George E. (ed.). 1995. *Technoscientific Imaginaries: Conversation, Profiles, and Memoirs*. Chicago: University of Chicago Press.

Martin, Katherine (ed.). 1999. *Women of Courage: Inspiring Stories from the Women Who Lived Them*. Novato, CA: New World Library.

Martin, Katherine and Judith Orloff. 2001. *Women of Spirit: Stories of Courage form the Women Who Lived Them*. Novato, CA: New World Library.

Martin, Molly (ed.). 1988. *Hard-Hatted Women: Stories of Struggle and Success in the Trades*. Seattle: Seal Press.

Mazumdar, Shudha. 1997. *Memoirs of an Indian Woman*. Armonk, NY: M.E. Sharpe.

Mellibovsky, Matilde. 1997. *Circle of Love Over Death: Testimonies of the Mothers of the Plaza De Mayo*. Willimantic, CT: Curbstone Press.

Moffitt, Gisela. 1993. *Bonds and Bondage: Daughter-Father Relationships in the Father Memoirs of German-Speaking Women Writers of the 1970s*. New York: P. Lang.

Morgan, Jill M., Eileen Gouge, Faye Kellerman and Diana Gabaldon (eds). 2000. *Father and Daughters: A Celebration of Memoirs, Stories, and Photographs*. Signet.

Morgan, Robin. 1996. *Sisterhood is Global: The International Women's Movement Anthology*. New York: Feminist Press.

———. 1970. *Sisterhood is Powerful: An Anthology of Writings from the Women's Liberation Movement*. New York: Random House.

Nakano, Mei T. 1990. *Japanese American Women: Three Generations 1890–1990*. Berkeley: Mina Press Publishing.

O'Keefe, Claudia (ed.). 1996. *Mother: Famous Writers Celebrate Motherhood with a Treasury of Short Stories, Essays, and Poems*. New York: Pocket Books.

O'Keefe, Claudia (ed.). 1999. *Forever Sisters: Famous Writers Celebrate the Power of Sisterhood with Short Stories, Essays, and Memoirs*. New York: Pocket Books.

Orndorff, Kata (ed.). 1998. *Bi Lives: Bisexual Women Tell Their Stories*. Tucson, Arizona: Sharp Press.

Paterson, Wendy Anne. 2001. *Unbroken Homes: Single-Parent Mothers Tell Their Stories*. New York: Haworth Press.

Penman, Sarah (ed.). 2000. *Honor the Grandmothers: Dakota and Lakota Women Tell Their Stories*. Minnesota Historical Society.

Personal Narratives Group (ed.). 1989. *Interpreting Women's Living—Feminist Theory and Personal Narratives*. Indiana: Bloomington.

Rodenberger, Lou Halsell (ed.). 2000. *Her Work: Stories by Texas Women*. Lightning Source.

Sa'Adadwi, Nawal. 1994. *Memoirs from the Women's Prison*. Berkeley: University of California Press.

Sahgal, Manmohini Zutshi. 1994. *An Indian Freedom Fighter Recalls Her Life*. Armonk, NY: M.E. Sharpe.

Scott, Nina M. (ed.). 1999. *Madres Del Verbo: Mothers of the Word: Early Spanish-American Women Writers: A Bilingual Anthology*. Albuquerque: University of New Mexico Press.

Siegel, Rachel Josefowitz and Ellen Cole (eds). 2000. *Jewish Mothers Tell Their Stories: Acts of Love and Courage*. New York: Haworth Press.

Rouhi, Shafii. 1997. *Scent of Saffron: Three Generations of an Iranian Family*. London: Scarlet Press.

Sarkar, Tanika. 1999. *Words to Win. The Making of Amar Jiban, a Modern Autobiography*. New Delhi: Kali for Women.

Solomon, Barbara (ed.). 1896. *American Wives: 30 Short Stories by Women*. New York: Mentor Books.

Sternsher, Bernard and Judith Sealander (eds). 1990. *Women of Valor: The Struggle Against the Great Depression as Told in Their Own Life Stories*. Lightning Source.

Stott, Michelle and Joseph O. Baker (eds). 1997. *Im Nonnengarten: An Anthology of German Women's Writing, 1850–1907*. Prospect Heights, IL: Waveland Press.

Sullivan, Soraya Paknazar. 1991. *Stories by Iranian Women Since the Revolution*. Austin, TX: Center for Middle Eastern Studies, The Univeısity of Texas at Austin.

Tarpley, Natasha. 1999. *Girl in the Mirror: Three Generations of Black Women in Motion*. Boston: Beacon Press.

Tharu, Susie and K. Lalita (eds). 1993. *Women Writing in India: 600 B.C. to the Present*. New York: Feminist Press at the City University of New York.

Traeder, Tamara and Carmen Renee Berry. 1998. *Girlfriends are Forever: Stories of Friendship*. Andrews McMeel Publishing.

Varma, Mahadevi. 1994. *Sketches from My Past: Encounters with India's Oppressed*. Boston: Northeastern University Press.

Vilensky, Simeon (ed.). 2001. *Till My Tale is Told: Women's Memoirs of the Gulag*. Bloomington: Indiana University Press.

Wachowich, Nancy. 2001. *Saqiyuq: Stories from the Lives of Three Inuit Women*. Montreal; Ithaca: McGill-Queen's University Press.

Walker, Keith (ed.). 1997. *A Piece of My Heart: The Stories of 26 American Women Who Served in Vietnam*. Novato, CA: Presidio Press.

Washington, Mary H. (ed.). 1990. *Black-Eyed Susans/Midnight Birds: Stories by and about Black Women*. New York: Anchor Books.

About the Editors and Contributors

The Editors

Leela Gulati was born in Mysore, India. She grew up in Baroda and was educated at the Maharaja Sayajirao University, where she began her teaching career. Later on she moved to Trivandrum and was associated with the Centre for Development Studies. Most of her work has focused on the issues of women, work and poverty, and she has tried to use the tools of the anthropologist to understand economic questions. She is known for the intensive use of case studies as a research methodology. These narratives that she has edited are also an extension of the same methodology to explore issues around women and social change. In recent years she has been interested in the study of Asian labour migration, both on women who stay behind and on those who migrate.

Jasodhara Bagchi is Chairperson, West Bengal Commission for Women, and Founder Director of the School of Women's Studies, Jadavpur University. She was born in 1937 and educated at Presidency College, Kolkata, Somerville College, Oxford, and New Hall, Cambridge. The larger part of her working life was spent at Jadavpur University, where she was Professor of English. In 1988 she became the Founder-Director of the School of Women's Studies at Jadavpur University, in which capacity she led the activities of the Centre until her retirement in 1997. She is also one of the founder-members of the feminist organisation Sachetana in Kolkata. Her focus areas of research include women's studies, women's writing, 19th-century English and Bengali literature, the reception of Positivism in Bengal, motherhood, and the Partition of India. Among her numerous authored, edited, and co-edited volumes are *The Changing Status of Women in West Bengal, 1970–2000: The Challenge Ahead* (2005), *The Trauma and the Triumph: Gender and Partition in India* (2003), *Thinking*

Social Science in India: Essays in Honour of Alice Thorner (2002), *Gem-like Flame: Walter Pater and the 19th-Century Paradigm of Modernity* (1997), *Loved and Unloved: The Girl Child in the Family* (1997), *Indian Women: Myth and Reality* (1995), and *Literature, Society, and Ideology in the Victorian Era* (1992). She initiated and spearheaded the pioneering Bengali Women Writers Reprint Series edited by the School of Women's Studies, Jadavpur University, which continues to bring out new editions of writers such as Jyotirmoyee Devi.

THE CONTRIBUTORS

Zarina Bhatty, former President of the Indian Association for Women's Studies, has researched, published and lectured extensively in India and abroad on Indian Muslim women's issues and on women in the unorganised sector. Her pioneering study on women in the *beedi* industry, undertaken and published by the ILO, received considerable recognition. Zarina Bhatty studied sociology at the London School of Economics and Political Science, and taught at Delhi University. She later worked as a Gender Specialist with USAID, IFAD and IDB.

Priti T. Desai obtained a Masters degree in Economics from the University of Bombay in 1956. She taught briefly at Miranda House, Delhi, and later worked in varied fields as reinsurance, neurological associations, foreign consulates, and finally administrative work in a management consultancy firm. She has co-edited the volume *Indelible Imprints—Daughters Write on Fathers*. She is an avid reader, fond of Indian classical music, and keenly interested in theatre.

Nabaneeta Dev Sen was born in 1938 in Calcutta into a family of well known poets—her father was Narendra Dev and her mother was Radharani Devi, who also wrote under the name Aparajita Devi. Dr Dev Sen obtained her Bachelor's in English from Presidency College, Calcutta. She was in the first batch of students of the Department of Comparative Literature, Jadavpur University, founded by Buddhadeva Bose, where she stood first in the Master's course. She went abroad for higher studies (M.A. with Distinction from Harvard; Ph.D. in Comparative Literature from Indiana University). She is now a Professor in the Comp. Lit. Dept. at Jadavpur University. Her hobbies are reading, records, and travelling—often unplanned.

Her first publication was a book of poems: *Pratham Pratyay* in 1959. *Ami Anupam*, her first novel, came much later: it was published in 1976 in the 'Puja Issue' of the *Ananda Bazar Patrika*. She now has many books to her credit in a variety of genres: short stories, essays, travelogues, poetry, fiction, children's literature, verse-plays, humour. Even her most scholarly essays are remarkable for the charming prose and sense of humour. She is one of the most popular authors in Bengal today. She has received numerous awards, including the Sahitya Akademi.

Carolyn M. Elliott is Professor of Political Science Emerita at the University of Vermont in Burlington, Vermont. She convened the first academic conference on Women and Development at Wellesley College, and subsequently served as Program Officer for Women's Studies at the Ford Foundation, New Delhi. She is a past president of the Association for Women's rights in Development, an international organisation for researchers, policy-makers and practitioners. She has held two Fulbright fellowships, one for research on politics in Andhra Pradesh and a second to direct the American Studies Research Center in Hyderabad. She has many publications on women's education, women and development, civil society and democracy, and the social bases of politics in India.

Arlie Hochschild is a Professor of Sociology at the University of California, Berkeley. She has published seven books, printed variously in 10 languages. Among them are *The Managed Heart*; *The Second Shift: Working Parents and the Revolution at Home*; *The Time Bind*; *When Work Becomes Home and Home Becomes Work*; and in 2003, *Global Women: Nannies, Maids and Sex Workers in the New Economy* (co-edited with Barbara Ehrenreich), and *The Commercialization of Intimate Life*.

Saroja Kamakshi has been closely associated with her younger daughter Malavika Sarukkai's dance career and, as artistic director, has been travelling extensively with Malavika's Company for more than two decades. From conceptualisation to the final presentation, she works closely with Malavika as creative collaborator and coordinator. With elder daughter Priya Sarukkai-Chabria, novelist and poet, she assists in editing, participates in discussions about concepts, and provides inputs from Sanskrit literature. As a freelance writer, Saroja Kamakshi had earlier contributed to leading publications, particularly to those of the Times of India group.

Maithreyi Krishna Raj retired as Professor and Director of the Research Centre for Women's Studies at the SNDT Women's University. She was also Professor at the Institute of Social Studies, The Hague, from 1992–94. Among her publications are *Women and Society; Essays in Women and Science; Population, Gender and Development;* and *Real Lives and Mythic Models*.

Vina Mazumdar is Chairperson, Centre for Women's Development Studies, New Delhi. She was educated at Calcutta, Banaras and Oxford. In her professional career, she has been a teacher of Political Science at the Universities of Patna and Berhampur, an Officer in the UGC Secretariat, and Fellow of the Indian Institute of Advanced Studies, Shimla. She was Member Secretary, Committee on the Status of Women in India, and later Director, Programme of Women's Studies, Indian Council of Social Science Research, from 1975–80. Dr Mazumdar was Founder-Director of the Centre for Women's Development Studies from 1980–91, and thereafter Senior Fellow at CWDS and J.P. Naik Fellow, ICSSR, for two years. She is one of the pioneers in women's studies in India, and a leading figure of the women's movement.

Vijaya Mehta is Executive Director of the National Centre for the Performing Arts. She is well known for her path-breaking experiments in Indian and international theatre.

Sushil Narulla was born into a Sikh family in Bannu, located in the North West Frontier Province of present day Pakistan. She was the only daughter among nine children. While in her teens she had to move to India with her mother and brothers as a result of the Partition. Her teenage years were spent in many of the refugee camps around Delhi.

Partition changed everything. The strict *purdah* rules of the frontier Sikh families had to be put aside. Sushil enrolled in college and cycled to and fro. She completed her Masters in Mathematics and retired as a principal of one of the higher secondary schools in Delhi.

Unfortunately she is no longer with us. This piece will remain a lasting memory to her life and struggles of many women like her.

Mary Roy started 'Pallikoodam', a Nursery to Grade XII school, which she still heads at the age of 70. A novelist and relentless campaigner for women's rights, Mary Roy has faced turbulent times with equanimity and come out successful.

Hema Sundaram had her early education in Chennai. She obtained her Masters degree in Political Science from the Utkal University, and her doctorate from the Mother Theresa Women's University, Kodaikanal, in Women's Studies. Dr Sundaram taught history and political science to undergraduate students at the Holy Cross College, Thiruchirappalli, Tamil Nadu, where she worked for 24 years. She has also designed a course on Women's Studies for undergraduates. Her special interest is classical Carnatic music, and she is also an activist with the local women's groups.